Tin-Can Canucks

A Century of Canadian Destroyers

S.D. Campbell

**Kay Cee
Publications
Calgary • Charlottetown**

Copyright © 2017 Sean Campbell

All rights reserved. No part of this book may be reproduced or transmitted in any form or by any means, electronic or mechanical, including photocopying, recording or by any information storage and retrieval system, without permission in writing from the copyright owner.

ISBN: 0-9691548-02-8
ISBN-13: 978-0-9691548-02-2

Cover Artwork:

"Grilse before the Gale" by Gerard Campbell

Campbell, S. D., 1974-, author
  Tin-can Canucks : a century of Canadian destroyers

/ S.D. Campbell.

Includes bibliographical references and index.
ISBN 978-0-9691548-2-2 (paperback)

1. Canada. Royal Canadian Navy. 2. Destroyers (Warships)--Canada--History--20th century. I. Title.

V825.5.C3C38 2017   359.3'2540971   C2016-904243-X

DEDICATION

To all Canadian destroyer crews, at sea, onshore and in greener pastures.

"On Patrol"

Out on the deep when the waves roll high,
When storm clouds scurry o'er sombre sky,
Plunging and rolling this way and that,
Scanning the seas for periscope's cap.

Steaming along when folks are at rest,
Scorning each danger with many a jest,
Searching for mine or submarine's lair.
By darkest night and the noonday glare.

Patrolling our beat on trembling keel,
With cheerful hearts and our nerves like steel,
Raging storm or foe — fear there is none;
Our duty's clear and it SHALL BE DONE.

We dream of our loved ones so far away,
'Tis them we're guarding each night and day,
Our glorious Empire to Britons dear,
Her honour's at stake, we'll show no fear.

We'll stick to our task till Vic'trys won,
Bring to his knees the treacherous hun,
Singing songs of the free and the Brave;
Britannia ever shall rule the wave.

Bertrand L. Twinn / 1916

CONTENTS

	Acknowledgments	i
	Foreword	iii
	Introduction	1
	Prologue: HMCS Grilse	8
1	The Early Years	14
2	The First Rivers	24
3	Towns from America	56
4	Later Rivers	80
5	Tribes of all Types	118
6	The Early Cadillacs	169
7	The Late Cadillacs	223
8	A New Tribe	249
9	Capabilities for the Future?	281
	Afterword: Lost and Gained	293
	Bibliography	297
	Index	314

ACKNOWLEDGMENTS

A book like this exists only because of the yeoman-like works of those authors, historians and archivists who have come before.

The books of Ken MacPherson, W.A.B. Douglas, Fraser McKee, Ron Barrie, Thomas G. Lynch, Richard Gimblett and James B. Lamb amongst many others have provided a foundation and inspiration for this volume. Many of these names will be familiar to those interested in Canadian Naval History—and if not, the bibliography can be used as a jumping off point for new readers of the genre. Other authors like Norman Freidman, Peter Hodges, Alan Raven, and Al Ross are also must-reads for any with interest in the ways of the world's navies—they certainly were for me.

Residing in Calgary has given me the fantastic opportunity to access records and artifacts through the Naval Museum of Alberta, including access to the Ken MacPherson photo collection. To the wonderful staff there—specifically to Brad Froggatt and Jason Nisenson, many thanks. Also thanks to Dennis McKay for giving me a 'lower deck' view of the RCN and Doug Bourne and Malcolm Butler for their added historical insights and generous praise.

Much of the final chapters of this book would have been impossible to put together without the assistance of Vice-Admiral Ron Lloyd and his staff—Commander Scott Robinson especially. Thank you again for your help.

I would also be remiss if I didn't thank my parents for their continued support, assistance and—most importantly—their example of how to get published.

Finally a heartfelt thank you (and much love) to my daughter Rhane, who has had the patience to tolerate her father's book writing—while baking cherry pies behind his back! It's only downhill from here sweetheart.

HMCS *St. Croix (I)* as built by the author.

FOREWORD

It is a real honour and privilege to have the opportunity to introduce *Tin-Can Canucks: A Century of Canadian Destroyers*. I need to begin by thanking Sean Campbell for dedicating his time, energy and effort to chronicle the individual histories of the 60-plus 'tin-can' destroyer-type warships that have served in the Royal Canadian Navy since our inception on 4 May 1910. The RCN has a rich institutional history of service to our country during times of crisis and conflict, but few Canadians are aware of the tremendous sacrifice of their sailors who have dedicated their lives in the service of their nation at sea. Sean's work is therefore a valuable contribution to better educate Canadians on an aspect of their history that they may not fully appreciate or be aware of.

Although the RCN has employed many ship-types, ranging from aircraft carriers and cruisers to frigates, corvettes and submarines, the history of the RCN is very much that of a destroyer Navy. From humble beginnings during the First World War with the converted steam-turbine yacht HMCS *Grilse* through to the present day, when HMCS *Athabaskan*— the last of the so-called 'Sisters of the Space Age'—has just recently been paid off, the core of the Canadian fleet always has been its destroyer force. Indeed, I was the Navigating Officer of her sister *Iroquois*, and I venture it would be difficult to find a sailor who joined before 1995 (when the *Halifax*-class frigates became the mainstay of the fleet) who had not served in a destroyer at some point in their career.

With that, it is clear from Sean's engaging text that the notion of what constitutes a 'destroyer' has evolved significantly over the century. From the 205-foot, 290-ton *Grilse* armed with two 12-pounder guns and a single 14-inch anti-ship torpedo tube, we see *Athabaskan* at more than twice that length (426 ft.) and fifteen times the displacement (4500 tons), armed with 29 vertically-launched SM-2MR Standard Missiles having a range in excess of 100 miles, carrying two of the venerable Sea King anti-submarine helicopters, and fitted to embark a flagship staff to command a multinational task force. The Canadian Surface Combatant shipbuilding program is aimed to incorporate many of the next generation of destroyer capabilities such as command and control, long range air defence, and robust anti-submarine warfare capabilities.

As Sean follows the RCN's history through the lens of our destroyers, he casts a light on many issues that are as relevant today as they were a hundred years ago. This is most aptly captured in the poem "On Patrol" penned late in 1916 by Canadian sailor Bertrand Twinn and reproduced on the dedication page to this book, about the mission of HMCS *Grilse*, every stanza of which is equally pertinent today (aside from the references to "Empire" and the "hun"). The leadership of the RCN, past and present, fully appreciate that our ships are large steel hulls, extremely complex and capable large steel hulls, but lifeless nevertheless. The true measure of a ship is really determined by the quality of its ship's company. "On Patrol" very much captures the timeless spirit of perseverance of the Canadian Sailor that is equally applicable over a century later.

Vice-Admiral M.F.R. Lloyd
Commander, Royal Canadian Navy
Ottawa, March 2017

INTRODUCTION
TIN-CANS[1] OF THE RCN

The story of the Canadian Destroyer begins with the convergence of two separate—and in their own way revolutionary—ideas: the self-propelled or locomotive torpedo, and the Naval Service of Canada.

Robert Whitehead was an Englishman working in Fiume (now Rijeka, Croatia) for the Austro-Hungarians in 1866, when he perfected a design by KuK Naval Officer Giovanni Luppis for a self-propelled torpedo. Whitehead's innovation was the development of a means to keep the torpedo running at a standard depth, ensuring it wouldn't crash-dive to the depths or wallow on the surface.

With the invention of a reliable locomotive torpedo it was immediately seen that the balance of power could easily shift from big-gun armored ships, to small, torpedo-carrying boats. Suddenly the mouse could kill the elephant—and at little cost.

---

[1] The destroyer, that ubiquitous 'tin-can' of the navy shares something of its name's history with Canada—the original Torpedo Boat Destroyer was of British origin, while using the term 'tin-can' for such ships was coined by the Americans during the two world wars. Founded by the British and influenced by the Americans—there's nothing more Canadian than that!

The first torpedo boat—HMS *Lightning*—was designed and built by a young marine engineer named John Isaac Thornycroft in 1876. His shipyard would become a familiar name for any interested in the origin of Canadian destroyers—but that would be decades in the future. Thornycroft's yard would build dozens of torpedo boats for the Royal Navy between 1876 and 1900. The most impressive being the 1st Class torpedo boat designed to steam on their own (rather than be launched from a mothership) and with a fair turn of speed, these boats haunted the nightmares of big-ship officers in nearly every navy. When the Royal Navy decided it needed something to catch or destroy such torpedo boats (as piloted by the French, Russians or Germans) they turned to Thornycroft and his chief rival Alfred Yarrow. These two shipyards would subsequently vie for Admiralty destroyer orders for over 85 years[2].

The first Torpedo Boat Destroyers (also known as TBDs, but eventually shortened to just 'destroyer') were launched in 1894 (two from Thornycroft, *Daring* and *Decoy*; two from Yarrow, *Havock* and *Hornet* and a final two from Laid, *Ferret* and *Lynx*) and were not much more than enlarged 1st class torpedo boats. Coal-powered, short-ranged and lightly armed (with between 1 and 3 torpedoes, plus small caliber guns) their size and strength belied the utility they would eventually have to the navies they served.

Within a decade, these early coal-powered, turtle-backed ships of under 350 tons had evolved to the 36-member River-class destroyers of over 550 tons which had proper forecastles to keep the seas in poor weather. Early Parson steam turbines were tried in some of these destroyers, and in 1907 the first of

---

[2] Both were merged with other British shipbuilders in 1977. Eventually, after privatization and industry consolidation Yarrow became part of BAE Surface Ships (who designed and built the latest British Destroyer, the Type 45), while Thornycroft was bought out by Vosper to eventually form the VT Group before merging with Babcock International in 2010.

the Tribal-class destroyers were ordered. These ships mated oil-fueled steam turbines to hulls displacing nearly (and in some cases over) 1,000 tons and with a speed of 33 knots.[3]

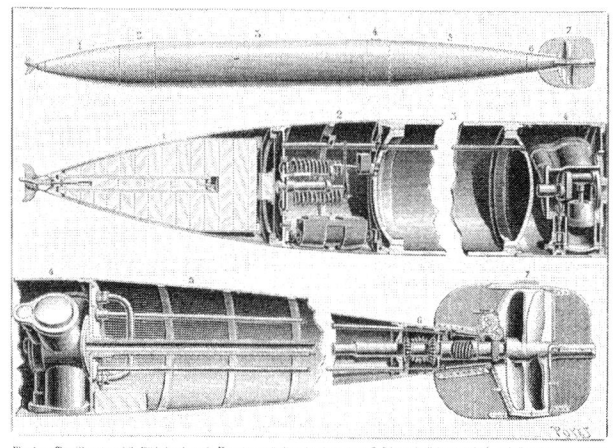

Whitehead torpedo mechanism
Mécanisme d'une torpille Whitehead
Louis Poyet; Revue "La Nature", 5 December 1891

These new types of TBDs were part of the Royal Navy's 'Fisher Revolution' which also saw the advent of the all-big-gun battleship HMS *Dreadnought* and the Battlecruiser. During that decade, Canada would see its own naval revolution.

In 1910 Sir Wilfred Laurier, the Prime Minister, and his governing Liberals, passed the Naval Service Bill which would establish the Naval Service of Canada. The intent was for the NSC to be a distinct naval force, used to protect the Dominion of Canada, but also to be placed under British control should the need arise. Robert Borden and his opposition

---

[3] (Smith, 1971) p. 22-106. These early River- and Tribal-class destroyers shouldn't be confused with the later British and Canadian classes of the same name as they predated those World War Two vintage destroyers by some 40 years.

Conservatives were very much against this approach—they felt that Canadian maritime interests were best served by funding construction of a Dreadnought-type battleship for the RN.

The Naval Service of Canada
CWM 19940001-980
Canadian War Museum

Regardless, the passage of the Naval Service Bill meant that Canada now had a Navy, and that meant the need for suitable ships and sailors to crew them. The man who would lead this infant navy was Rear-Admiral (later Sir) Charles Kingsmill, who had headed up the Marine Service of the Department of Marine and Fisheries after he retired from the Royal Navy in 1909. The Admiral was well acquainted with British warships large and small, with his first sea-command being the composite gunboat HMS *Goldfinch* and his last being the pre-dreadnought HMS *Dominion*. At the time he became Director of the Naval Service he was 55 years old.

Canada's fleet at the outset was quite small and it didn't take long for the Navy to start looking at destroyers—the Admiralty notes Canadian interest in purchasing several of the repeat *Acorn*-class destroyers which were on order for the 1910-1911 naval estimates[4]. Sadly, politics intervened.

The 1911 Federal election saw Laurier and his Liberals swept from office by Robert Borden and his Conservatives. The man who became Canada's 8th prime minister had been a vocal opponent to a Canadian Naval Service—indeed he had worked to block both the Naval Service Act and campaign for a Canadian contribution towards the construction of a Dreadnaught Battleship as the Dominion's naval contribution to the British Empire's protection (Australia and New Zealand had both taken a similar route). Now in power, Borden discovered the same challenges that had stymied Laurier's desire to build a Navy[5]—a Navy which was now in existence and which he could not dissolve without looking as if he was electing to open Canada's coasts to attack.

In the end, Canada's Naval Service would spend the next several years existing on a razor's edge—never quite sure of its support from either the government or the Canadian people. At the same time, support from the British Admiralty would shift depending on the Admiralty's (lack of) policies around defense of the Empire. Between its formation and World War One, the Canadian Naval Service would consist of the cruisers HMCS *Rainbow* and HMCS *Niobe*; a pair of former Royal Navy sloops, *Algerine* and *Shearwater*; the fisheries protection and customs' ships HMCS *Canada*, HMCS *Constance*, HMCS *Curlew;* and a handful of smaller vessels. One of the last acquisitions prior to the outbreak of war was HMCS *Margaret*—an armed

---

[4] (Friedman, British Destroyers: From Earliest Days to the Second World War, 2009) p. 123 These ships were also known as the *Acheron*-class or the I-Class (1911). During World War One, one of these destroyers, HMS *Ariel*, saw action at Heligoland Bight, Dogger Bank, and Jutland and famously rammed and sank U-12 in March of 1915.

[5] For more detail on the origin and struggles of the nascent RCN, see "The Naval Debates, 1909-1914" in (Johnston, Rawling, Gimblett, & MacFarlane, 2011)

customs cruiser designed and built by Thornycroft's Woolston yard for the Canadian government which, in addition to a pair of quick-firing guns, had a bow specially shaped and reinforced for ramming opposing vessels.[6]

For all of that, the Canadian vessels were lightly armed and the two cruisers were obsolete and ill-equipped to meet even token attacking forces. Add to that a shortage of crew, torpedoes and other essentials for a fighting vessel, and it became clear that the Canadian navy was a long way from being a full-spectrum fighting force—even protecting Canada's coasts and naval facilities like Halifax proved to be challenging for a Naval Service poorly supported by its Government.[7]

Thus on the eve of the Great War, Canada had little in the way of defense against surface raiders, and even less to protect her from submarines[8]. What the Royal Canadian Navy did have however, was an unwavering belief in the British Empire (and Canada's place in it) and the righteousness of its cause. Led by Admiral Kingsmill, they would be ready to take on the enemy however he appeared in Canadian waters. It would be this esprit de corps that would sustain them through the hard lying ahead—and they knew it.

---

[6] (Barnaby, 1964) p. 60

[7] (Hadley & Sarty, 1991) p. 74

[8] The closest thing to an ASW force that Canada had were two ex-Chilean submarines purchased in Seattle by the Premier of British Columbia and smuggled to Esquimalt just days before hostilities erupted. These were subsequently acquired by the Canadian Government for the Naval Service.

TIN CAN CANUCKS

A quote from wartime poet and sailor Bertrand L. Twinn's[9] 1916 poem (published in a 1916 HMCS *Grilse* greeting card), "On Patrol" sums up their fierce dedication to Canada—and the Empire:

We dream of our loved ones so far away,
'Tis them we're guarding each night and day,
Our glorious Empire to Britons dear,
Her honour's at stake, we'll show no fear.

---

[9] ("On Patrol" rare HMCS Grilse 1916 poem, 2016) Bertrand Lawrence Twinn was born in 1887 near London, England. During World War One he served as a clerk for the Royal Canadian Navy—having previously served with the Royal Navy before emigrating to Canada sometime before the war. He also authored an ode to HMCS *Grilse*, called "The Assassin by Night (Ode to the *Grilse*)" reproduced in this book's end papers.

PROLOGUE
HMCS GRILSE

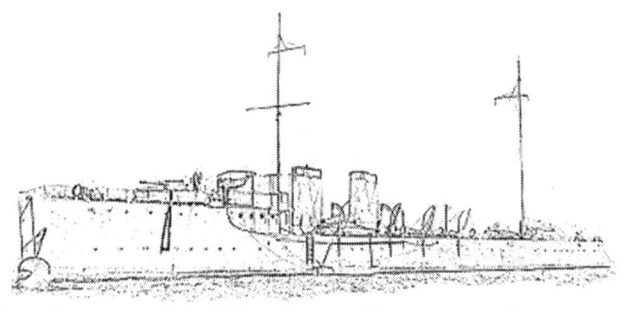

Length[1]:	205'[2]	Laid Down:	1912
Beam:	18' 6"	Launched:	15-05-1912[2]
Draft:	9.2'	Commissioned[3]:	15-07-1915
Displacement:	287 tons	Paid Off:	10-12-1918
Armament:	2 × 12pdr LA guns; one 14" Torpedo Tube		

Only five years old, facing the prospect of German U-boats in

---

[1] All specifications are per (MacPherson & Barrie, Ships of Canada's Naval Forces: 1910-2002, 2004) unless otherwise noted

[2] (The Turbine Driven Yacht Winchester, 1912)

[3] All commissioning dates are the date commissioned into the Royal Canadian Navy

Canadian waters—and without destroyers for protection—the RCN set about acquiring private yachts for use as patrol and escort vessels. One of these was a 202-foot steam turbine yacht by the name of *Winchester*. To avoid running up against the Americans' neutrality, several Canadian yacht owners privately purchased boats from Americans and then traded them to the RCN. This is the manner in which *Grisle* came to fly the white ensign in 1915.

SY *Winchester* was one of a family of fast steam yachts used for commuting by P.W. Rouss. She was designed by Cox & Stevens and built by Yarrow along the sleek torpedo boat destroyer lines—which in conjunction with her Parson's steam turbines could drive her up to 34 knots in good weather.

In an odd quirk of fate, Mr. Rouss commissioned the construction of another yacht named *Winchester* (the fourth), only to have it pressed into service with the US Navy in 1917—and she would later see wartime service with the Canadian Navy in 1940 as HMCS *Renard*[4]. In all, three of the four *Winchesters* owned by Rouss would see military service with various navies at least once in their life.

Although not a destroyer in the truest sense, having been designated a Torpedo Boat, she was tasked with many of the same escort and patrol duties in Canadian waters as Royal Navy torpedo boat destroyers (those of an earlier vintage than the frontline fleet's destroyers represented by the M and R classes[5]). In that respect, she could be seen as the precursor of the navy's destroyer force.

She arrived in Canada and was commissioned the middle of July 1915. After arriving at the Canadian Vickers shipyard in

---

[4] HMCS *Renard* herself had an interesting career and unusual fate—she was to become an electrical generator for a Cape Breton coal mine after WW2, but instead sank at her moorings in 1949; See (McKee, The Armed Yachts of Canada, 1983)

[5] (Friedman, British Destroyers: From Earliest Days to the Second World War, 2009) p. 129

Montreal, she was converted from a luxury yacht to a torpedo boat by the addition of a pair of 12-pounder (3-inch) quick-firing guns and a 14-inch torpedo tube (located aft in place of the former salon/deckhouse). Additionally, care was taken to remove the ship's fine china and other luxury items, keeping them safely ashore—although the wood fittings and other decor remained, leaving one to wonder how difficult life aboard the ship was in good weather![6]

Although she saw no U-boat during the war, *Grilse* was much in demand as an escort for convoy's arriving and departing Halifax (a major Royal Navy base at the time). By October of 1915 she was patrolling off Cape Breton where she hunted for a reported U-boat in and around Little Bras d'Or Bridge and took part in an abortive U-boat trap off Cape Dauphine. In the winter of 1915-1916 *Grilse* was loaned to the British Commander-in-Chief North America and West Indies station based in Bermuda. She would spend her time in the Caribbean undertaking anti-submarine patrols out of Jamaica. Her trip south was complicated by her high fuel consumption (3000 gallons—over 11,000 litres—of fuel oil a day at cruising speed) which left her almost out of oil 150 nautical miles out of Bermuda. She had used more than 13,000 gallons of fuel oil in her passage, leaving *Grilse* to be towed in to Ireland Island Bermuda by the cruiser HMS *Cumberland*. After several quiet months in fine weather she returned to Canada—again short of fuel and needing to be towed into port.

Her patrols off Cape Breton during 1916 once more showed her lack of fuel economy and so she was pulled from her posting at Sydney, Nova Scotia, to report back to Halifax where she would be reserved for escorting important vessels into and out of the port—with the stipulation that she couldn't exceed 13 knots, as a means of limiting her oil consumption.

---

[6] And conversely, how damaging the splinters from such fittings would be under shellfire.

Once again she was loaned to the Royal Navy for the winter, and setting out for Bermuda with extra barrels (some 2,000 gallons) of oil lashed to her upper deck, *Grilse* departed Halifax December 11th, 1916. She would never complete her passage to the Caribbean. Running into a gale near Sable Island, the former yacht nearly foundered as she was repeatedly swept by green seas. The oil barrels were jettisoned, but several crew members were lost when they were washed overboard. These included one of the signalmen who was attempting to repair the radio antenna damaged by the gale. Later, when one of the engine room skylights was smashed open, the sea poured in—some four feet of water being shipped into the engine room, giving the vessel a 20° list to starboard. Through dogged determination, a long night of bailing, and not a little luck *Grilse* made it into Shelburne, Nova Scotia on December 14th, with little left in the way of freeboard. In addition to the men washed overboard she had lost 3 lifeboats and a torpedo reload (including the warhead but excluding the gyro[7]).

Refitted and back to sea by May 10th, 1917 she returned to her anti-submarine patrol work, but thankfully would see no further calamities. She was likely laid up during the winter of 1917-1918 with a caretaker crew (her thin steel hull wouldn't have fared well against thick maritime ice).

Grilse's one chance to hunt a U-boat came in August 1918 when U-156 torpedoed the tanker *Luz Blanca*, 35 miles south of the Sambro lightship. When word reached Halifax it was clear a fast torpedo boat like *Grilse* was needed—however as she was in dock for repairs her replacement on the harbour entrance patrol, the American torpedo boat USS *Tigley* was dispatched. Despite a dogged search for the submarine, U-156 escaped. Later the same month—once she was out of dockyard hands—*Grilse* was ordered to test Halifax's shore

---

[7] (McKee, The Armed Yachts of Canada, 1983) p. 39

defenses. The night of August 19th she quietly sailed past the picket boats and army forts. In passing undetected she showed just how vulnerable the harbour was to German submarines.[8]

The next month U-155—the former merchant submarine *Deutschland*—arrived off Halifax and laid eight mines near the Sambro light vessel and another six southeast of Peggy's Cove, Nova Scotia on September 17th. One of these broke free of its mooring and was discovered by *Grilse* and her crew on the 18th. It was promptly destroyed by gunfire—one of the few times *Grilse* would have fired a shot in anger. Regardless, the armed yacht's war was winding down.[9]

By the Armistice *Grilse* saw little use—her thirsty machinery and overall fragility had made her very expensive for upkeep and for the limited local patrols which she had been undertaking. Subsequently she was paid off and an attempt was made to sell her. An initial offer was received from John Simon of Pictou for $1,025, but the Captain of Halifax Dockyard thought it "too absurd for consideration." *Grilse* was still with the navy when the 'true' destroyers *Patriot* and *Patrician* joined the ranks of Canada's naval vessels in 1920.

Grilse was sold to Solomon Guggenheim in 1922, for $25,000. Upon receipt of the vessel he had her towed to the United States and fitted out as a fast luxury yacht once more. Renaming the yacht *Trillola*—the same as his estate on Long Island Sound—Guggenheim took her around to major yachting events in the area until 1938. On September 21st of that year she foundered while secured alongside his jetty in Roslyn, Long Island Sound during a hurricane. Guggenheim was apparently in the process of trying to sell her, and so was delighted that he could now collect insurance money on the former Canadian torpedo boat.

Eventually the US Coast Guard demanded that

---

[8] (Hadley & Sarty, 1991) p. 256 & 264

[9] (Sarty, 1988) p. 122

Guggenheim remove her from where she lay and he turned her over to a local salvage firm for no cost. *Grilse* was still on the yacht register as late as October 1941. By then the former *Winchester*, ex-*Grilse*, ex-*Trillola* had been raised and scrapped.[10]

---

[10] (McKee, The Armed Yachts of Canada, 1983) p. 40

1

THE EARLY YEARS
AFTER THE GREAT WAR

In the years after the end of the Great War, the Royal Canadian Navy faced an existential threat brought about by the three-fold problems of anti-war sentiment, growing governmental financial constraints, and a poor public image—the latter helped neither by the Halifax explosion nor the Army's high profile '100 days' offensive, both coming at the close of the war.

Here the Navy found itself at first with too many ships and not enough crew—for the Royal Navy had gifted Canada with two destroyers, a light cruiser and a pair of submarines, after hostilities ended; at the same time as the RCN was demobilizing. Shortly after however, the Navy faced an even more insoluble problem—too little money to keep even the crew and ships they had.

The Canadian navy was founded when the Naval Service Bill of 1910 received royal assent on May 4th, 1910, and received its Royal designation from King George V on August 29th, 1911. Yet it took Canada ten years before a destroyer was given the appellation HMCS. The first—*Patriot* and *Patrician*—were a gift to the Dominion from England after the first world war, and along with the cruiser HMCS *Aurora*, replaced the elderly HMCS *Rainbow* and HMCS *Niobe*, which had been the bulk of the Canadian fleet to that time. Sadly, depression-era budget cuts saw *Aurora* paid off and scrapped, leaving *Patriot* and *Patrician* the only warships in Canadian service until the purchase of HMCS *Vancouver* (ex-HMS *Torbay*) and HMCS *Champlain* (ex-HMS *Toreador*) in 1934. These then replaced the elderly *Patriot* and *Patrician* and would serve as the destroyer force while Canada's first new-built destroyers were constructed in England.

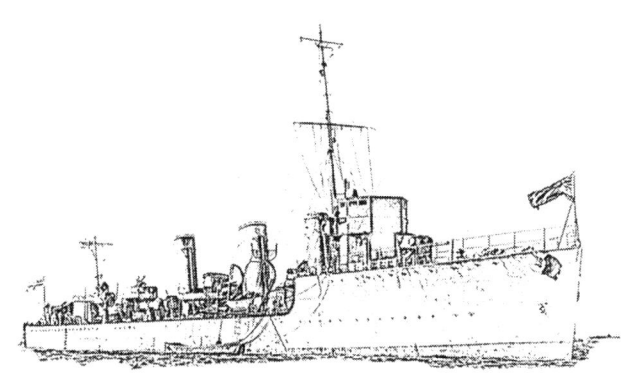

HMCS Patriot (Thornycroft M-class)

Length:	274'	Laid Down:	07-1915
Beam:	27' 6"	Launched:	20-04-1916
Draft:	10' 6"	Commissioned:	01-11-1920
Displacement:	1004 tons	Paid Off:	21-10-1927

Armament: 3 x 4" LA guns, four 21" torpedo tubes, 2 x 2pdr AA guns

Patriot, like her sister *Patrician*, was a WW1 vintage destroyer of the M class. Unlike other M-class destroyers they were not built to Admiralty specification, but instead were 'specials' ordered from Thornycroft[1] to the company's own design.

Both destroyers saw service during the Great War—*Patriot*

---

[1] It's interesting to note that Thornycroft ship-builders appear rather often in the history of Canadian destroyers—fully 20% of all Canadian ships of that type were built by the firm

having sunk the U-boat U-69 in July 1917 after an observer aloft in the destroyer's kite balloon saw the submarine at some 28 miles. *Patriot* had served with the 14th Destroyer Flotilla of the Grand Fleet, and by 1920 she and *Patrician* were in need of reconditioning before being gifted to Canada. The cost to make *Patriot* seaworthy was estimated at £6,105 with the work taking an estimated four weeks. More extensive work to bring *Patriot* to full fighting efficiency would take £7,321 and five weeks in dockyard hands. This second option was selected for both destroyers.[2]

The two destroyers would be fitted with an oil-fired galley (to replace the former coal-fired unit and its need for coal), an enclosed bridge to protect those conning the ship from the Canadian weather, and an electric motor launch for harbor use. Steam heat would not be provided as of yet—electrical radiation being used instead[3]. *Patriot* and *Patrician* were commissioned into the Royal Canadian Navy—along with the cruiser HMCS *Aurora*—on November 1, 1920 at Devonport.

Surveyed in January 1921—the year after commissioning in the RCN—both destroyers appeared in good shape, although it was obvious that *Patriot's* regular maintenance had been somewhat neglected as she wasn't as well off as her sister. Regardless she was "...in all respects stable and seaworthy."[4]

In August 1921 both *Patriot* and her sister took part in a training exercises designed to test Halifax harbor defenses. *Patriot* was on the opposing force and was directed to attempt to enter the harbor through a 'ruse de gurre'—that of pretending to be a member of the defending forces needing urgent repair. While she fooled the port war signal station at Camperdown, she was intercepted by an inspection vessel

---

[2] (Schleihauf, Summer 2000)

[3] (Johnston, Rawling, Gimblett, & MacFarlane, 2011) p. 755

[4] (Schleihauf, Summer 2000)

which alerted the shore batteries—who subsequently 'shelled' and 'sank' *Patriot* with blanks.

September of 1921 saw *Patriot* used to tow Alexander Graham Bell's hydrofoil HD-4 on Bras d'or Lakes—a feat later commemorated by the commissioning of the Canadian Force's experimental hydrofoil HMCS *Bras d'Or* in 1972.

After Bell's death, *Patriot*'s then Commanding Officer[5] (CO) Lieutenant H.E. Reid remained in contact with F.W. Baldwin who continued Bell's Hydrofoil work[6]. Baldwin's subsequent model was designed as a high-speed gunnery target. Even after Lt. Reid's *Patriot* scored 60 4" gunfire hits, it was still in operational condition. Baldwin's targets would see heavy use by the Navy during the Second World War, as the RCN's exponential growth nearly overwhelmed available training resources.

Patriot was assigned to the east coast—based out of Halifax—and was the only operation naval vessel on that coast after the budget cuts of 1922. She would spend most of her time training new naval recruits and members of the Royal Canadian Naval Volunteer Reserve (the so-called 'wavy navy')

By the late 1920s *Patriot* and *Patrician* were coming to the end of their useful lives and *Patriot* was decommissioned in 1927. She would be sold for £3,110 to Thomas W. Ward Ltd. in 1929 for breaking up.[7]

---

[5] To reduce the confusion between the ranks of Captain or Commander and the position of Captain as commander of a vessel I have elected to use the term Commanding Officer or CO rather than the other terms.

[6] (Vice-Admiral H. E. Reid Dead, 1962)

[7] (Schleihauf, Summer 2000)

HMCS Patrician (Thornycroft M-class)

Length:	274'	Laid Down:	06-1915
Beam:	27' 6"	Launched:	5-06-1916
Draft:	10' 6"	Commissioned:	01-11-1920
Displacement:	1004 tons	Paid Off:	01-1928

Armament: 3 x 4" LA guns, four 21" torpedo tubes, 2 x 2pdr AA guns

Like *Patriot*, HMCS *Patrician* had served with the Grand Fleet during the Great War but as a member of the 13th Destroyer Flotilla rather than the 14th. Not as successful a hunter as *Patriot*, she appeared to be in better shape as her refit prior to transfer to the RCN cost only £6,610. An additional £887 per destroyer was required in September of 1920 to fit them with a complete set of awnings and other equipment suitable for their winter training cruises to Bermuda. She and her sister commissioned in Devonport the 1st of November 1920.

During her 1921 survey she was adjudged in better shape than her sister, and was found to be more economical in fuel consumption—getting 9 miles per ton of fuel while steaming at 11 knots; a mile more per ton than *Patriot*.[8]

After the naval budget cuts of 1922, *Patriot* and *Patrician* were the only sea-going warships in the RCN. *Patrician* was ordered to the west coast in 1922, and like her sister she spent

---

[8] (Schleihauf, Summer 2000)

nearly 5 years training officers and men of the naval reserve.

On 12 December 1924, she was sent to patrol for and intercept a group of bank thieves who had robbed a bank in Canada and were attempting to escape by boat to the United States. The search was ultimately unsuccessful.

In the spring of 1927 *Patrician* took part in a different sort of interdiction mission. The destroyer would undertake patrols on the west coast for halibut poachers—Canadian or American registered vessels which were fishing halibut out of season. In a similar vein the ship sent an armed landing party to search for a seal poacher thought to be operating around Aristazabel Island.[9]

Similar to *Patriot*, *Patrician* was worn out by the end of 1927 and no longer of economical use. She was decommissioned and eventually sold for breaking in 1929. Unlike her sister who was broken up in Wales, *Patrician* would face the scraper's torch where she had spent her last few years—British Columbia[10].

---

[9] (Johnston, Rawling, Gimblett, & MacFarlane, 2011) p. 832

[10] Part of this first Canadian destroyer still survives; HMCS *Patrician*'s wheel is currently on display at the Naval Museum of Alberta, in Calgary.

HMCS Vancouver (Thornycroft S-class)

Length:	276'	Laid Down:	11-1917
Beam:	27' 6"	Launched:	07-12-1918
Draft:	10' 6"	Commissioned:	01-03-1928
Displacement:	1087 tons	Paid Off:	25-11-1936

Armament: 3 x 4" LA guns, four 21" torpedo tubes, 1 x 2pdr AA gun

In November of 1927 the Canadian Government announced its intention to order a pair of modern destroyers from England. These ships (*Saguenay* and *Skeena*—see Chapter Two) would take some time to design and construct, and so the RCN elected to lease a pair of Great War vintage destroyers to cover the time between the decommissioning of *Patriot* and *Patrician* and the commissioning of *Saguenay* and *Skeena*.

HMCS *Vancouver* had served in the Royal Navy as HMS *Toreador*. She was one of the S-Class, a small destroyer designed late in the war. Like *Patriot* and *Patrician* the two S-class destroyers were 'Specials'; built to a slightly different design by Thornycroft. They were descendants of the earlier M-Class (like *Patriot* and *Patrician*) and were quite similar in many ways, but were visually distinguished by having two rather than three funnels and a raised platform for the forecastle 4-inch gun.

In Canadian service she was named for explorer George Vancouver (1757-1798)—like her sister *Champlain* she was one of the first ships with names associated with Canada. *Vancouver* was based in Esquimalt and she took over *Patrician*'s training and patrol duties; continuing even after *Saguenay* and *Skeena* were commissioned.

TIN CAN CANUCKS

In 1931 Canada was asked by the British Foreign Office to send a naval vessel to El Salvador to show the flag and protect British interests during the post-coup tensions and the La Mantza peasant uprising and ensuing military crackdown. *Vancouver* and *Skeena* were dispatched to two different ports, with *Vancouver* arriving at Port La Union in January 1932. Although she was ordered to land an armed party by the British Charge d'Affairs, no such party was landed—the order being countermanded by Commander (D). By January 25 she had moved to Acajutla, a tiny village that was the terminus of the British-owned railway connecting to San Salvador. Both destroyers would depart at the end of the month, while the military junta would maintain control of El Salvador for another 60 years.

By 1935 the two S-class ships were in poor shape; a 1934 naval engineer survey indicated that of the two destroyers would need a refit costing over $80,000 each—with another $50,000 to make them fit for a North Atlantic crossing to return them to England. Ultimately the British—who had no interest in retaining the ships as operational units and feared for the safety of their crews should they be sailed home—agreed that the *Vancouver* and *Champlain* could be scrapped in Canada with their guns and other military supplies turned over to the RCN.[11]

Vancouver was decommissioned in November of 1936, and broken up the next year.

---

[11] (Johnston, Rawling, Gimblett, & MacFarlane, 2011) p. 946

HMCS Champlain (Thornycroft S-class)

Length:	276'	Laid Down:	11-1917
Beam:	27' 6"	Launched:	06-03-1919
Draft:	10' 6"	Commissioned:	01-03-1928
Displacement:	1087 tons	Paid Off:	25-11-1936

Armament: 3 x 4" LA guns, four 21" torpedo tubes, 1 x 2pdr AA gun

HMCS *Champlain* was a Thornycroft S-Class destroyer like HMCS *Vancouver* and, like her sister, wasn't launched before the Great War ended. Commissioned as HMS *Torbay* and placed in reserve in 1920, this destroyer was selected to join the RCN while *Skeena* and *Saguenay* were being built. Named for Samuel de Champlain (1574-1635) HMCS *Champlain* was commissioned into Canadian service in 1928 and based out of Halifax as the east coast destroyer.

Beginning in 1929 *Champlain* and *Vancouver* began participating in a winter peacetime cruise to the Caribbean Sea. This tradition would continue through to the outbreak of the Second World War and would include other destroyers as the Royal Canadian Navy expanded.

In January 1931, en route to the Caribbean, *Champlain* ran into a gale which required her to reduce speed to the minimum to maintain steerage—according to the revolution counters this was 8 knots, but the ship was moving only about 4 knots through the raging waters. Three days later *Champlain* arrived in St. David's having—like *Grilse* twelve years before—lost her rigging and deck fittings and with severe damage to boats and bridge. Luckily there were no casualties.

The following year, while in Trinidad, *Champlain*'s Gunner (Torpedo) responded to a disturbance related to the Danish ship MS *Stensby*. Apparently the *Stensby*'s chief tally clerk had been distributing food to the locals through an open porthole. The ship's Chief Officer responded by brandishing his revolver and in the ensuing incident two men were injured. Responding to *Stensby*'s siren, the party from *Champlain* arrived on the scene and sentries were posted at the gangway with orders to ensure nobody left the *Stensby* until local police arrived to take maters in hand[12].

In August 1934 *Champlain* took part in the Jacques Cartier Quartercentenary at Gaspe; she was joined by HMCS *Saguenay*, at the time the other east coast destroyer.

It wasn't cheap to run destroyers and in the interwar years the RCN faced many budgetary challenges and upkeep costs never seemed to go down. *Champlain* on her own had gone from costing almost $70,000 per year in 1928 to peak at nearly $220,000 per year in 1931. The newer destroyers would cost almost $390,000 per year each by the late 1930s, just to stay operational[13].

By that time *Champlain* and her sister were deemed too worn for further service and in no shape for an Atlantic crossing. She would be decommissioned in November 1936 and broken up in 1937. The ship's armament was removed and stored for future use, when war—already on the horizon—broke out.

Champlain and *Vancouver* were completed too late for the previous war, and decommissioned and scrapped before the next, but they had had their part to play. The training they had provided would form the nucleus of a larger RCN in World War Two.

---

[12] (Johnston, Rawling, Gimblett, & MacFarlane, 2011) p. 900

[13] Ibid. p. 948

2

THE FIRST RIVERS
PREPARING FOR WAR

By the late 1920s the Royal Canadian Navy was in a better position financially, and while the regular navy was small, the RCNVR system was well on its way to developing the reserve forces the navy would need with the advent of war.

One of the promising signs of this newly-renewed RCN was the order of two destroyers from Thornycroft based on the then-current Admiralty A-class, with some modifications to support service in northern climes.

HMCS *Skeena* and *Saguenay* also marked a departure in the naming of Canadian destroyers. Part of the Navy's goal with the RCNVR system was to make the navy more visible in Canada's various provinces and cities, as a way of instilling better understanding amongst Canadians as to the Navy's duties and values; and to foster a pride in the service the Navy and her sailors rendered to the country.

In a similar manner, there was a conscious choice by the RCN to name the next generation of Canadian destroyers after regional rivers across Canada. Thus *Skeena* would be named for the Skeena River, which is the second longest river entirely within British Columbia. *Saguenay* would then be named for the Rivière Saguenay in Quebec, which runs from Lac St. Jean to the St Lawrence River.

These two destroyers would be the first ships specifically built for the Royal Canadian Navy, with HMCS *Skeena* assigned to the East Coast and HMCS *Saguenay* to the west, once commissioned in 1931.

Although neither of these first two River-class destroyers survived to see the end of the conflict, HMCS *Saguenay* and HMCS *Skeena* paved the way for an expanded Canadian destroyer force and laid the groundwork for traditions still in practice today. The 'Rolls-Royce Destroyers' showed that Canada's Navy understood the value of quality over quantity. The investment made in these destroyers would be echoed decades after they were gone, in the development of the 'Cadillac of Destroyers' (the *St. Laurent*-class and successors) and the later 280-class destroyers, the last of which, HMCS *Athabaskan* is still in service today. It wouldn't be the last time the world looked upon Canadian destroyers and saw the very best of the breed.

HMCS Saguenay (River-class)

Length:	320'	Laid Down:	27-09-1929
Beam:	32' 6"	Launched:	11-07-1930
Draft:	10'	Commissioned:	22-05-1931
Displacement:	1337 tons	Paid Off:	30-07-1945

Armament: 4 x 4.7" LA guns, eight 21" torpedo tubes, 2 x 2pdr AA guns

As noted before, in November 1927, the Canadian Government announced its intention to purchase two new destroyers to be built to Canadian specification in the United Kingdom. In February of 1928 two Canadian officers reviewed the plans for the new British *Acasta* (or A-class) destroyers. Several design changes were requested, including a more streamlined bridge structure and oil heating[1]. The Canadian High Commission requested tenders for the construction of these destroyers on June 4, 1928 and by September, 14 British shipyards had responded, all of whom offered the necessary 'Canadianized' fittings without appreciable extra cost. Of those 14 Yarrow's was the cheapest, but didn't quite meet the RCN's stated specifications. Thornycroft's bid was the next lowest at about £10,000 more, but their proposed machinery was much more compact and efficient. Thornycroft landed the contract to build HMCS *Saguenay* and *Skeena*, with both being laid down in late 1929 at Thornycroft's Woolston Works, Southampton. The total cost of the destroyers—including armament—would be £3,350,132.[2]

Initially *Saguenay* had an experimental set of four-bladed propellers fitted—although they seemed to reduce vibration at speeds up to 32 knots, they were unsuccessful at full power, requiring more horsepower for a lower top speed than *Skeena*.[3] Triple-bladed screws would be fitted before service with the RCN. The design and construction of *Saguenay* and her sister *Skeena* was carried out under the direction of Engineer-Commander R.C. Phillips, RCN, MEIC—at the time, the principle technical officer of the Naval Service of Canada.[4]

---

[1] (Friedman, British Destroyers: From Earliest Days to the Second World War, 2009) p. 203

[2] (Johnston, Rawling, Gimblett, & MacFarlane, 2011) p. 901

[3] (Barnaby, 1964) p. 97

[4] (The Engineering Journal, 1931) p. 521

Saguenay would be the first made-to-order RCN warship when she was commissioned May 22, 1931 at Portsmouth under the command of Commander P. W. Nelles, RCN.[5] After her sister's commissioning the two sailed for Halifax, and in September of 1931 she sailed up the Saguenay River to visit Chicoutimi.

Together with *Champlain* she took part in the Jacques Cartier[6] Quartercentenary at Gaspe in August 1934, and in 1936 she escorted Great War veterans across the Atlantic to France for the dedication of the Vimy Memorial at Vimy Ridge. Along with her sister she would represent Canada at King George VI's coronation the following year, and in May 1939 she would escort the King and Queen up the St. Lawrence to Quebec City, on their Canadian tour. This would be one of her last peacetime assignments.

Six days after the declaration of war, *Saguenay* and another of the River-class destroyers HMCS *St. Laurent* joined the escorting forces of convoy HX 1—the first fast convoy from Halifax to England. She spent the rest of the year and the early part of 1940 on patrol, first from Kingston Jamaica and later from Halifax. In October 1940 she was assigned to Escort Group 10 based out of Greenock in Scotland. Two months later, while escorting convoy HG 47 from Gibraltar to England, she was torpedoed by the Italian submarine *Argo* west of Ireland. Commander G.R. Miles, RCN took over form the

---

[5] Nelles would eventually reach the rank of Admiral and hold the position of Chief of the Naval Staff from 1934 to 1944. Often blamed for the RCN's failings early in the war, Nelles presided over a navy that underwent explosive growth under the most trying of circumstances. Removed from his position as head of the RCN, he was promoted and assigned as Overseas Naval Attaché to coordinate RCN operations for Operation Overlord. He retired in 1945.

[6] Indeed, her wartime crest carried a representation of Jacques Cartier, even though some in the Royal Navy felt it looked like "some sort of Red Indian"; (Lynch & Lamb, 1984) p. 115

office-of-the-watch Lieutenant R.B. Warwick, RCNVR. Minutes later Warwick spotted the submarine almost a kilometer away. At this point Lt. Warwick jumped from the bridge down to the 'B' gun (some 10-12 feet below) and directed the gun crew to fire a pair of 4.7-inch shells, which straddled but didn't strike the *Argo*, after which the submarine immediately dived[7].

The torpedo had shattered the destroyer's bow and killed 21 men, yet despite it all she made Barrow-in-Furness four days later under her own power. She wouldn't be fit for service again until May of 1941.

She put to sea to take part in screening the Home Fleet capital ships during the hunt for the *Bismarck*. After this she was recalled to Newfoundland, arriving in St. John's on June 7, 1941. In July she would escort Winston Churchill—aboard HMS *Prince of Wales*—from the conference with President Roosevelt in Placentia Bay to Iceland where she was detached to return to Newfoundland.

1942 was a hard year on the destroyer—it started in January when she suffered extensive storm damage which left her barely able to make it back to St John's, where she was laid up for three months for repairs. In November she was hit by the Panamanian freighter *Azra*, severing her stern and causing the depth charges to detonate. The explosion sank the freighter, but luckily there were only two fatalities between both ships.

Deemed too expensive to repair, her stern was sealed off and she was converted to a stationary training vessel and tender to HMCS *Cornwallis*. Ultimately paid off after VE Day, the first made-to-order Canadian destroyer went to International Iron & Metal in Hamilton for breaking in 1946.[8]

---

[7] (Douglas, Sarty, & Whitby, No Higher Purpose: The Official Operational History of the Royal Canadian Navy in the Second World War, 1939-1943, 2004) p. 122

[8] (MacPherson & Butterley, River Class Destroyers of the Royal Canadian Navy, 2008) p. 14

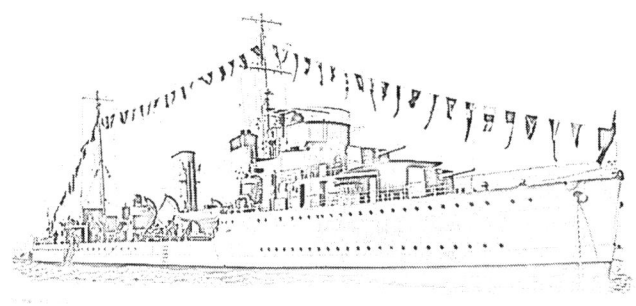

HMCS Skeena (River-class)

Length:	320'	Laid Down:	14-10-1929
Beam:	32' 6"	Launched:	10-10-1930
Draft:	10'	Commissioned:	10-06-1931
Displacement:	1337 tons	Paid Off:	25-10-1944

Armament: 4 x 4.7" LA guns, eight 21" torpedo tubes, 2 x 2pdr AA guns

Like her sister HMCS *Skeena*, she was designed and built by Thornycroft at its Woolston yard in Southampton. The design of the Canadian destroyers tended to follow the recent Royal Navy designs, although Thornycroft would use the Teddington model water tank (part of the National Physical Laboratory) to test and refine the hull lines; these tests also provided design data that would be used for future British destroyers.

In addition to the oil heating, *Skeena* and *Saguenay* also had strengthened bows and forward plating to provide additional protection against ice—it had been calculated that there could be up to 50 or 60 tons of snow and ice built up on the upper decks and rigging. Additional stability was provided to ensure such occasions wouldn't end in disaster. Additional ventilation for working in tropical weather (like winter cruises to Bermuda), and other items like automatic electric fresh-water and salt-water services, caused the two Canadian ships to be dubbed the 'Rolls-Royce destroyers' when they reached Portsmouth.[9] The first Canadian warship to be named *Skeena*

---

[9] (Barnaby, 1964) p. 96

had just set a standard the later *Skeena* would need to live up to. She made 36 knots on her trials in the Firth of Clyde.

Commissioned at Portsmouth a little less than a month after *Saguenay*, she sailed under the command of Commander V.G. Brodeur,[10] with Engineer Commander G.L. Stephens RCN, MEIC as her chief engineer. Stephens had been the Assistant Canadian Overseer for building during the ship's construction.[11] Upon reaching Canada in July, *Skeena* would tarry in Halifax for only a month before she sailed for Esquimalt to take her place with HMCS *Vancouver* as the west coast destroyer division.

Along with *Vancouver* she took part in showing the flag in Acajutla, San Salvador during the 1932 peasant uprising. Ultimately no intervention was required on the part of the Canadian ships, and before she left to resume her winter training cruise with *Vancouver*, *Skeena* played host to local British subjects.

In January of 1936, *Skeena* departed on her spring cruise to the Caribbean. At this time her Commanding Officer was H.E. Reid, RCN—former CO of HMCS *Patriot*, and recently returned from a posting in command of a RN destroyer on the China Station—and the second-in-command was Lieutenant Commander H.N. Lay. Lay had previously been second-in-command of HMCS *Vancouver* and on similar cruises previously, when *Vancouver* and *Skeena* reached Acapulco the crew would go to Tropical Routine—due to the heat such a routine would see the crew turn out at 0600 to begin work until noon and then undertake a more relaxed 'make and mend' in the afternoon.[12]

---

[10] Ibid p. 97

[11] (The Engineering Journal, 1931) p. 518

[12] Originally in the days of sail, the Royal Navy would provide regular, if occasional 'make and mend' sessions where the crew could make and mend their uniforms (which at the time weren't issued to them). In more modern parlance it's an

TIN CAN CANUCKS

When Lt. Commander Lay proposed this to the CO, Reid denied the request—telling Lay "I don't think you are working the ship's company hard enough." Lt. Commander Lay—who had already mentioned to the Coxswain that he would propose the switch to a tropical routine for the crew; and the crew had expected this regardless as it had been the routine previously—was obliged to order the crew to fall in at 1315. However at about 1255 the Coxswain—apparently somewhat ashen—reported to Lay that the crew were refusing to fall in. They had locked themselves in their mess and refused to work; the classic signs of a mutiny. Lt. Commander Lay and the Coxswain were able to enter the forward mess deck through an ammunition passageway, and the second-in-command found himself facing some belligerent-looking seamen. Luckily the situation was defused when the crew—after expressing their displeasure at having to work in the hot sun in the afternoons—was informed by Lt. Commander Lay of the seriousness of a mutiny and the possible punishment to mutineers. The crew fell in after Lay promised he would not report the mutiny 'officially' to the CO and would try to persuade Commander Reid to approve going to the Tropical Routine.

Although Commander Reid was none too pleased with Lay's insistence, the CO promise not to act on the report of the mutiny (an assurance Lay extracted before he told his CO about what had happened), Reid acquiesced and the ship went to Tropical Routine the next day.[13]

Skeena would represent Canada (with her sister *Saguenay*) at

---

afternoon off.

[13] (Lay, 1982) p. 85 Lay apparently told the crew he expected the Captain could signal a British cruiser (also in Acapulco harbor) to send over its detachment of 100 Royal Marines to put down the mutiny and arrest the mutineers, after which he made the point that per regulations "The penalty for mutiny is death or other such punishment..." H.N. Lay would retire from the RCN as a Rear Admiral.

the coronation of King George VI in May of 1937. The year after, *Skeena* moved bases to Halifax as HMCS *Fraser* took up her duties in Esquimalt. One of her last peacetime assignments was to escort the King and Queen from Cape Tormentine, New Brunswick to Charlottetown, Prince Edward Island (and after to Pictou, Nova Scotia) during their royal visit of June 1939.

When war erupted three months later, *Skeena* was in Halifax; the next day she welcomed aboard the British Commander-in-Chief, America and West Indies Station, along with his staff; and sailed to Bermuda to debark them there. She arrived home the day after Canada declared war, and joined her sister *Saguenay* along with HMCS *Fraser*, HMCS *Restigouche*, HMCS *Ottawa*, and HMCS *St. Laurent* as Halifax Force. This organization acted as local escort for fast convoys out of Halifax Harbour to England until late May, when *Skeena*, *Restigouche* and *St. Laurent* sailed from Halifax to join Western Approaches Command in Britain—HMCS *Fraser* had also been seconded to the Royal Navy, but she sailed from Bermuda, having been on an escort mission in Jamaica.

Skeena would spend the remainder of 1940 posted as a convoy escort/convoy rescue or on anti-submarine patrols, first with Western Approaches and later with Northern Escort Force, and saw herself based out of Plymouth, Rosythe, Greenock, Liverpool, and Londonderry (the soon-to-be-famous endpoint for the 'Newfie-Derry Run'—convoy sailings from Newfoundland to Londonderry). During her service with Escort Group 10, *Skeena* was involved in a minor collision with the Polish destroyer *Blyskawica* on the Clyde in December. *Skeena* would return to Canada for refit in March of 1941.

Upon return to sea duty in June she joined the Newfoundland Escort Force. As she was usually the most senior command she would often take the lead as Senior Officer Commanding the escort and was in that role when Canada's first U-boat kill was made by the corvettes HMCS *Moose Jaw* and HMCS *Chambly* in September of 1941. *Skeena's* own first blood would come almost a year later when she and

HMCS *Wetaskiwin* sank U-588 in June of 1942. *Skeena's* CO, Lieutenant K.L. Dyer, RCN would subsequently earn much praise for his tactical innovations while escort commander— including a procedure called 'Major Hoople'[14].

Throughout the remainder of 1942 and much of 1943 *Skeena* remained a North Atlantic convoy escort and on antisubmarine patrol. During this period—save for a 3-month refit in Halifax in the winter of 1942/43— *Skeena* escorted 22 convoys, crossing the Atlantic more than 20 times—a distance of over 64,000 kilometers.

The night of July 5-6, 1944 *Skeena* was with EG-12 during Operation Dredger. The goal of the operation was to engage and defeat the escort vessels accompanying Nazi U-boats into and out of Brest, France. That night EG 12, led by HMCS *Qu'Appelle*, jumped four minesweepers escorting 2 U-boats—3 escorts were sunk in the brief exchange and the fourth and its charges scattered. *Skeena*, having gotten her share of the action, had her CO Lieutenant Commander P.F.X. Russel take over as senior officer after *Qu'Appelle's* commanding officer was wounded (and the ship heavily damaged). The follow-up Operation Kinetic—a strike against German ships trying to supply a garrison in Auiderne Bay ended with a collision between *Qu'Appelle* and *Skeena* that left both in dry-dock for several weeks.[15]

By the fall *Skeena* had been transferred to EG 11 and was

---

[14] (Douglas, Sarty, & Whitby, No Higher Purpose: The Official Operational History of the Royal Canadian Navy in the Second World War, 1939-1943, 2004) p. 557. Essentially, this maneuver was meant to expose U-boats as they drew near to attack. When the SOE signaled 'Major Hoople', the escort would fire starshell and flares to illuminate the side of the convoy under attack; hopefully exposing the attacking submarines on the surface to be engaged by the escort. Ultimately this was to make up for a lack of radar in Canadian escort vessels; and with better equipment the procedure was discontinued. See Also (Milner, 1990) p. 181

[15] (German, 1990) p 173

back on the convoy routes. Sadly, on October 24 1944 while EG-11 took shelter in Reykjavik, Iceland from a Gale, *Skeena* would drag her anchor (the bottom of the harbor was more volcanic ash than rock) and be driven up on the rocks. Fifteen men were lost when they attempted to reach the shore by carley float. The rest of the officers and crew were rescued, but *Skeena* was judged a total loss. Her hulk was sold in 1945 to a local resident who ultimately had her scrapped in place.

As we've seen, the Canadian government ordered its first new-construction ships in 1929. These two destroyers, *Saguenay* and *Skeena* were named after Canadian rivers, setting a pattern for the naming of nearly all Canadian destroyers until 1970. These two would form the basis of the Canadian River class destroyers—a class made up of fourteen near-sisters either based on British A-I class designs (like *Skeena* and *Saguenay*) or transferred British ships belonging to those classes. Pre-war the RCN could only boast seven of these River-class destroyers—*Saguenay*, *Skeena* and the C-Class vessels which are described below. The remainder, transferred after hostilities began, are covered in Chapter Four.

As the threat of war with Germany increased throughout the 1930s, Canada would purchase an additional half-flotilla[16] of modern destroyers from Britain, to increase her ability to protect her coasts and work with the British battle fleet—and most importantly to Britain, assist the Royal Navy in convoy escort should war break out.

---

[16] British policy throughout the 20s and 30s was to build a flotilla of 9 destroyers a year (8 standard hulls, plus one flotilla leader); the C-class consisted only of 5 however, as the order had been cut in 1930, in a show of good-faith prior to negotiations for the 1930 London Naval Treaty (where the British were hoping to bring in a ban on submarines)

HMCS Assiniboine (River–class (C))

Length:	329'	Laid Down:	18-10-1930
Beam:	33'	Launched:	29-10-1931
Draft:	10' 2"	Commissioned:	19-10-1939
Displacement:	1375 tons	Paid Off:	08-08-1945

Armament: 4 x 4.7" LA guns, eight 21" torpedo tubes, 2 x 2pdr AA guns

HMCS *Assiniboine* was originally built as HMS *Kempenfelt* by the shipyard of J. Samuel White & Co. and on commissioning into the RN in 1930 joined the 2nd Destroyer Flotilla of the Home Fleet. *Assiniboine*, being the destroyer leader for the 1929-30 destroyer building program was built to a slightly different design. Initially the design saw the bridge lowered by two-and-a-half feet from the B-Class destroyer leader.[17] The final design would carry only four 4.7-inch guns (the previous class' leader carried a fifth between the funnels). *Assiniboine* was also the first British destroyer to ship an auxiliary diesel generator in its forward boiler room—all previous such generators had run on petrol.[18]

By the time of her commissioning in 1939 both Britain and Canada were already at war with Nazi Germany—war having been declared a little more than a month before. *Assiniboine* reached Halifax on November 17, 1939 and immediately took up escort duty with convoy HX 9. In conjunction with HMCS *St. Laurent*, she escorted the cruiser HMS *Emerald* into Halifax

---

[17] (Friedman, British Destroyers: From Earliest Days to the Second World War, 2009) p. 207

[18] Ibid. p 210

November 20th. *Emerald* was carrying gold bullion from the Bank of England; she would eventually carry £58 million to North America by August 1940.[19]

In December, 'Bones'—the nickname given her by her crew—relieved *Saguenay* in Kingston, Jamaica and took up patrols for German merchant vessels attempting to sail homeward from the Caribbean. In March of 1940 MV *Hannover* was stopped by the cruiser HMS *Dunedin* and the German crew set their own vessel alight. The cruiser and destroyer shared both firefighting and towing duties until *Hannover* made port in Kingston on March 13. The prize ship would eventually enter service with the RN as the first escort carrier HMS *Audacity*.

After this adventure *Assiniboine* came home for a short refit before resuming local escort duties. Early in 1941 she would sail in company with HMCS *Restigouche* along with three town-class destroyers to Greenock where she would join EG 10. After repairs from a collision in the spring of 1941, *Assiniboine* joined the hunt for *Bismarck* as an escort for the British battleship HMS *Repulse*. Needing to refuel in Iceland placed her off the chess board for the *Bismarck's* final gambit and she was ordered back to Greenock. Her brushes with greatness (or at least great events) were to continue when she was part of the screening force (once again with *Restigouche*) for the battleship HMS *Prince of Wales* on its voyage to bring Prime Minister Winston Churchill to the Atlantic Charter meeting. During this duty *Assiniboine* had the privilege of transporting Churchill from the battleship to the Reykjavik jetty and back while at the Iceland port.[20]

While part of escort group C-1 in August of 1942, *Assiniboine* was escorting the slow convoy SC-94 when it was

---

[19] (MacPherson & Butterley, River Class Destroyers of the Royal Canadian Navy, 2008) p. 66

[20] Ibid p. 68

attacked by the U-boat wolf-pack *Steinbrink*—which included U-210 who had escaped Lt. Dyer's HMCS *Skeena* in June. In a fog bank *Assiniboine* and U-210 played a game of hide and seek until U-210 "suddenly appeared out of the mist…some fifty yards away and about to cross [*Assiniboine's*] bow."[21]

A short, sharp gun action then took place between the Canadian destroyer and the surfaced U-boat. At point blank range *Assiniboine's* 4.7-inch guns couldn't depress enough to hit the submarine; however the crew used the ship's machine guns to clear away those Germans manning the submarine's 88mm deck gun. The Germans manned their 20mm guns instead and holed *Assiniboine's* superstructure in several places, setting petrol tanks on her deck alight. *Assiniboine's* CO, Acting Lieutenant Commander J.H. Stubbs, RCN turned to his second-in-command[22] Lieutenant R.L. Hennessy and said "Get that fire out," Pointing to the flames and smoke aft of the bridge. The fire was blocking both companionways from the bridge[23], so Lt. Hennessy jumped from the back of the bridge to the foremast and climbed down to the main deck to direct the damage control parties—for which he would receive the

---

[21] (Douglas, Sarty, & Whitby, No Higher Purpose: The Official Operational History of the Royal Canadian Navy in the Second World War, 1939-1943, 2004) p. 506. This quote is from official naval historian Dr. Gilbert Tucker who was aboard *Assiniboine* at the time.

[22] Again, to avoid confusion that might arise from the different British and American terms for a ship's second-in-command ('First Lieutenant' and 'Executive Officer' respectively) both of which the RCN has used, the officer holding that position is simply called the second-in-command.

[23] It also trapped CPO Max Bernays, who was at the helm, alone in the wheelhouse. He remained at his station, calmly following Stubbs' helm orders and earned himself the Conspicuous Gallantry Medal. (Douglas, Sarty, & Whitby, No Higher Purpose: The Official Operational History of the Royal Canadian Navy in the Second World War, 1939-1943, 2004) p. 506

DSC.[24]

Meanwhile Lt. Cmdr. Stubbs cut *Assiniboine* inside U-210's turning circle by reversing his inside screw and put the wheel hard over. He then attempted to ram the desperately dodging U-boat (indeed, Stubbs could see the German captain giving helm orders) but missed several times, until one of *Assiniboine's* 4.7-inch shells hit home, destroying the bridge and killing the U-boat's commander. The German engineering officer then attempted to dive, but before U-210 could complete the maneuver *Assiniboine's* bow crashed into the submarine abaft the conning tower. With no hope of escape the U-boat surfaced and the crew abandoned ship. *Assiniboine* rammed the stricken vessel once again and dropped a final pattern of depth charges, but U-210's fate was sealed and she sank after a thirty-minute fight for her life. *Assiniboine*, suffering from some flooding below the waterline and with 13 wounded and one crew member dead, returned to St. John's, Newfoundland for repair.[25]

This wouldn't be the ship's only skirmish with a surfaced U-boat. In February 1943, while crossing to Londonderry to join escort group C-3, she again fought a German submarine; the results of which required four months to repair. By August of 1944 she had moved onto patrols of the English Channel, taking part in a surface action with three armed trawlers. She would later be part of a screening force for the battleship HMS *Warspite* while it shelled Brest in September 1944, and would subsequently be in Iceland with EG 11 when HMCS *Skeena* dragged her anchors and wrecked. In the last year of the war *Assiniboine* suffered more damage, colliding with SS *Empire Bond* in the English Channel in February, and suffering a boiler

---

[24] (MacPherson & Butterley, River Class Destroyers of the Royal Canadian Navy, 2008) p. 73

[25] (Douglas, Sarty, & Whitby, No Higher Purpose: The Official Operational History of the Royal Canadian Navy in the Second World War, 1939-1943, 2004) p. 507

room fire in July. Considering her age and material state, the destroyer wasn't worth repairing and was towed to Sorel on August 8, 1945.[26]

Paid off and sold for scrap, *Assiniboine* would fail to arrive in Boston when she went aground off East Point, Prince Edward Island while being towed to the breakers. She was being towed stern first around the Island by HMCS *York* when the tow broke in a strong southerly gale; the sea then drove her up on a sandbar the night of November 7, 1945.

Amazingly, the seven-man skeleton crew aboard her made it off, and after asking for directions from a rather surprised local resident[27], they headed for the town of Souris, PEI for their trip home. *Assiniboine's* wreck was left where it grounded, opposite the easternmost tip of South Lake, five kilometers west of the East Point Lighthouse. Six days later, a Nor'easter refloated her briefly, allowing her to swing westward over the sandbar and ground high up the beach. She would move no more.

Over time, locals would attempt to salvage parts of the ship as it lay on the rocks, laying claim to valuable brass and copper piping, but also items like one of the ships compasses, a lamp and a heavy bench from a crew's mess that for years was used in the East Point schoolhouse.[28] Some of the 'treasures' were still labeled HMS *Kempenfelt*—the ship's original name in the Royal Navy.

There is also a story—perhaps apocryphal—of a man who was crushed trying to salvage one of the screws he had wanted

---

[26] (MacPherson & Butterley, River Class Destroyers of the Royal Canadian Navy, 2008) p. 72

[27] (MacIntyre, 1997) This was Bernard Cheverie, who while duck hunting discovered the men walking up the beach—with a warship grounded behind them!

[28] Ibid. When he wrote his article, Mr. MacIntyre was in possession of said mess bench.

to sell as scrap brass.[29]

The destroyer 'Bones' remained visible well into the late 1950s.

HMCS Fraser (River–class (C))

Length:	329'	Laid Down:	01-02-1930
Beam:	33'	Launched:	29-09-1931
Draft:	10' 2"	Commissioned:	17-02-1937
Displacement:	1375 tons	Lost:	25-06-1940

Armament: 4 x 4.7" LA guns, eight 21" torpedo tubes, 2 x 2pdr AA guns

The ship that was to become HMCS *Fraser* was commissioned as HMS *Crescent* on April 21, 1932 joining the 2nd Destroyer Flotilla of the home fleet. Like her sister HMS *Cygnet* (HMCS *St. Laurent*) she was built by Vickers-Armstrong Ltd.—the only private firm to build more than one of the C-class destroyers. She and *Cygnet* would both be commissioned into the RCN at Chatham Dockyard in 1937.

The ship's luck may well have started off poor, as she collided with her sister HMS *Comet* (HMCS *Restigouche*) at Chatham in July of 1932, which saw her under repairs until the end of August. Her RN career included a deployment to the West Indies in 1934 and the Red Sea and Indian Ocean during

---

[29] (Watson, 2001) p. 147

the Abyssinian Crisis in 1935-36.[30]

She and *Cygnet* were sold to the Canadian Navy for £400,000 and prior to commissioning in the RCN they would both be refitted with ASDIC (sonar) in 1937. She was posted to the Canadian west coast for a little under two years when, at the declaration of war, she was ordered from Esquimalt to Halifax. She spent the winter in Halifax before being posted to Bermuda and then to Plymouth in June of 1940. Although she missed the 'Dunkirk Miracle', she was participating in other evacuations of Allied troops from the French coast when she unexpectedly crossed the bow of the cruiser HMS *Calcutta* and was rammed and cut in two while leaving the port of St. Jean de Luz. The bow, severed just forward of the bridge, sank immediately with no hope of escape for the crew in the forward messes. 45 crewmen were killed. The remainder of the ship showed no signs of sinking on its own and had to be scuttled by sister *Restigouche*.[31]

Amazingly, after the collision the bridge superstructure of the destroyer ended up sitting on the *Calcutta's* forecastle. *Fraser's* Commanding Officer Commander W. B. Creery, RCN, his second-in-command, the officer-of-the-watch, and 3 ratings simply stepped off the wreckage and onto the cruiser's bow. *Calcutta* would return to Plymouth with the bridge wreckage still on deck.[32] Tragically, many of the survivors of *Fraser's* collision with *Calcutta* would later be assigned to the similarly ill-fated HMCS *Margaree*.

---

[30] (English, Amazon to Ivanhoe: British Standard Destroyers of the 1930s, 1993) p. 48

[31] (MacPherson & Butterley, River Class Destroyers of the Royal Canadian Navy, 2008) p. 32

[32] (Douglas, Sarty, & Whitby, No Higher Purpose: The Official Operational History of the Royal Canadian Navy in the Second World War, 1939-1943, 2004) p. 100. Creery would subsequently command an Armed Merchant Cruiser and post-war served as the Vice-Chief of Naval Staff, having attained the rank of Rear Admiral.

HMCS Restigouche (River-class (C))

Length:	329'	Laid Down:	12-09-1930
Beam:	33'	Launched:	30-09-1931
Draft:	10' 2"	Commissioned:	15-06-1938
Displacement:	1375 tons	Paid Off:	06-10-1945

Armament: 4 x 4.7" LA guns, eight 21" torpedo tubes, 2 x 2pdr AA guns

HMCS *Restigouche* (known to her wartime crew as 'Rustyguts'[33]) was first launched in 1931 and later commissioned as HMS *Comet* at Portsmouth Naval Dockyard in 1932. Like her sisters she was assigned to the 2nd Destroyer Flotilla of the Home Fleet upon commissioning. During this time she was in a collision with HMS *Crescent* (HMCS *Fraser*) and suffered damage to her propellers. She stayed in home waters until assigned to the Red Sea in 1935/36, coming home for duty with the Non-Intervention Patrol off Spanish ports in the Bay of Biscay during the Spanish Civil War.

After a stint as a plane guard to HMS *Glorious* in the Mediterranean in 1937, she would be turned over to the Canadian Navy and commissioned as HMCS *Restigouche* in 1938.[34]

---

[33] (MacPherson & Barrie, Ships of Canada's Naval Forces: 1910-2002, 2004) p. 49

[34] (English, Amazon to Ivanhoe: British Standard Destroyers of the 1930s, 1993)

She and HMCS *Ottawa* sailed for Canada September 6, 1938 and visited several Canadian ports before arriving in Esquimalt. There she and the three other Western Division destroyers would escort the King and Queen from Vancouver to Victoria and back during their visit in May of 1939. In August of that year, *Restigouche* was at the Canadian Pacific exhibition when sisters *St. Laurent* and *Fraser* (who were also at the exhibition) were ordered to the East coast with all due haste—war would be declared within days. *Restigouche* and *Ottawa* would again sail together to the east coast in November, meeting HMAS *Perth* in the Caicos Islands to refuel before transiting the Panama Canal on November 27th. Another refueling in Jamaica would lead them onto Halifax by December 7. From there she would undertake local escort work until May of 1940.

With France on the verge of collapse, *Restigouche*, *St. Laurent*, and *Skeena* were sent to British waters to bolster her defenses. *Restigouche's* Commanding Officer at the time was Lieutenant Commander H.N. Lay who was Senior Officer amongst the three destroyers. Lt. Commander Lay and his fellow ship's commanding officers had been instructed not to inform the remaining officers or crew that they were destined for British waters—an active war zone—until the Canadian ships were well out to sea. There was some shock amongst *Restigouche's* crew when they were told they were not bound for the West Indies, as some had expected.[35]

Once in Plymouth, *Restigouche* had her aft torpedo tubes replaced by a 3-inch AA gun and her Pom-Poms replaced by quadruple AA machine gun mounts. In this fit she saw service on the French coast, at one time engaging a German shore battery at St. Valéry-en-Caux. She would be on hand when, during the evacuation of troops from St. Jean de Luz, HMS *Calcutta* cut HMCS *Fraser* in half in a collision. *Restigouche*

---

p. 46

[35] (Lay, 1982) p. 105

rescued 11 of *Fraser's* officers and 90 other members of the crew and then scuttled the hulk with demolition charges.[36] Arriving in Plymouth on the 26th of June, *Restigouche* had some of her crew detailed to assist in the take-over of French ships in Plymouth—France having capitulated to the Nazis.

The next several months would see *Restigouche* undertaking patrol, rescue, and convoy duties from Plymouth and Rosyth, before heading to Halifax for a refit. After this she dabbled with local escort for a short time, before returning to the UK with four Town-class destroyers (including HMCS *Columbia* and HMCS *St. Francis*) to take up her duties with the Clyde Escort Force until May of 1941. She crossed the Atlantic once more to assume a position with HMCS *Ottawa* in the Newfoundland Escort Force in June. She was quickly sidelined with mechanical defects requiring repair in Halifax. Once those were complete, she embarked a film crew from MGM studios who were filming the crossing of a troop convoy.[37] After this diversion she was assigned to the screening force for HMS *Prince of Wales*—along with HMCS *Assiniboine* and HMCS *Saguenay*[38]—which was transporting Churchill to Placentia Bay, Newfoundland for the Atlantic Charter conference. While refueling in Placentia she grounded briefly, emerging with damage to her screws and requiring repair work in St. John's.

Late in the year, while escorting convoy ON 44, *Restigouche* encountered a gale which caused extensive damage to the deck and hull. While being repaired over Christmas of 1941 problems were discovered in her port steam turbine and she was kept in dockyard hands until the following March. She

---

[36] (MacPherson & Butterley, River Class Destroyers of the Royal Canadian Navy, 2008) p. 57

[37] Ibid p. 58

[38] (Douglas, Sarty, & Whitby, No Higher Purpose: The Official Operational History of the Royal Canadian Navy in the Second World War, 1939-1943, 2004) p. 220

returned to the North Atlantic run for several convoys before problems in one of her propeller shafts (a legacy of the Placentia Bay grounding) sidelined her again. Repairs lasted until September. Apparently at some time during this period *Restigouche's* CO, Lieutenant Commander D.W. Piers, RCN—who had relieved Lt. Commander Lay in June of 1941—'purchased' a HF/DF set for installation aboard the ship with a bottle of scotch. Thanks to that 'wee dram' *Restigouche* became the first Canadian destroyer so fitted.[39]

Between September 1942 and April 1944 she sailed as escort with Escort Group C-4 on 22 convoy escort missions, including SC 107 which lost nearly half of its ships and a pair of convoys, to and from Algeria in support of Operation Torch (the North Africa Landings). In April 1944 she joined HMCS *Qu'Appelle*, HMCS *Skeena*, and HMCS *Saskatchewan* as part of EG 12 who were to patrol the west end of the English Channel after the D-Day landings. EG 12 engaged U-boats and their escorts several times, luckily avoiding the new German acoustic torpedo—a weapon specially designed to kill escorts and destroyers—but did suffer light casualties in one skirmish in early July. After a temporary deployment to EG 14 where she rescued survivors from U-243 (sunk by aircraft), she and the rest of EG 12 fought a sharp surface action against a German coastal convoy in late August. *Qu'Appelle* and *Skeena* ended up colliding during this gun battle and the latter required *Restigouche* to escort her to Plymouth. *Restigouche* then joined HMCS *Chaudière* and HMCS *Kootenay* in EG 11 and was present when they sank U-621 on August 18, 1944.

She sailed with HMCS *Ottawa* to Saint John, New Brunswick for a refit, and afterwards escorted a small convoy to Halifax where further work was undertaken. Back at sea for

---

[39] (MacPherson & Butterley, River Class Destroyers of the Royal Canadian Navy, 2008) p.61. Canadian destroyers assigned to England were well known for lacking modern electronics and sensors due to shortage of such equiptment in Canada. This likely wasn't the first or last such 'trade' made during wartime.

working-up, *Restigouche* suffered a severe electrical fire, repairs from which laid the ship up until February of 1945. From then to the end of the war she served with Halifax's Local Escort Force.

After some final crossings to and from the Clyde to repatriate Canadian naval personnel, *Restigouche* was paid off at Sydney, Nova Scotia on October 6, 1945. The next year she was sold to International Iron & Metal Co. and scrapped.[40]

HMCS Ottawa (River–class (C))

Length:	329'	Laid Down:	12-09-1930
Beam:	33'	Launched:	30-09-1931
Draft:	10' 2"	Commissioned:	15-06-1938
Displacement:	1375 tons	Lost:	13-09-1942

Armament: 4 x 4.7" LA guns, eight 21" torpedo tubes, 2 x 2pdr AA guns

The first Canadian destroyer to carry the name HMCS *Ottawa* was launched as HMS *Crusader* at Portsmouth Naval Dockyard in 1931. Like her sister HMS *Comet* (later HMCS *Restigouche*) she was commissioned into the Royal Navy in 1932 and assigned to the 2nd Destroyer Flotilla of the British Home Fleet. She served with the Home Fleet until the Abyssinian Crisis in 1935, when she was deployed to the Mediterranean. From then until her transfer to the RCN she saw various duties, including transporting the C-in-C Home Fleet and acting as tender to the battleship HMS *Royal Oak* during torpedo trials, and attending the carrier HMS *Courageous* as a

---

[40] Ibid. p. 60

plane guard.[41]

She was commissioned as HMCS *Ottawa* at Chatham Dockyard in the same ceremony as HMCS *Restigouche*. Together they visited several Quebec and Maritime ports, and on October 12 departed Halifax to transit the Panama canal and join the other two destroyers of the Western Division— HMCS *Fraser* and HMCS St. *Laurent*—in Esquimalt. In February and March of 1939 this half-flotilla, joined by the two Eastern Division destroyers, joined the RN's 8th Cruiser Squadron in the Caribbean for exercises and training. Later in the spring, *Ottawa* and her sisters escorted the King and Queen from Vancouver to Victoria and back during their May 1939 state visit.

In August of 1939, war was imminent and *Fraser* and *St. Laurent* were ordered to the east coast with all due haste. In November, *Ottawa* and *Restigouche* would join them. The Canadian destroyers would act as local escorts until late May 1940 when four of *Ottawa's* sisters were deployed to British home waters. *Ottawa* was unable to join them immediately as she was undergoing repairs for damage sustained in an April collision with the tug *Bansurf*. It wasn't until late August that *Ottawa* would escort the troop convoy TC 7 to Britain. Here she was sent to the Clyde to act as a local escort there. On September 25th she had just departed the convoy OB 217 when she was ordered back—SS *Sulairia* and SS *Eurymedon* had been torpedoed and *Eurymedon* was still afloat but shipping water; her captain and two other officers refused to abandon the vessel. *Ottawa* took aboard the other survivors and sprinted off to catch up with the convoy. The next day she was ordered back to *Eurymedon* which was still afloat—and now surrounded by boats from *Sulairia*. *Ottawa* took aboard the kit-and-kaboodle and headed for Greenock with an extra 118 souls

---

[41] (English, Amazon to Ivanhoe: British Standard Destroyers of the 1930s, 1993) p. 49

aboard.[42]

She spent a fortnight having her aft torpedo tubes replaced with a 3-inch AA gun, and then resumed her duties escorting convoys mostly in transit to and from the middle east. In early November *Ottawa* and HMS *Harvester*[43] were dispatched to aid the freighter *Melrose Abbey* which reported being attacked by gunfire from a submarine on the surface. The pair made several depth charge attacks with no apparent results. Sunrise revealed a large oil slick spreading across the water and the destroyers departed the scene. This was the last sign of the Italian submarine *Faa Di Bruno*—a 'kill' not awarded to *Ottawa* until 1984 after closer review of both Italian and Admiralty records.

Ottawa would continue convoy escort operations out of Greenock until she was posted with her sister River-class destroyers to the Newfoundland Escort Force—newly established and to which *Ottawa* was assigned in June of 1941. Between June of 1941 and September of 1942 *Ottawa* cycled between mid-ocean escort and local escort before joining the Newfie-Derry run.[44]

September 5, 1942 saw *Ottawa* assigned to convoy ON 127, departing Londonderry for St. John's, Newfoundland. Leading the escort was Lieutenant Commander A.H. Dobson, DSC, RCN aboard HMCS *St. Croix* as Senior Officer, Escort (SOE). On September 10 the convoy was found and attacked by the

---

[42] (MacPherson & Butterley, River Class Destroyers of the Royal Canadian Navy, 2008) p. 50

[43] *Harvester* was an H-Class destroyer originally built for Brazil as *Jurura* but taken over by the Royal Navy when hostilities began. She was a near-sister to HMS *Hero*—the destroyer that would eventually be commissioned in the RCN as HMCS *Chaudière*

[44] (MacPherson & Butterley, River Class Destroyers of the Royal Canadian Navy, 2008) p. 51

13-boat wolf-pack *Vorwärts* around early to mid-afternoon local time. Two tankers—*Sveve* and *F.J. Wolfe*—and a freighter—*Elisabeth van Belgie*—were torpedoed immediately by U-96. Once survivors were rescued, Dobson sent the corvette HMCS *Sherbrooke* to sink the *Sveve* and *F.J. Wolfe* by gunfire, as the freighter remained afloat and under control. He also positioned *Ottawa* astern to deter the attacking U-boat from shadowing the convoy.

The night that followed was one of confusion as the escort fought to scatter the wolf-pack, or at least force it to stay submerged and thus unable to follow the convoy. Several more merchant ships were torpedoed that night. Throughout the 11th and 12th the convoy struggled on, having 3 more merchant ships struck by torpedoes. The convoy was diverted to a more westerly course the night of the 12th, in the hope it would reach air-cover sooner. Help had also been sent in the form of the British WW1-vintage destroyer HMS *Witch* and HMCS *Annapolis*—another Canadian Town-class destroyer like *St. Croix*. These two ships arrived the night of the 13th and Dobson positioned them ahead of the convoy with HMCS *Ottawa*. The sea was calm by this point, and the night clear, with *Ottawa* making ten knots and waiting for the two fresh destroyers to arrive. Her Commanding Officer, Acting Lieutenant Commander C.A. Rutherford, RCN was on the bridge and her second-in-command Lieutenant T.C. Pullen, RCN was aft at his action station near the depth charges.

Just after midnight *Ottawa's* older 286P radar detected what was believed to be *Witch* and *Annapolis*, and making a challenge was hailed by *Witch* less than a kilometer away. *Ottawa* altered to port to avoid a collision. At that moment, the so-far invisible stalker—U-91—struck. Two torpedoes impacted the ship forward. Pullen witnessed the explosion and heard debris falling onto the deck. *St. Croix* dashed to the scene and into U-91's sights but the torpedo fired at *St. Croix*, struck *Ottawa* instead, finishing her off. Lt. Pullen and 68 others were rescued but five officers—including Lt. Cmdr. Rutherford—and 109 other crewmen were lost.

Tragically, *Ottawa* may have avoided her fate had she a better radar outfit. Type 286 was known for its limitations, and the centimetric set Type 271 likely would have detected the skulking U-boat. Before she sailed with ON 127, *Ottawa's* Gunnery and RDF officer Lieutenant L.B. Jenson was notified by the dockyard that a new Type 127 set was to be installed aboard the ship. When it arrived alongside, Jenson informed the CO. Lt. Cmdr. Rutherford—apparently under the impression that Jenson had ordered the installation himself—countermanded the modification order and had it canceled; *Ottawa* sailed with her obsolete radar.[45] Lt. Jenson survived the sinking of HMCS *Ottawa*, having been picked up by the British corvette HMS *Celadine*, which made port in St. John's three days later.[46]

HMCS St. Laurent (River–class (C))

Length:	329'	Laid Down:	01-12-1930
Beam:	33'	Launched:	29-09-1931
Draft:	10' 2"	Commissioned:	17-02-1937
Displacement:	1375 tons	Paid Off:	10-10-1945

Armament: 4 x 4.7" LA guns, eight 21" torpedo tubes, 2 x 2pdr AA guns

HMS *Cygnet* was the first of the C-Class destroyers to be completed (although she was one of the last to be laid down), and was one of the two destroyers built by the Vickers-

---

[45] (Douglas, Sarty, & Whitby, No Higher Purpose: The Official Operational History of the Royal Canadian Navy in the Second World War, 1939-1943, 2004) p. 515

[46] (Jenson, 2000) p. 141 & p. 207. Jenson would subsequently be assigned to HMCS *Algonquin* as her second-in-command while the destroyer was completing at the Clydebank yard of John Brown & Co. Ltd. in early 1944

Armstrong Ltd. Shipyard at Barrows-in-Furness; HMCS *Fraser* being the other. Vickers was only one of two private firms to build C-class destroyers, and the only firm to receive two orders.[47] After commissioning, *Cygnet* joined her sisters in the 2nd Destroyer Flotilla of the Home Fleet and spent a significant amount of time in dockyard hands under repair or modification, until a deployment to the West Indies in 1934. On return she again shuttled between repair and refit at Devonport, until detached from the home fleet to the Red Sea in 1935/36 during the Abyssinian Crisis. After a stint on Non-Intervention Patrol off the coast of Spain and some time in reserve at the Nore, she was refitted to Canadian specifications and commissioned in the RCN as HMCS *St. Laurent* in early 1927.[48]

She sailed to Barbados with HMCS *Fraser*, where the two met HMCS *Saguenay* and HMCS *Skeena* March 24, 1937. *Fraser* proceeded independently to Esquimalt while *St. Laurent*, *Saguenay* and *Skeena* sailed to Halifax. In May *St. Laurent* proceeded up her eponymous river to visit Montreal, Quebec City, and Chicoutimi. That summer she undertook additional courtesy calls to various Maritime ports. The following year she and HMCS *Skeena* switched home ports, with *Skeena* returning from Esquimalt and *St. Laurent* joining the Western Division at that Vancouver Island port. Later in the year *Fraser* and *St. Laurent* were joined by sisters *Ottawa* and *Restigouche* whom the RCN had recently acquired. All six River-class destroyers undertook a West Indies winter cruise in early 1939.

In May, *St. Laurent* and the three other Western Division destroyers escorted the King and Queen to and from Vancouver Island during their visit to British Columbia. In August as war loomed, the Western Division was in Vancouver

---

[47] (English, Amazon to Ivanhoe: British Standard Destroyers of the 1930s, 1993) p. 45

[48] Ibid p. 50

for the Canadian Pacific Exhibition. *St. Laurent* and *Fraser* were ordered to Halifax with all due haste and were passing eastward through the Panama Canal when war was declared on Germany September 10. Arriving in Halifax on the 15th, *St. Laurent* and *Fraser* commenced wartime duties as local escort to the first convoys of the HX series. In October *St. Laurent* escorted the 'Detached Squadron'—including HMS *Emerald* which was carrying gold bullion from the Bank of England to Canada. Subsequently, in November she escorted HMS *Ascania* to Halifax—the vessel was carrying another £2 million of gold. December saw her act as local escort for the troop convoy TC 1 which was carrying 7,400 men of the 1st Canadian Division to England.[49]

France's imminent collapse had the four River-class destroyers in Halifax posted to British waters, and *St. Laurent* took up her post with Western Approaches Command in May of 1940. She arrived off Northwest Ireland July 2nd to render assistance to MV *Arandora Star* which had been torpedoed. *St. Laurent* was able to rescue some 857 passengers and German and Italian POWs. After picking up survivors from SS *Conch* the first of December, she and HMS *Viscount* were detailed to assist in the rescue of crewmen from the merchant cruiser HMS *Forfar*[50]. On their way to aid *Forfar*, *St. Laurent* undertook a long hunt for the Italian submarine *Argo* which had torpedoed her sister HMCS *Saguenay* earlier that day.

With HMCS *Skeena* she departed Greenock for Halifax the end of February 1941 and put in for refit there until July, when

---

[49] (MacPherson & Butterley, River Class Destroyers of the Royal Canadian Navy, 2008) p. 37

[50] HMS *Forfar*, prior to being taken into service by the Royal Navy in 1939, had been SS *Montrose*—a liner in service to Canadian Pacific Steamships Company. Launched in 1920, she was sunk December 2nd, 1940 by U-99 under the command of Otto Kretschmer—who would become the most successful U-boat commander of the war.

they were both assigned to the newly-formed Newfoundland Escort Force. She would spend much of the next three years assigned to Escort Group C-1 as a mid-ocean escort and making the Newfie-Derry run.

In December 1942 *St. Laurent* sailed from the UK with the convoy ONS 154, bound for St John's. The first attack on the convoy came on Boxing Day, by the U-boats of the wolf-packs *Spitz* and *Ungestüm*, and on the 27th *St. Laurent* and three corvettes—HMCS *Battleford*, HMCS *Chilliwack*, and HMCS *Napanee*—were able to hunt and sink U-356; but the remaining 17 U-boats sank 14 ships—with a loss of nearly 500 souls—before the convoy was clear of the wolf-packs.

Lieutenant Commander G. S. Windeyer, RCN, CO of *St. Laurent* was SOE for ONS 154, and despite the sinking of U-356 the unfolding disaster over the five-day attack appears to have broken him. His second-in-command Lieutenant F.C. Frewer, RCN relieved Lt. Cmdr. Windeyer of duty on New Year's Day and took command of *St. Laurent*. By then HMS *Fame* had arrived to take over the role of SOE.[51] Ultimately, command of *St. Laurent* would pass to Commander H.F. Pullen, RCN (one-time second-in-command of HMCS *Ottawa*) who assumed command January 20, 1943.[52]

In May, while still with C-1, *St. Laurent* and the USN support group based around the escort carrier USS *Bogue* were assigned escort duties with ON 184. When *Bogue's* aircraft sank U-569, *St. Laurent* was johnnie-on-the-spot to collect 25 German survivors. She returned to Dartmouth, Nova Scotia in August for a long refit and wouldn't be back to sea for work-ups before the end of the year.

In March of 1944 *St. Laurent*, back with EG C-1, joined the slow convoy SC 154 en route to Londonderry from Argentia,

---

[51] (Douglas, Sarty, & Whitby, No Higher Purpose: The Official Operational History of the Royal Canadian Navy in the Second World War, 1939-1943, 2004) p. 576

[52] (MacPherson & Barrie, Ships of Canada's Naval Forces: 1910-2002, 2004) p. 49

Newfoundland. On March 6 the Swedish vessel MV *San Francisco*—carrying a cargo of flax seed and pit props (wooden sections for shoring up mines, trenches or other delvings)—had a fire break out, setting the cargo alight. *St. Laurent*, at this time commanded by Lieutenant Commander G.H. Stephen, RCNR, sent over a firefighting party and after a grueling seven-hour battle against the flames, the freighter was moving once again. As she raced to catch up with the rest of the convoy, her HF/DF operators picked up a U-boat transmission between her and the convoy. Lt. Cmdr. Stephens plotted the position some thirty miles behind the convoy—and there he caught U-845 on the surface recharging her batteries. The German dove immediately and *St. Laurent* began her attack. She was joined by HMCS *Owen Sound* and HMCS *Swansea* as well as HMS *Forrester*, and after a hunt of several hours the destroyer was able to drive U-845 to the surface. The U-Boat was struck several times by shells from the escorts and by midnight was badly damaged and taking on water. *St. Laurent* sailed past and as Lt. Cmdr. Stephen looked down he saw "…a red glow in the conning tower as though there was a fire burning below inside the boat."[53] The remaining crew of U-845 scuttled her and abandoned ship. In the end there were forty-five survivors.[54]

A month later *St. Laurent* was assigned to EG-11 which was tasked with protect shipping in the English Channel during the Normandy invasion. There she was teamed with four other River-class destroyers, HMCS *Chaudière*, HMCS *Gatineau*, HMCS *Kootenay* and HMCS *Ottawa (II)*.[55] They spent six weeks,

---

[53] (Easton, 1966) p. 226 Easton, then CO of HMCS *Matane* heard the Radio Telephone (RT) traffic from the escorts during the attack.

[54] (Douglas, Sarty, & Whitby, A Blue Water Navy: The Official Operational History of the Royal Canadian Navy in the Second World War, 1943-1945, 2007) p. 420

[55] These four River-class destroyers were later models than *St. Laurent*—all having been acquired from the RN after the start of hostilities, with some being

starting the end of May, based out of Plymouth, patrolling the western Channel. After a respite in Londonderry, *St. Laurent* was detailed to the Bay of Biscay where she narrowly missed being struck by a German glider-bomb. On August 13 she picked up survivors from U-270 which had been sunk by aircraft.

October saw *St. Laurent*, *Assiniboine*, *Chaudière*, and *Skeena* based out of Reykjavik, Iceland. The intent was to block access to the Atlantic by U-boats that had fled the Biscay coastal bases for Norway. During a wild gale on October 24th *Skeena* dragged her anchors and piled up on the rocks of Videy Island with a loss of 15 crew. Afterwards *St. Laurent* dispatched a party to assist in removing ammunition and stores from the wrecked destroyer.

In November *St. Laurent*, *Chaudière* and HMCS *Qu'Appelle* sailed back to Canada as extra escorts with the convoy ON 267, and upon arrival *St. Laurent* went into refit in Shelbourne, Nova Scotia, emerging in March of 1945 to join the Halifax Local Escort Force after a short work-up in Bermuda with HMCS *Restigouche*. After VE day she spent some time between Newfoundland, Canada and Scotland repatriating troops. Finally she and HMCS *Ottawa (II)* arrived in Sydney in late September to de-store and be paid off.

HMCS *St. Laurent*, the first of the C-Class to be completed was the last of her class to go to the ship breakers. She was sold to International Iron & Metal Co. of Hamilton, Ontario and broken up at Levis, Quebec in 1947.[56]

---

replacements for war losses.

[56] (MacPherson & Butterley, River Class Destroyers of the Royal Canadian Navy, 2008) p. 42

3

TOWNS FROM AMERICA
DESTROYERS FOR BASES

In contrast to the new, or nearly new Rivers, shortly after the outbreak of war, the Canadian Navy received six obsolescent ex-USN 'flush-deck' destroyers. These six were members of a class that in British and Canadian service was known as the Town-class—notwithstanding the fact that the Canadian ships were all named for rivers[1]. Their complex history stemmed from a shortage of British destroyers early in the war.

When war broke out the Royal Navy found that it lacked enough destroyers to cover all the myriad tasks those versatile ships needed to be employed at. Convoy escort was one specific duty that needed additional ships, but without shipyard capacity—or time—to build the necessary escorts immediately, the Royal Navy had to look elsewhere.

---

[1] The British ships were named for towns in England and the United States that shared names (Burnham for instance) —a way to show solidarity between the two countries. Canadian ships, despite being of the same class were named for rivers along the border of Canada and the United States, thus maintaining the RCN tradition of naming destroyers for rivers. HMCS *Annapolis* was an odd duck being named for the Annapolis valley in Nova Scotia—a name shared by the US Naval Academy in Maryland

These ships were part of the destroyers-for-bases deal, which saw the RN receive 50 barely-used but nearly obsolete destroyers in exchange for rights to military bases in British overseas holdings. They were cantankerous and uncomfortable—never having been designed for North Atlantic service. Well known for mechanical breakdowns and turning circles the size of a battleship, they were far from ideal. Their one great strength was that they were available.

There were three major classes of the flush-decks of which two, the *Wicks*- and *Clemson*-classes were represented by the Canadian Towns. Within those classes, there were several sub-classes, noted in the ship description, depending on which American shipyard designed and built them. Based on its class or sub-class, one Town could differ greatly from another in terms of fuel capacity, and therefore range and endurance as well as speed and maneuverability. Many too, differed in quality of construction, and as can be seen this could impact their durability during hostilities.

All had a distinctive profile—unlike contemporary British destroyers they had no forecastle, but instead a continuous upper deck gently sloping towards the stern. They also had a separate funnel for each of their four boilers. Taken together they were known amongst American crews as 'Four-Stack Destroyers', or 'Flush-deck with Four-Pipes.'[2]

Prior to being taken over by the Royal Navy, the ships were made seaworthy (several had been in reserve and two had been stricken from the US Navy List)[3], were stored and crewed by a USN crew and sailed to Halifax. There they met their British crews and a two-day overlap was provided to allow the British to see and get comfortable using the unfamiliar equipment. After this handover period the US Navy colors were struck, the White Ensign raised, and the ships commissioned. The

---

[2] (Alden, 1989)

[3] (Hague, 1990) p. 10

ships were thoroughly inspected in Halifax, and depending on their condition, were detailed to Devonport for a refit to bring the ships up to convoy escort standards. Several would remain in Canadian waters, as they were considered too unsafe for a full Atlantic crossing.

Over the course of their service lives the Town-class saw a series of modifications which tended to reduce the torpedo broadside and the gun armament and increase the depth charge facilities. In almost all cases the bridge superstructure was rebuilt, as the original American bridges had been designed for service in the Pacific and couldn't cope with the severe North Atlantic weather.[4] All the Towns had issues with their fuel oil; they were inefficient steamers requiring careful management of fuel expenditure, and often corroded rivets allowed sea water into the oil fuel tanks, contaminating it and reducing the available bunkerage even further. Some vessels saw one (or more) of the boilers removed, to be replaced by added fuel tanks.

Six of the Town-class destroyers listed here are those officially transferred to Canada and named after Canadian rivers. A further two (HMCS *Hamilton* and HMCS *Buxton*) were transferred to the RCN after this initial group, and retained their British town names. In all, the crews tended to be a mix of RCN and RN personnel.

---

[4] Indeed in one case (HMS *Roxborough*) the bridge was crushed by a wave, killing both the CO and second-in-command as well as 9 others. (Hague, 1990) p. 77

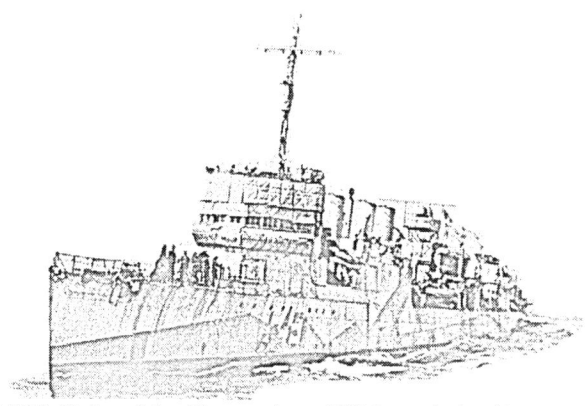

HMCS Columbia (Town-class (*Wickes*-subclass))

Length:	314' 3"	Laid Down:	30-03-1918
Beam:	30' 6"	Launched:	04-07-1918
Draft:	8' 6"	Commissioned:	24-09-1940
Displacement:	1069 tons	Paid Off:	17-03-1944

Armament: 1 x 4" LA guns, three 21" torpedo tubes, 1 x 12pdr AA guns, Hedgehog ASW mortar

HMCS *Columbia* began life as USS *Haraden*, built by Newport News Shipbuilding in 1918. She was a *Lamberton* sub-class ship—designed by Bath Iron Works—with Thornycroft boilers. She was assigned to U.S. Naval Forces in European waters, arriving in the Adriatic in July of 1919. Here she remained until October, before returning to Norfolk, Virginia. From spring of 1920 to spring of 1922 she operated either as part of a reserve unit or on training operations. She was decommissioned by the US Navy 17 July 1922.[5]

She had a brief commission in the USN again in 1939, before being handed over to the Royal Navy who then gave her to the RCN. She remained in Halifax until January of 1941 when she crossed the Atlantic to refit in Devonport. She then served with Escort Group E-4 out of Greenock, until being assigned to the newly formed Newfoundland Escort Force in

---

[5] (Mooney, James L; Naval Historical Center, et al.)

June of 1941.

In March of 1942 she was assigned to the Western Local Escort Force (WLEF) after repairs in Halifax—likely her low radius and increasing number of defects prompted this reassignment. She did however render aid to a sister with the Royal Navy when in January 1943 she towed HMS *Caldwell* into Halifax from St. John's.[6] *Caldwell* had suffered extensive weather damage in a winter storm that had left her adrift for three days before HMS *Wanderer* was able to tow her into St. John's. It was found that repairs couldn't be done with the facilities in that small port and eventually *Caldwell* was towed to Boston.[7]

She saw a major refit in Saint John, New Brunswick in February, and afterwards rejoined WLEF as a member of first Escort Group W-4 and then W-10. Little more than a year later, while she was coming into the small port of Morton Bay, Newfoundland in the fog and with her Radar out, she rammed a cliff[8], crushing her bow and ending her days as an escort. Towed to St. John's, she lay unrepaired until made sea-worthy at Bay Bulls, Newfoundland in May. *Columbia* was then assigned to Liverpool, Nova Scotia as ammunition and stores hulk. She was paid off in June of 1945 and sold for scrap in August.[9]

---

[6] (MacPherson & Barrie, Ships of Canada's Naval Forces: 1910-2002, 2004) p. 55

[7] (Hague, 1990) p. 34

[8] Technically this wasn't a grounding incident as she never touched bottom.

[9] (Hague, 1990) p. 47

HMCS Annapolis (Town-class (*Little*-subclass))

Length:	314' 3"	Laid Down:	04-07-1918
Beam:	30' 6"	Launched:	19-09-1918
Draft:	8' 6"	Commissioned:	24-09-1940
Displacement:	1069 tons	Paid Off:	04-06-1945

Armament: 1 x 4" LA guns, three 21" torpedo tubes, 1 x 12pdr AA guns, Hedgehog ASW mortar

HMCS *Annapolis* was first christened USS *Mackenzie* when launched in 1918 by Mrs. Percy J. Cotton. She was a member of the *Little* sub-class, Built by Union Iron Works based on the Bethlehem design, using Yarrow Boilers and Curtis turbines. This sub-class was less successful than the Bath Iron Works design, and nearly 60 of the Yarrow-boilered flush-deckers were scrapped in 1936 due to their boilers being too worn out to be worth repairing. This may explain why *Annapolis* had her number 4 boiler burn out shortly after her transfer to the RCN—a combination of old, fragile Yarrow boilers and new, inexperienced RCN crew may have made it almost inevitable.

Mackenzie spent two years with the USN Pacific Fleet's Destroyer Squadron 2 (DESRON2) and Destroyer Squadron 4 (DESRON4) until placed in reserve in May of 1922.

She was commissioned into the Royal Canadian Navy as HMCS *Annapolis* at Halifax the end of September 1940. As noted above, she almost immediately suffered severe damage to her number 4 boiler. She was under repair at Halifax until February of 1941 and emerged with only three stacks—

number 4 boiler and its associated funnel having been completely removed.[10] It's unclear as to whether she ever received additional bunkerage capacity with a new fuel tank in place of the missing boiler, as some British Towns did[11], but considering her subsequent services—none of which required any great radius of action—it seems unlikely.

Due to her reduced power from only three boilers, *Annapolis* spent the rest of her war in Canadian waters exclusively with local escort forces. She and HMS *Witch* came to the aid of convoy ON 127 in September of 1942—her sister HMCS *St. Croix* was Senior Officer Escort (SOE)—and was on hand when HMCS *Ottawa* was sunk by U-91.[12]

By 1944 more modern escorts were becoming available in greater numbers, and so *Annapolis* was relegated to training duties at HMCS *Cornwallis* in April of that year. She also acted as escort for British submarines transiting from Halifax to Digby, Nova Scotia.[13] She was finally decommissioned in early June of 1945 and sold to Frankel Brothers for breaking. She left Halifax for the last time, being towed to Boston for scrap on June 22, 1945.

---

[10] (Hague, 1990) p. 21

[11] (Friedman, British Destroyers: From Earliest Days to the Second World War, 2009) p. 260

[12] (Douglas, Sarty, & Whitby, No Higher Purpose: The Official Operational History of the Royal Canadian Navy in the Second World War, 1939-1943, 2004) p. 520

[13] 'Friendly' submarines required escort through Allied controlled waters so as to avoid being taken as U-boats and sunk. This did still happen however as the case of HMS P514, sunk by HMCS *Georgian* in June of 1942 sadly showed. For details see (Perkins, 2000) p. 110

HMCS Hamilton (Town-class (*Wickes*-subclass))

Length:	314' 3"	Laid Down:	17-08-1918
Beam:	30' 6"	Launched:	21-02-1918
Draft:	8' 6"	Commissioned:	06-07-1941
Displacement:	1069 tons	Paid Off:	08-06-1945

Armament: 1 x 4" LA guns, three 21" torpedo tubes, 1 x 12pdr AA guns, Hedgehog ASW mortar

Before becoming HMS (and then HMCS) *Hamilton* this ship was USS *Kalk* built by Fore River Shipyard—a *Little* sub-class ship with Yarrow boilers. She commissioned into the USN at Boston 29 March 1919, under the command of Lieutenant Commander N.R. Van der Veer, USN. In May she left Boston for Newfoundland—her first visit to what was to be a common port of call when she joined the RCN twenty-one years later. She acted as mid-Atlantic rescue cover for the first flight from Newfoundland to the Azores of USN seaplane NC-4. Afterwards she returned to Boston and then sailed for Europe, arriving in Brest in late July 1919. She would serve in various European waters until returning to the United States in late January 1920.

Arriving in February, she undertook training with the reserves of the 1st Naval District, and joined Destroyer Squadron 3 (DESRON3) in operations between Cape Cod and Charleston. As part of the Washington Conference agreement in February of 1922, *Kalk* was sent to Philadelphia and decommissioned 10 July 1922 to be placed in reserve.

She was recommissioned by the USN in 1940, taking up Neutrality Patrol duties in the Atlantic in July of that year. Selected for transfer to the Royal Navy, she was recalled to Charleston.[14]

Commissioned into the Royal Navy as HMS *Hamilton* (for Hamilton, Bermuda) in September of 1940, she collided with her sister HMS *Georgetown* at St. John's in October. She was taken to Saint John, New Brunswick for repair, and while undocking there October 26, she ran aground necessitating another 6-months in dockyard hands. As she had been in Canada for so long, she was then subsequently transferred and commissioned into the Royal Canadian Navy in July of 1941 and assigned to WLEF.

After escorting a single convoy, *Hamilton* was again in a collision, this time with the Dutch submarine O-15 while moored in Halifax Harbour, where both had been tied up to buoys in the same trot. *Hamilton* was preparing to depart and had steam up when full power was accidentally applied to one turbine. The destroyer broke her moorings and crashed into O-15. The collision punctured a main ballast tank, and while the submarine took on a significant list, the Dutch crew was able to keep the boat afloat. Damage turned out not as serious as expected and O-15 was repaired in Dartmouth fairly quickly.[15]

Like many Town-class destroyers, *Hamilton* was painted in several different camouflage schemes throughout her service—including some experimental ones. In December of 1941 one would have found her wearing a rather wild, cubist scheme based on one of the designs from war artist Rowley Murphy.[16]

Hamilton resumed her local escort duties, joining Escort

---

[14] (Mooney, James L; Naval Historical Center, et al.)

[15] (Perkins, 2000) p. 108

[16] (Raven, Royal Navy camouflage of WW2, 1972)

Group W-4 in June 1943. That August she was assigned to HMCS *Cornwallis* at Annapolis, Nova Scotia and was relegated to training duties in the Bay of Fundy. [17] At some point during 1943 she sported gunshield art depicting Donald Duck, his cap aloft, hammering a partially surfaced Nazi U-Boat—considering her career, *Hamilton's* artwork was aspirational at best.[18] She remained in her training role until paid off June 8, 1945.

Later that year she and her sister HMCS *St. Francis* were sold to Frankel Brothers (who were acting as agents for Boston Iron & Metal Co.) The two left Sydney, Nova Scotia under tow by MV *Foundation Security* bound for the breakers in Boston. At some point during the trip *Foundation Security* collided with another ship and the tow parted. One of the two flush-decker hulks was taken under tow by USCGC *Hornbeam* and beached, becoming a total loss; while the other apparently sank off Sakonnet Point, Rhode Island.[19]

---

[17] (MacPherson & Barrie, Ships of Canada's Naval Forces: 1910-2002, 2004) p. 56

[18] (Lynch & Lamb, Gunshield Graffiti, 1984) p. 64

[19] (Hague, 1990) p.52

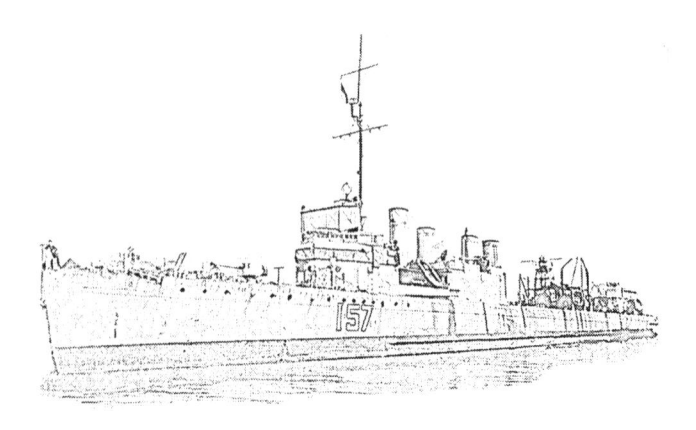

HMCS Niagara (Town-class (*Wickes*-subclass))

Length:	314' 3"	Laid Down:	08-06-1918
Beam:	30' 6"	Launched:	31-08-1918
Draft:	8' 6"	Commissioned:	24-09-1940
Displacement:	1069 tons	Paid Off:	15-09-1945

Armament: 1 x 4" LA guns, three 21" torpedo tubes, 1 x 12pdr AA guns, Hedgehog ASW mortar

First commissioned as USS *Thatcher*, she was a *Little* subclass ship with Yarrow boilers built by Fore River Shipyard. She was launched by Ms. Doris Bentley the grand-niece of Admiral Henry K. Thatcher[20] after whom the ship was named. Her first CO was Lieutenant Commander F.W. Rockwell, USN, who would later command the 16th Naval District in the Philippines at the opening of World War 2. *Thatcher* was assigned to the Atlantic fleet and took part in the transatlantic flights of the Curtis NC-4 flying boat in May of 1919. She was posted not quite midway along the flight path, and while at sea provided radio and visual bearings on the flying boats as they flew to Lisbon, Portugal.

In 1921 *Thatcher* was transferred to the west coast as part of

---

[20] Adm. Thatcher was an American Civil War veteran who had been instrumental in the capture of Mobile, Alabama in 1865

the Pacific Fleet based out of San Diego, California. There she conducted exercises and training cruises until laid up in reserve June 7, 1922.

The destroyer recommissioned in the USN December 18th, 1939 under the command of Lieutenant Commander H.R. Richter, USN and was sent to the East Coast upon completing working up. She took up Neutrality Patrols in the Gulf of Mexico and further up the coast, until transferred to the Royal Canadian Navy in September 1944 and commissioned as HMCS *Niagara*.

Now under the White Ensign, she crossed the Atlantic in November, arriving at Devonport for refit the end of that month. She completed her post-refit work-up in April of 1941 and was assigned to EG 4 at Greenock, sailing with convoy ON 306 on April 5.

She returned to Canadian waters for assignment to the Newfoundland Escort Force in June of 1941. In August she was off the coast of Iceland to take aboard the German crew of U-570. The U-boat had surrendered to a 269 Squadron (RAF Coastal Command) Lockheed Hudson the day before, after the bomber's depth charges had panicked the green crew.[21]

Niagara joined WLEF in March 1942 as a member of Escort Group W-9, moving to W-10 in October. During this period she took part in rescuing the crew of the American merchantman *Independence Hall* off Sable Island on March 9, and recovering two boats and their survivors from the freighter *Rio Blanco* the following month.

Boiler problems sidelined *Niagara* in Halifax from May to July of 1942 but she returned to WLEF after repairs. Transferred to Escort Group W-2 in May of 1943, it was

---

[21] While the U-Boat commander ensured the submarine's Enigma machine had been destroyed, the capture was still a coup for the Allies. After a thorough inspection the British commissioned her into the Royal Navy as HMS *Graph*; while on patrol in October 1942 she fired on and nearly sank U-333.

found that her continuing defects were hindering her ability to carry out her duties. With that in mind she was reassigned as a torpedo firing vessel for the training of Torpedo Branch personnel in Halifax in January of 1944.

She was listed for disposal September 15th 1945, placed on the sale list June 27th 1946, and ultimately broken up the end of 1947.[22]

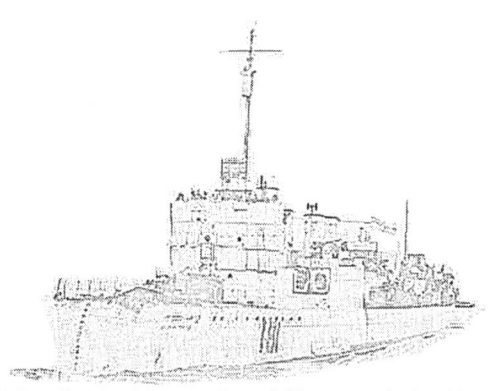

HMCS St. Croix (Town-class (*Clemson*-subclass))

Length:	314' 3"	Laid Down:	11-09-1918
Beam:	30' 6"	Launched:	31-01-1919
Draft:	8' 6"	Commissioned:	24-09-1940
Displacement:	1190 tons	Lost:	20-09-1943
Armament:	1 x 4" LA guns, three 21" torpedo tubes, 1 x 12pdr AA guns, Hedgehog ASW mortar		

If there was a uniquely tragic Canadian destroyer it would be HMCS *St. Croix*. She was originally launched as USS *McCook* by Mrs. Henry C. Dinger at the Bethlehem Shipbuilding Corporation shipyard in April 1919. Commissioned into the USN with Lieutenant Commander G.B Ashe in command, she spent two quiet years with

---

[22] (Hague, 1990) p. 68

Destroyer Force, Atlantic Fleet before being sent to Philadelphia for decommissioning. She was placed in the Atlantic Fleet Reserve until recommissioning in December 1939.[23] Shortly after, she was selected for transfer to the Royal Navy.

At first commissioned into the Royal Navy as HMS *McCook* at Halifax in September of 1940, due to manpower shortages the RN transferred her to Canada and she became HMCS *St. Croix*. On October 19th, 1940 her Commanding Officer, Commander H. Kingsley, RCN, received the orders which would send his ship to war: "Being in all respects ready for sea, HMCS *St. Croix* will sail in consort with HMCS *St. Francis* to join convoy HX 82 for local escort leaving Halifax at 0800 20th October 1940." This first foray was an inauspicious start—she withstood heavy weather poorly on the night of October 21st and spent the next 3 weeks in dockyard hands for repairs. It would set the tone for *St. Croix*—the hard luck destroyer.[24]

Not all repairs could be fully completed in Halifax, and so *St. Croix* set out for refit in Devonport from St. John's on November 30th. She was turned back however, having run into a hurricane en route. Finally reaching Halifax on December 18th, 1940 she was again placed under repair until the middle of March 1941. For this reason she never sailed to Britain for a complete refit as intended, but was kept in Canadian waters—first with the Newfoundland Escort Force and then the 21st Escort Group.

Her first major refit was completed in St. John's in April of 1942—she had entered dock in September of the previous year. After this she joined the Mid-Ocean Escort Force (MOEF). During the wolfpack attack on convoy ON 113 in late July 1972—an action in which the Canadian destroyer HMCS *Ottawa* was sunk—she attacked and sank the German

---

[23] (Mooney, James L; Naval Historical Center, et al.)

[24] (Bercuson & Herwig, 2011) p. 38 & p. 64

Type VIIC U-boat U-90. She would enter dock again that fall for a five-week refit in St. John's starting in November.

St. Croix finally made it to Britain when she escorted convoy HX 222 across the Atlantic in January 1942, after which she undertook working up at Tobermory between January 22nd and February 17th—this was part of the Royal Navy's intensive instructional effort focused on remediating the persistent training deficiencies in Canadian escorts. This paid off for *St. Croix* in early march of 1943, as she and the corvette HMCS *Shediac* attacked and sank the German submarine U-87 while escorting the convoy KMS 10 from Britain to Gibraltar. *St. Croix* subsequently acted as part of the escort for the North African convoy MKS 9 before returning to Halifax for repairs in June of 1943.

In August of 1943 she returned to England once more to join the anti-submarine offensive in the Bay of Biscay, and was involved in the running action between a German wolfpack and the combine convoys ON 202 and ONS 18, on September 19th 1943. This battle—which ran throughout several nights with increasing Allied losses—saw one of the first successful deployments of the German acoustic torpedo (known to the Allies as GNAT). *St. Croix* was one of the first ships sunk by such a torpedo[25], when on the night of the 20th U-305[26]

---

[25] Countermeasures against an acoustic homing torpedo were in active development by the National Research Council as many expected the Germans to develop such a weapon. While it came too late for *St. Croix* and the other escorts sunk in the battle for ON 202 and ONS 18, within weeks the RCN would deploy the CAT (Canadian Anti-Torpedo) countermeasure—'two lengths of pipe, carried side by side which banged together...in the water' (Zimmerman, 1989) p. 96

[26] U-305 was thought to have been sunk by the British destroyer HMS *Wanderer* on January 7th, 1944 but more recent research casts doubt on this, instead indicating the submarine may have fallen victim to one of its own GNATs. See (Niestlé, 2007). A narrative of HMS *Wanderer's* hunt can be found in (Bercuson & Herwig, 2011) p. 315 and (Whinney, 1986) p. 11

torpedoed the old destroyer twice. Although most of the crew got off and were rescued by the British frigate HMS *Itchen* before the destroyer sank, *Itchen* herself was sunk two nights later with heavy loss of life. Of HMCS *St. Croix's* crew of 147, only one man survived—Leading Stoker William Allen Fisher of Alberta.[27]

HMCS St. Clair (Town-class (*Wickes*-subclass))

Length:	314' 3"	Laid Down:	25-03-1918
Beam:	30' 6"	Launched:	04-07-1918
Draft:	8' 6"	Commissioned:	24-09-1940
Displacement:	1069 tons	Paid Off:	23-08-1944
Armament:	1 x 4" LA guns, three 21" torpedo tubes, 1 x 12pdr AA guns, Hedgehog ASW mortar		

The destroyer that would become HMCS *St. Clair* was laid down as a *Little* sub-class ship with Yarrow boilers. Built by Union Iron Works of San Francisco, she was commissioned into the US Navy as USS *Williams* at the Mare Island Naval Yard in March of 1919.

June of that year found her in the Azores en route to Gibraltar where she received information on minefields still extant in the Adriatic, which she conveyed to Commander, naval Forces, and Eastern Mediterranean. Her tour of duty in

---

[27] (Hague, 1990) p. 80

these waters took her to Split in the Kingdom of Serbs, Croats and Slovenes (eventually to become Yugoslavia), Gallipoli and Trieste.

She arrived home in New York City the 1st of August 1919 and was eventually posted back to the Pacific Fleet, operating out of San Diego until decommissioned and placed in reserve there in June of 1922.

She was recommissioned into the US Navy early November of 1939 and after refitting at Mare Island, operated in the San Diego area before being sent east in February 1940. *Williams* made passage through the Panama Canal after having 'manned the rail' at Balboa, Panama in President Roosevelt's honor, as he was informally inspecting the Canal Zone at the time. *Williams* arrived in Key West, Florida the end of February. She would spend the next several months on Neutrality Patrol along the Atlantic seaboard, before arriving in New York to conduct training cruises for Naval Reserve crewmen throughout the summer. She went into refit at Boston one last time before departing to Halifax for transfer to the RCN.[28]

As HMCS *St. Clair*, she briefly served as local escort out of Halifax before voyaging across the Atlantic as an escort with convoy HX 91. She was assigned to EG 4, part of Western Approaches Command based out of Greenock. Arriving on the Clyde in December 1940 she started her refit there and only transferred to Devonport for its completion in January of 1941. *St. Clair* didn't finish refitting until March of that year, but after working up she rejoined EG 4. While the hunt for the *Bismarck* was going on she was diverted to search duties, and in late May was one of three destroyers attacked by German bombers west of Galway, Ireland. *St. Clair* and HMS *Tartar* rescued survivors after HMS *Mashona* was capsized by the bomb attack. After picking up all the *Mashona* survivors, *St. Clair* sank the hulk.

---

[28] (Mooney, James L; Naval Historical Center, et al.)

TIN CAN CANUCKS

Posted back to Canada to join Newfoundland Escort Force, she made the trek as escort to convoy ON 328 and arrived in St. John's June 7, 1941. Her service with NEF was short, as she collided with the oiler *Clam* ten days later, damage from which necessitated repairs which sidelined her until December. Afterwards she joined WLEF, and in late January 1942 rescued survivors from the merchantman *Nyholt*.[29]

Through 1942 and 1943 she remained with WLEF, serving with Escort Group W-2, save for a short stint attached as tender to HMCS *Cornwallis* during the summer of 1943. In December of that year she was withdrawn from escort duties and assigned to St. Margaret's Bay as depot ship for the RN submarines that had been detailed to be 'clockwork-mice' for RCN anti-submarine training.

Finally in May of 1944 she went to Halifax for repairs and was subsequently paid off in August. Used as a firefighting and damage control training hulk for the Damage Control School, she was moved to the Bedford Basin and her remains could still be found there as late as the 1950s.[30]

---

[29] (Hague, 1990) p. 79

[30] (MacPherson & Barrie, Ships of Canada's Naval Forces: 1910-2002, 2004) p. 56

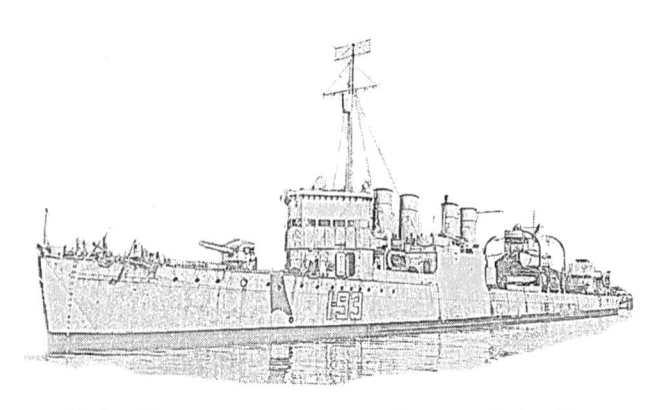

HMCS St. Francis (Town-class (*Clemson*-subclass))

Length:	314' 3"	Laid Down:	04-11-1918
Beam:	30' 9"	Launched:	21-03-1919
Draft:	9' 3"	Commissioned:	24-09-1940
Displacement:	1190 tons	Paid Off:	11-06-1945
Armament:	1 x 4" LA guns, three 21" torpedo tubes, 1 x 12pdr AA guns, Hedgehog ASW mortar		

USS *Bancroft* was built by Bethlehem Shipbuilding Corporation at their Fore River shipyard in Quincy, Massachusetts and on March 23, 1919 was launched by Ms. Mary W. Bancroft—the great granddaughter of George Bancroft (former Secretary of the Navy), after whom the ship was named.

Commissioned into the US Navy on June 30, 1919, she immediately joined the Atlantic Fleet and took part in fleet exercises and training, until placed in reserve commission in November of that year. Ultimately she was placed out of commission in Philadelphia on July 11, 1922.

Bancroft was recommissioned into the USN and assigned to the Atlantic Squadron in December of 1939, after which she was transferred to the Royal Canadian Navy in Halifax on September 24, 1940, and commissioned as HMCS *St. Francis*— the same day as her sister HMCS *St. Croix*, ex-USS *McCook*.[31]

---

[31] (Mooney, James L; Naval Historical Center, et al.)

She spent the remainder of 1940 doing local escort work out of Halifax. Following the German Cruiser *Admiral Scheer*'s attack on convoy HX 84 and its sinking of the armed merchant cruiser HMS *Jervis Bay*, *St. Francis* was detailed to join the search for the raider, but the German cruiser slipped away.

Leaving Halifax for Greenock the first of January of 1941, she made the Clyde later that month. In addition to a host of other changes—like the modifications to her bridge to stiffen it against winter North Atlantic weather—she also received a new coat of paint.

In 1941 Town-class destroyers were being given a camouflage scheme based partly on the original scheme proposed by Peter Scott—a British naval officer and painter. The modified Peter Scott scheme still used large areas of white, but also had areas of dark grey based on the idea (soon debunked) that this camouflage color had utility in the dark, and reduced visibility from searchlights. Additionally there were vertical panels fore and aft, which were meant to foreshorten the apparent length of the hull and provide a false impression of the ships inclination—this was a modification to the scheme only found on the Town-class.[32] Ultimately it was discovered that this camouflage wasn't of any use in the North Atlantic against U-boats, and so gave way to the more common Western Approaches Camouflage scheme with its blue and green and white combination.

After her refit at Greenock and having worked-up at Tobermory she was assigned to EG 4 of Western Approaches Command, with whom she served until June, when she was posted back to the Western Atlantic and the Newfoundland Escort Force.[33]

She underwent a minor refit in Pictou in July, and was continuously employed as a mid-ocean escort until she went to

---

[32] (Raven, Royal Navy camouflage of WW2, 1972)

[33] (MacPherson & Barrie, Ships of Canada's Naval Forces: 1910-2002, 2004) p. 58

Halifax for a major refit in early December of 1942. Apparently, at this time *St. Francis* underwent significant modification, having her number 4 boiler and associated funnel removed and replaced with 470 tons of additional fuel bunkerage. It's not entirely clear if this was done because the boiler had been burned out like HMCS *Annapolis*, or if it was a result of sea-going experience with the other Town-class destroyers in commission.[34] At the same time, she had her bridge superstructure plated in and strengthened. Returning to service with the Mid-Ocean Escort Force (MOEF) in April 1943 she was back in dockyard hands in November for urgent repairs, which were completed at Shelbourne, Nova Scotia.

Badly worn like most of her sisters, and being replaced by newer escorts, *St. Francis* was reassigned to HMCS *Cornwallis* in Annapolis, Nova Scotia as a static training vessel. Here she spent the remainder of her useful life, until decommissioned in Sydney in June and 1945 and turned over to Crown War Assets Disposal Commission. Sold to Frankel Brothers for breaking up in Boston, she and ex-HMS *Hamilton* were wrecked while under tow after a collision with another vessel off Rhode Island in July of 1945.

---

[34] (Hague, 1990) p. 81

HMCS Buxton (Town-class (*Clemson*-subclass))

Length:	314' 3"	Laid Down:	20-04-1918
Beam:	30' 9"	Launched:	10-10-1918
Draft:	9' 3"	Commissioned:	04-11-1943
Displacement:	1190 tons	Paid Off:	02-06-1945
Armament:	1 x 4" LA guns, three 21" torpedo tubes, 1 x 12pdr AA guns, Hedgehog ASW mortar		

HMCS *Buxton* began life as USS *Edwards*. She was built by Bethlehem Shipbuilding Corporation at its Squantum, Massachusetts shipyard and named after Midshipman William W. Edwards. Edwards was an officer of the US Navy during the War of 1812, assigned to USS *Argus*, when he was killed in action against HMS *Pelican* 14 August 1913. The ship bearing his name was launched 10 October 1918 by Ms. Julia Edwards Noyes, Midshipman Edwards uncle's great granddaughter. USS *Edwards* was commissioned on April 24, 1919 under the command of Commander P.L. Wilson, USN.

In May 1919 *Edwards* was assigned to transport seaplane spares to St. John's, Newfoundland, as part of the historic first transatlantic seaplane flight by the US Navy. Later that month she sailed to European waters to take up duties with the Food Administration, reporting to the Commander of US Naval Forces in Europe. After arriving in Gibraltar she joined the escort of USS *George Washington*, the former ocean liner carrying President Woodrow Wilson to Brest, France. Subsequently *Edwards* visited England and Germany before arriving back in the United States in late August.

In September she was transferred to the Pacific Fleet, and

upon arrival at San Diego she was placed in reduced commission with a minimal complement. In February of 1920 she moved to Puget Sound Navy Yard, only to return to San Diego a year later, still in reserve and only occasionally at sea for gunnery practice. Finally in June of 1922 she was placed out of commission.

Edwards was recommissioned in December of 1939, to take up Neutrality Patrol duties. She underwent an overhaul on the west coast before traveling east in March of 1940, making port in Galveston, Texas. She continued to patrol the Gulf of Mexico until the fall of 1940 when she was selected for transfer to the Royal Navy, and was handed over in Halifax on October 8, 1940.[35]

Commissioned into the Royal Navy as HMS *Buxton*, she set out to cross the Atlantic on her way to Devonport for refit, when she was delayed in St. John's, Newfoundland with serious defects. Back to Halifax she went, and repairs weren't completed until March 1941. Further defects arose and ultimately *Buxton* would go to Boston for a two-month refit starting in July. Upon her return she was assigned for local escort work until she joined the troop convoy TC 14, and crossed the Atlantic headed for the Clyde to join EG-26. She wasn't with that posting long before more defects cropped up and she was in Chatham dockyard for repairs and refit in November 1941, not to emerge until February 1942. While working up after this period, she grounded and subsequently those repairs kept her idle until the end of May.

Finally back at sea, she joined Escort Group B-6, undertaking convoy and individual ship escort duties out of Liverpool until August 1943, when she was posted back to Canada to join the Western Local Escort Force (WLEF) out of Halifax. WLEF held the operational responsibility of escorting convoys between the ports of New York and Halifax out to

---

[35] (Mooney, James L; Naval Historical Center, et al.)

the Western Ocean Meeting Point (WOMP) which was east of St. John's, Newfoundland, where WLEF handed off responsibility to the Mid-Ocean Escort Force (MOEF).[36]

HMS *Buxton* served on this route for several months until her persistent defects required she return to Boston for a three-month refit in December. In March 1943 she rejoined WLEF as part of the newly-formed Escort Group W-1, but finally her ongoing mechanical issues and defects drove the RN to offer *Buxton* to the Royal Canadian Navy for static training purposes. In this manner she joined the RCN as HMCS *Buxton* on 4 November 1943—the last of the Canadian Towns commissioned.[37] She arrived at Digby, Nova Scotia in December, and continued to serve as a static training vessel until decommissioned and sold for scrap 16 January 1945. She was broken up in Boston that same year, after an undistinguished wartime career in which she appeared to spend more time in dock under repair, than at sea.

---

[36] (Hague, 1990) p. 32

[37] (MacPherson & Barrie, Ships of Canada's Naval Forces: 1910-2002, 2004) p. 54

4

LATER RIVERS
HOSTILITIES ONLY DESTROYERS

As noted in Chapter Two, after the First World War the Royal Navy reviewed its existing destroyer force and its projected needs for a future conflict, in an attempt to rationalize its procurement policy. Starting with two prototype destroyers built by the venerable shipbuilders of Thornycroft and Yarrow between 1925 and 1927—HMS *Amazon* and HMS *Ambuscade* respectively—the Admiralty's Director of Naval Construction (DNC) laid out a pattern for the new generation of 'standard' destroyers.

These became known as the A – I classes. Each year, beginning with the A-Class in 1927, a flotilla of eight destroyers and one destroyer leader would be laid down. Alternative years would see these ships fitted either with ASDIC (sonar) or anti-mine sweeps known as Two-Speed Destroyer Sweep (TSDS)—although all destroyers would be designed to accommodate ASDIC in a time of war.[1]

Each flotilla would thus consist of ships that were

---

[1] (Friedman, British Destroyers: From Earliest Days to the Second World War, 2009) p. 194

homogenous, in design, in name (all destroyer's in a flotilla would have names starting with that flotilla's letter designation, hence the C-Class destroyer HMS *Crescent* or the D-Class destroyer HMS *Decoy*—although some of the destroyer leaders, like HMS *Kempenfelt* broke this pattern in the first several flotillas) and in equipment fit, thereby allowing for a consistency in strategic and tactical deployment—not to mention easing crew training.

Canada's early River-class destroyers were either based on an existing standard design—*Saguenay* and *Skeena* were much like the A- and B-Class—or were standard destroyers; Canada having purchased the 'freak' half-flotilla C-class. Wartime losses early in the conflict reduced the destroyers available to the RCN (and by extension the Royal Navy).

Meanwhile, Britain continued to build these standard types, each year with some minor changes or improvements—the most common being the ongoing AA weaponry fit experiments—but essentially the same as the previous flotilla, up until the I-class of the 1935-36 program. There was a break with the construction of the two flotillas of Tribal-class destroyers ordered in 1936 (see the next chapter) before a new standard design was developed for the J- and subsequent classes from the 1936-37 program and onward.[2]

Due to construction time, destroyers ordered in 1936 were likely to commission only in 1939, and the outbreak of war brought the same sort of demands on destroyers as had been made two decades before. The older destroyers of the D-, E-, F-, G-, H- and I-classes would have to soldier on doing fleet work (as opposed to the convoy work undertaken by the Canadian destroyers) until the 1936 and later flotillas entered service.

As these new British destroyers joined the Royal Navy , and

---

[2] For a more thorough and complete description of the J-, K-, N-, L-, M-, O-, P- and war emergency classes and their genesis see Friedman, British Destroyers and Frigates: The Second World War and After, 2008

as Canada's own losses mounted, there was a move to replenish and strengthen Canadian destroyer numbers by converting former late-model pre-war standard fleet destroyers into escort destroyers, and lending (or giving) them to the RCN.

In this manner Canada would receive an additional seven River-class destroyers. Functionally they were identical to the earlier River-class destroyers, with some differences in profile and radar fit—although most of them, having been refit in the UK before being handed over to Canada, were likely to have more up-to-date electronics and better AA batteries than their Canadian-based sisters. This was an added bonus enjoyed both by the RCN brass and the destroyer crews themselves.

While these seven 'new' River-class destroyers were veterans of the early fighting—some, like *Saskatchewan*, had quirks thanks to serious battle damage not fully repaired—they were solidly built and far less prone to breakdowns than the Town-class destroyers. But, like the Town-class, one of their major advantages was that they were available.

HMCS Kootenay (River–class (D))

Length:	329'	Laid Down:	25-06-1931
Beam:	33'	Launched:	07-06-1932
Draft:	10' 2"	Commissioned:	12-04-1943
Displacement:	1375 tons	Paid Off:	26-19-1945
Armament:	3 x 4.7" LA guns, four 21" torpedo tubes, 7 x 20mm Oerlikon AA guns, Hedgehog ASW Mortar		

The second British destroyer to carry the name HMS *Decoy* was also built by Thornycroft—this one at the Woolston yard rather than Chiswick. Due to the depressed economic times, *Decoy* and her sister D-class destroyer *Daring* were the only ships to be built in the Woolston yard in 1932.[3] After commissioning and working up, HMS *Decoy* sailed to the Mediterranean to join the 1st Destroyer Flotilla there in April of 1933. Following this she was posted to the Persian Gulf for two months in the fall of the year, returning to Malta for new torpedo tubes at the end of 1933. She remained in the Mediterranean until recalled to Devonport for refit in the fall of 1934, after which she sailed to Hong Kong to take up duty there.

---

[3] (Barnaby, 1964) p. 100 In point of fact, Sir John I. Thornycroft, at the 1931 Annual General Meeting of Thornycroft's shareholders, expressed their good fortune at having landed these two orders "...in the face of the keenest competition." Few British shipyards were busy in those days.

Decoy remained on the China Station, posted to first the 8th Destroyer Flotilla and later the 21st Destroyer Flotilla, until the outbreak of war in 1939. Throughout that period, from 1935 to 1939 she led a busy life, being temporarily posted to the Red Sea during the Abyssinian Crisis, based out of Aden and Perim. Once the Crisis ended, she visited Mombasa and other East African ports on her way back to Hong Kong. Based from there, she undertook local patrols around the island and up the China coast, refitting in Hong Kong in early 1936, and then further repairs and fumigations (!) in the spring of the next year, after completing a tour of South East Asia the first few months of 1937. In August of 1938 she carried a representative of the British Government to Tsing-Tao, who was to apologize for incidents where liberty men had insulted the Japanese Flag.[4]

Upon the declaration of war in September 1939, *Decoy* and her flotilla (led by HMS *Duncan*) transferred west to the Mediterranean where they were active in contraband control. *Decoy* went to Malta for refit in December, and at that time it was discovered that she was suffering corrosion of the bulkheads between her engine room and her aft boiler room. This had the effect of her being declared unseaworthy.[5] Four weeks of continuous overtime work by the dockyard saw her funnels replaced, defects in her feed pumps made right, and a full hull survey completed.

She was transferred to Freetown for a four-month tour with the 20th Destroyer Flotilla in early 1940, before returning to the Mediterranean and joining the 10th Destroyer Flotilla in

---

[4] (English, Amazon to Ivanhoe: British Standard Destroyers of the 1930s, 1993) p. 55

[5] As that bulkhead separated the large open space of the turbine room from the smaller space of the aft boiler room (which contained a single boiler), if the bulkhead was pierced and those two spaces flooded, the ship would find itself still afloat but in grave danger.

May of that year. Later that month *Decoy* and sister ship HMS *Defender* met convoy US 2 in the Red Sea. They escorted this Australian troop convoy to the Suez. On the night of June 20th she, along with HMS *Dainty*, HMS *Hasty*, and HMAS *Stuart*, shelled Bardia; after which she took up further escort and patrol duties, including the cruisers HMS *Orion* and HMAS *Sydney* during their bombardment of Scarpanto in September. In November, she was struck by a bomb during an air raid at Alexandria, with damage done to Y-mount 4.7-inch gun as well as the upper and main decks. The ship's bottom was penetrated between frames 146 and 153. She sailed to Malta for permanent repairs, having those completed the first of February 1941—which also repaired additional bomb damage received in late January.

HMS *Decoy* was one of the many destroyers involved in the evacuations from Crete and Greece, during which she took minor bomb damage from a near miss at the end of May 1941. During this time she was joined by HMS *Hero* on a mission to evacuate the King of Greece from Crete, as well as land troops at Suda Bay—the two would work again together later in the war as HMCS *Kootenay* and HMCS *Chaudière*. She ran a regular route from Tobruk to Alexandria between July and November of 1941, again suffering a near miss while returning to Alexandria early July 1941. On completion of repairs she joined the escort for convoy ME 10 from Malta to Alexandria. Subsequently assigned to the Eastern Fleet, *Decoy* joined the 2nd Destroyer Flotilla, and by the end of March 1942 she had joined the escort for Force B south of Sri Lanka. Without organic air cover, the Eastern Fleet spent much of its time avoiding Japanese carrier forces.

After a brief stint operating once more from Freetown, *Decoy* finally returned home to Greenock for refit the end of October 1942. She had not been in home waters since 1934, and was long overdue for a refit. This was undertaken at the

Palmers Shipbuilding yard on the Tyne[6] between November 3, 1941 and April 12, 1942, after which she commissioned into the Royal Canadian Navy as HMCS *Kootenay*.[7]

Kootenay—transferred as a gift to Canada—began workups at Tobermory, which, once completed led to her assignment to Escort Group C-5—the famous 'Barber Pole Brigade.'—and her joining the Newfie-Derry Run for the next year. The escort duties weren't without their challenges as the North Atlantic Weather was just as foul as ever—*Kootenay* suffering severe storm damage in June 1943—even if the U-boats had been dealt a strong check in May of 1943 and had been withdrawn from the Atlantic to a great extent.

In April of 1944 *Kootenay* was reassigned to EG 11 to serve beside her sister River-class destroyers HMCS *Chaudière*, HMCS *Gatineau*, HMCS *Ottawa (II)*, and HMCS *St. Laurent*. They were tasked with patrolling the English Channel, and dealt with the expected U-Boat attacks during and after the Normandy Invasion.

At some point during this assignment *Kootenay* was patrolling between Isle of Wright and Land's End and was encountering thick fog patches. While in one of these, her Radar detected several large contacts, and *Kootenay* went to action stations and sped towards the contacts, making her challenge. When she broke out of the fog she found herself faced by several capital ships. Luckily they were British, as she would have been unlikely to successfully engage the likes of HMS *Rodney* or HMS *Warspite* on her own.[8]

---

[6] Palmers shipyard on the Tyne was where *Decoy's* sister ship HMS *Diana* had been built—she too would serve in the RCN, as the star-crossed HMCS *Margaree*.

[7] (English, Amazon to Ivanhoe: British Standard Destroyers of the 1930s, 1993) p. 56

[8] (MacPherson & Butterley, River Class Destroyers of the Royal Canadian Navy, 2008) p. 89

Her patrolling started June 6, but it would be a month after D-Day before *Kootenay* saw actual combat action. July 6 she and *Ottawa* moved to assist HMS *Stattice* which had an ASDIC contact near Beachy Head. After a prolonged attack by the three warships, they eventually cornered and sank U-678. Then on August 18, *Kootenay* and *Ottawa* again teamed up, and with *Chaudière* sank U-621 at the mouth of the Gironde River, followed two days later by the successful hunt for U-984 west of Brest.

By this point EG 11 was withdrawn to Londonderry, but a defective feed pump again sidelined *Kootenay* and she diverted to Plymouth for repairs. At Devonport the feed pump was repaired, but other defects were discovered and *Kootenay* sailed with convoy ONS 254 west, leaving Londonderry on September 17th, 1944 to St. John's, Newfoundland and then onto Halifax. When she arrived at that port on September 27th it would be the Canadian destroyer's first landfall in Canada. She was in refit at Shelbourne, Nova Scotia until February 1945, after which she returned across the Atlantic with convoy HX 345, arriving in Londonderry April 2. After working up at Tobermory she returned to EG 11 and was at sea for a final short patrol when war ended in Europe.

She returned to Canada the end of May, with a collection of Canadian service members aboard on their own return home. She then undertook similar 'trooping' runs between St. John's, Newfoundland and Quebec City over the next three months. Having completed six such round trips, she was paid off October 26, 1945 in Sydney, Nova Scotia and eventually sold for breaking in 1946 to International Iron and Metal Co. of Hamilton Ontario. *Kootenay* was finally scrapped in Lévis, Quebec later that year.[9]

---

[9] (MacPherson & Butterley, River Class Destroyers of the Royal Canadian Navy, 2008) p. 88

HMCS Margaree (River–class (D))

Length:	329'	Laid Down:	12-06-1931
Beam:	33'	Launched:	16-06-1932
Draft:	10' 2"	Commissioned:	06-09-1940
Displacement:	1375 tons	Lost:	22-10-1940

Armament: 4 x 4.7" LA guns, eight 21" torpedo tubes, 2 x 2pdr AA guns

After the loss of HMCS *Fraser* in 1940, the Canadians began negotiations for a suitable replacement almost immediately. The ship selected was HMS *Diana* which had been built by Palmers Shipbuilding Co. Ltd. Hebbrun-on-the-Tyne.[10] Launched in June 1932 and commissioned the end of that year, *Diana* joined the rest of her flotilla (at that time the 1st Destroyer Flotilla) first in the Mediterranean from January 1933 to August 1934, and then posted to the China Station a year later as the 8th Destroyer Flotilla.[11] While in the Mediterranean she had been detached to the Red Sea and the Persian Gulf from September to November of 1933. Arriving in the Far East in January 1935, she would remain there until the outbreak of war in 1939.

During this time, she once again saw detached service to the Red Sea and Persian Gulf from September of 1935 to June 1936—during the Abyssinian Crisis. *Diana* also visited Bombay in May and June of 1936, east Africa that June and

---

[10] (English, Amazon to Ivanhoe: British Standard Destroyers of the 1930s, 1993) p. 59

[11] (MacPherson & Butterley, River Class Destroyers of the Royal Canadian Navy, 2008) p. 77

July, and finally returned to Hong Kong in August. While on the China Station in 1937-1938, she took part in stopping a potential mutiny aboard the vessel *Fausang* and investigated a pirate attack on the Turnout Island lighthouse. [12]

By 1939 *Diana* was assigned to the 21st Flotilla which, on the declaration of war was transferred to the Mediterranean. She spent November of 1939 in dock at Malta for repairs for corrosion—not unlike her sister HMS *Decoy* (who would eventually become HMCS *Kootenay*). She returned to British Home Waters in December and joined the 3rd Destroyer Flotilla in the Norway Campaign. She entered the Royal Albert Dock in London in July of 1940 for refit, prior to her transfer to the RCN.

She was commissioned as HMCS *Margaree* September 6, 1940 while still in the Royal Albert Docks—this was at the height of the London Blitz. As she was the replacement for the lost HMCS *Fraser*, many of her officers and crew came from having previously served on that vessel. She was posted to Western Approaches Command's North Escort Force, and arrived in Londonderry October 20, 1940 to take up immediate assignment as escort to fast convoy OL 8. She was to be the only escort for this convoy of five ships bound for Canada, amongst whom was the troop transport MV *Port Fairy*. OL 8 was 400 miles west of Ireland when rain blew in, severely reducing visibility. *Margaree* was 2 or 3 kilometers ahead of the lead ship in the convoy. The second-in-command Lieutenant P.F.X. Russelll, who had taken first watch at 8:00 p.m. called for a reduction in speed to allow the convoy to catch up, to maintain visibility. When he went off duty at midnight, he detailed the situation to his relief and retired below.[13] An hour

---

[12] (English, Amazon to Ivanhoe: British Standard Destroyers of the 1930s, 1993) p. 60

[13] (Douglas, Sarty, & Whitby, No Higher Purpose: The Official Operational History of the Royal Canadian Navy in the Second World War, 1939-1943, 2004) p. 116

later, rain squalls blew in reducing visibility further. Suddenly at 1:25 a.m. the watch-keeper on *Port Fairy* spotted *Margaree* just off the starboard bow, and very close. Inexplicably, at 1:29 *Margaree* suddenly turned hard to port and right across *Port Fairy's* bows. The transport reversed its engines, put her rudder hard over to port and let out three blasts of its horn. Suddenly aware of the danger *Margaree* took evasive action but it was too late.[14]

Port Fairy's towering stem tore through the smaller ship's bridge, severing her bows from the rest of her and ripping *Margaree's* forward plating from her frames. The destroyer's bow sank instantly, taking the crew in the forward messdecks (the majority of whom had been off duty and asleep) with it. The commanding officer, Commander J.W.R. Roy, RCN was in his sea cabin below the bridge and he and 140 other men were lost.

Thirty-six men survived the collision, mostly off-duty officers, engine room personnel and those on watch on the quarterdeck. Lieutenant W.M. Landymore was one of those who had survived a similar collision between HMCS *Fraser* and HMS *Calcutta* and now the *Margaree* collision. Lt. Landymore ran forward to survey the bridge, but found it "...knocked off as straight as a die, there wasn't anything—just a piece of a bulkhead." By this time *Margaree* had fetched up against the stopped *Port Fairy*, and the transport's crew helped thirty men scale the distance form *Margaree* up and over the side of *Port Fairy*—while the ships ground together as they rose and fell in the stormy waters. Two men, including Able Seaman Al Jones of Vancouver fell between the two ships and were crushed to death.[15]

---

[14] A Board of Inquiry into the destroyer's loss could come to no clear conclusions as to what had caused *Margaree's* final fatal turn, or why she had not seen *Port Fairy*—none of the bridge watch survived the collision to provide evidence as to what happened.

[15] (MacPherson & Butterley, River Class Destroyers of the Royal Canadian Navy,

Lt. Russell, two other officers, and a rating stayed aboard *Margaree's* hulk to ensure the depth charges had their safeties set—to avoid detonating below *Port Fairy* should *Margaree's* remains sink beneath the transport.[16] Once assured of the depth charges safety, the four men made it off *Margaree* on a Carley float which *Port Fairy* was unable to recover for nearly an hour. *Margaree's* hulk stayed afloat until daybreak on October 22nd even though *Port Fairy* had put twenty-six 4-inch shells into her from the merchantman's deck gun. A demolition party tried to board her, but as *Margaree's* magazines were nearly alight, they elected to keep their distance. *Margaree* finally slipped beneath the waves after taking another ten 4-inch rounds from *Port Fairy*.[17]

2008) p. 79

[16] This would happen when HMCS *Saguenay* sank the freighter *Azra* in November of 1942, after the freighter collided with the destroyer and severed her stern. The depth charges on the plummeting stern went off and sank *Azra*

[17] (Douglas, Sarty, & Whitby, No Higher Purpose: The Official Operational History of the Royal Canadian Navy in the Second World War, 1939-1943, 2004) p.117

HMCS Gatineau (River–class (E))

Length:	329'	Laid Down:	23-03-1933
Beam:	33' 3"	Launched:	29-05-1934
Draft:	10' 10"	Commissioned:	03-06-1943
Displacement:	1405 tons	Paid Off:	10-01-1946

Armament: 3 x 4.7" LA guns, four 21" torpedo tubes, 6 x 20mm Oerlikon AA guns, Hedgehog ASW mortar

Unique amongst the Canadian River-class destroyers, HMCS *Gatineau*—built as HMS *Express* by Swan Hunter & Wigham Richardson Wallsend-on-Tyne—had been originally fitted as a minesweeper, and had twin sponsoons aft for the mine rails (never carried in Canadian service). She would be the sole E-Class destroyer to serve in the RCN.

HMS *Express* was commissioned into the Home Fleet November 6, 1934 and assigned to the 5th Destroyer Flotilla. She had her gun mounts adjusted at Sheerness between December 1934 and January 1935. During the Abyssinian crisis she was detached to the Mediterranean Fleet at Alexandria where she served until March 1936, after which she returned to Portsmouth for a refit until May. After refitting she was posted back east to Gibraltar for two months, returning to home waters for the remainder of 1936. The first three months of 1937 *Express* undertook Non-Intervention Patrols off the Spanish coast, returning to the UK for a brief period of repairs and then two months of minelaying trials.

Having completed a refit in Portsmouth in October 1937 she suffered a fire in her forward boiler room, which caused extensive damage to her electrical cables, necessitating further repairs. She spent some time in home waters and patrolling out of Gibraltar, until returning to Portsmouth to operate as a minelayer from August to October 1938. After a short refit there she returned to Gibraltar, and on March 21, 1939 she escorted the ferry Cote D'Azur and its passengers—the French President and his retinue—to Britain for a state visit.

She was relieved of duty with the 5th Destroyer Flotilla by the J-Class destroyer HMS *Janus*, and was selected for conversion to a Boys' Training Ship and aircraft co-operation vessel, but ultimately these plans fell through.

When war broke out she was assigned to Immingham and joined the 20th Destroyer (Minelaying) Flotilla on its formation. Her first offensive minefield was laid at a suspected exit of the German mine barrage in the North Sea. Subsequently she and HMS *Esk*, HMS *Intrepid*, and HMS *Ivanhoe* laid 240 mines in the Ems estuary the night of December 17th, and another barrage of 164 off the Hook of Holland with the same comrades (less *Intrepid*) the 15th of May. Prior to the operation off the Hook of Holland, *Express* had collided with a trawler and had to be repaired in Hartlepool in April.

During the 'Miracle of Dunkirk' *Express* made six trips, evacuating over 3,500 troops, and was the second-last vessel to leave Dunkirk.

On August 31, 1940, *Express* was one of several destroyers laying a defensive minefield 40 miles off Texel. At just past 11:00 p.m. that day she struck a mine just abreast her B-mount. Everything forward frame 52 was demolished and 4 officers and 53 other crew were killed. It took some two and a half hours before she was mobile again—and then only backwards. She spent several hours plodding back to British waters stern first (having unfortunately left behind 9 of her men who would be taken prisoner once rescued), before she was found by HMS *Kelvin* and HMS *Jupiter*. She was first taken in tow by *Kelvin*, but the tow broke after some 90 minutes and she was then taken in tow by HMS *Jupiter* to Hull, where she arrived early evening September 9.

Her reconstruction at Chatham would last until October of

1941. After passing trials post-repair, she joined HMS *Eclectra* to escort HMS *Prince of Wales* to the Far East. They left the Clyde October 25, 1941 and sailed to join HMS *Repulse*, her savior HMS *Jupiter* and sister HMS *Encounter*. When Imperial Japanese Navy carrier strikes sank *Prince of Wales* and *Repulse*, *Express* was able to rescue nearly a thousand of the 2,081 men who survived the sinkings. She then took over escort duties for 'China Force' between Singapore and Java, but in February suffered a boiler room fire that caused extensive damage to her electric cabling, fuel tanks, and bulkheads. She continued operations until she could be repaired and refitted in Simonstown between late April and Late June 1942; thus missing the Battle of the Java Sea and the attack on Trincomalee, Sri Lanka.

After returning to duty, she joined the Eastern Fleet's 12th Destroyer Flotilla, and she served as an escort to the aircraft carrier HMS *Illustrious* during the landings at Majunga, Madagascar in September of 1942. She returned to England in February of 1943 and went into refit at Liverpool until June 2, 1943. Upon her emergence she was commissioned into the Royal Canadian Navy as HMCS *Gatineau* on June 3, 1943, having been given to Canada as a gift.[18]

Gatineau completed her work-ups at Tobermory and was then assigned to Escort Group C-2 in Londonderry to join convoy ON 191 as escort on July 2. As the German U-Boats had suffered a serious check in May of 1943, *Gatineau* found her convoy escort work reasonably quiet until the combined convoy action of ON 202/ONS 18 in September of that year.

The U-boats had returned to the Atlantic with a vengeance—and a new weapon. The Acoustic torpedo (known to the British as the GNAT) carried a new danger; it was able to target a vessel based on the noise made by that

---

[18] (English, Amazon to Ivanhoe: British Standard Destroyers of the 1930s, 1993) p. 74

ship's screws. As escort vessels ran faster than merchantmen, their screws made more noise at speed—the GNAT was designed to kill escorts. And it did that well.

Between September 20 and September 23 20 U-boats attacked the combined convoy. The success of the GNAT could be seen in the fact that only six of 63 merchantmen were lost. The convoy escort lost three ships sunk (including HMCS *St. Croix*) and one damaged. The loss of *St. Croix* was especially bitter, as she and her Commanding Officer Lieutenant Commander A.H. Dobson, DSC, RCN has been a successful U-boat killing team for a Town-class destroyer.

Escort Group C-2 began to be employed as a support group in December of 1943. In this manner it didn't escort convoys directly, but instead joined convoys specifically to hunt down U-boats detected by ASDIC (sonar) or other means, thereby freeing up the close escort vessels to continue with the convoy. In March of 1944 C-2 joined convoy HX 280 which had been attacked by a substantial wolf pack. *Gatineau* made ASDIC contact with one of them the morning of March 5, and after a 32 hour hunt, U-744 was sunk. *Gatineau* however couldn't enjoy this success as she had already been called away to assist another convoy under attack.[19]

She joined Escort Group 11 in Londonderry in late April with her River-class sisters, HMCS *Chaudière*, HMCS *Kootenay*, HMCS *Ottawa* and HMCS *St. Laurent*. These five were detailed to patrolling the west end of the English Channel during the lead-up to D-Day and after the invasion. Starting June 5 they kept a sharp eye out for U-boats attempting to attack shipping vital to landing and supporting the Normandy Invasion. *Gatineau* didn't stay long however—she left in early July bound for Halifax, to have urgent boiler repairs completed. She would be in refit there until March of the next year, after which

---

[19] (MacPherson & Butterley, River Class Destroyers of the Royal Canadian Navy, 2008) p. 96

she sailed across the Atlantic once more to work-up in Tobermory before re-joining EG 11 (now consisting of HMCS *Assiniboine* and HMCS *Saskatchewan* along with veteran member HMCS *Kootenay*).

EG 11 continued their patrols for the remainder of the war and after, until all U-boats had been surrendered (or scuttled) and accounted for. *Gatineau* would head home to Canada after this—briefly stopping in Greenock to embark repatriated Canadian naval personnel. She made two subsequent round trips to Greenock on similar 'trooping' runs before she was assigned to the Canadian West Coast to become a training ship for HMCS *Royal Roads* in August. Despite this plan, and an oceanographic survey she took part in in November, she was laid up and decommissioned January 10, 1946.

Apparently sold for scrap and broken up in late 1946, there is some indication she may have been scuttled as a breakwater in Royston, British Columbia in 1948.[20]

---

[20] (MacPherson & Barrie, Ships of Canada's Naval Forces: 1910-2002, 2004) p. 51

HMCS Qu'Appelle (River-class (F))

Length:	329'	Laid Down:	21-08-1933
Beam:	33' 2"	Launched:	12-10-1934
Draft:	10' 10"	Commissioned:	08-02-1944
Displacement:	1405 tons	Paid Off:	27-05-1946

Armament: 4 x 4.7" LA guns, eight 21" torpedo tubes, 2 x 2pdr AA guns

HMCS *Qu'Appelle* and her sister HMCS *Saskatchewan* were both built by John Brown & Co. Ltd. at their Clydebank shipyard. She was launched as HMS *Foxhound* in October 1934, and upon commissioning in the Royal Navy the end of June, joined the Home Fleet's 6th Destroyer Flotilla.

She would operate off Vigo and Corunna between November of 1936 and January 1937, and after a short refit in Sheerness, was based out of Gibraltar for February and March of 1937. This was followed by operations out of the Biscay ports in May and June, and again from August to October of 1937. She returned to Chatham for a refit late in 1937, and then it was back to patrol duties from Gibraltar and Oran the first three months of 1938. She would then return to home waters where she would remain based for the rest of 1938 and 1939.

She suffered propeller damage, after striking the submerged submarine HMS *Seahorse*, while she was en route from Rosyth to Invergordon, late September 1938. As the damage to the starboard propeller was minor, she continued to Invergordon and received repairs at Sheerness in November and December of that year.

Having remained with the 6th Destroyer Flotilla since 1935,

she was still a part of it when it was renumbered to the 8th Destroyer Flotilla in April of 1939. When war broke out *Foxhound* found herself in Home Waters as part of the Home Fleet.

The 8th Flotilla was escorting the aircraft carrier HMS *Ark Royal* on September 14th, when the carrier was attacked by U-39. *Foxhound*, her destroyer leader HMS *Faulknor*, and sister HMS *Firedrake* hunted down and sank the submarine. *Foxhound* rescued and took prisoner the U-boat's entire crew.

Later in the year *Foxhound* rescued the survivors of the Swedish vessel *Orania*, which had been torpedoed by U-50 sixty miles north-east of the Shetland Islands.

The next year found *Foxhound* heavily involved in the Norwegian Campaign, where in the Second Battle of Narvik she engaged and sank the German destroyer *Diether von Roeder* inside Narvik Harbour on April 13th 1940.[21] In May she escorted HMS *Warspite* to Gibraltar, returning to escort the vessels carrying the occupying force to Iceland. She remained in those waters for a month before joining Force H at Gibraltar, and subsequently took part in the July attacks against the French Fleet in Oran Harbour[22].

Foxhound underwent refit in Sheerness between August and October of 1940, returning to Force H and the 8th Destroyer Flotilla once complete. Over the next ten months she took part in three operations, ferrying supplies to Malta as well as shelling Genoa in January 1941, and escort duties between Gibraltar and West Africa. She joined her 8th flotilla sisters in sinking U-138 west of Gibraltar in June of that year. After

---

[21] While April 13, 1940 was a Saturday, it was apparently still an unlucky day for *Diether von Roeder* and her crew.

[22] (MacPherson & Butterley, River Class Destroyers of the Royal Canadian Navy, 2008) p. 107. She had entered the harbour before the attacks, carrying Captain C.S. Holland on his mission to negotiate the handover of the French Fleet to the British and avoid bloodshed, but the French Admiral refused to see him.

undergoing a three-month refit she undertook some escort duties until reassigned to the 2nd Destroyer Flotilla in the Mediterranean early in 1942. By April of that year she was sent east to reinforce the Eastern Fleet, and served on the South African Station for a year. Afterwards she served with the 4th Destroyer Flotilla based out of Freetown on the West African Station.[23]

In August of 1943 she returned to Britain for refit and conversion to a long-range escort. After this she was handed over to the RCN and commissioned as HMCS *Qu'Appelle* on February 8, 1944—having put in some 240,000 miles of war service already.

Completing workups in Tobermory she briefly joined Escort Group 6 in Londonderry, before being reassigned as senior officer with EG 12 in April. There she joined the River-class destroyers HMCS *Restigouche*, HMCS *Saskatchewan*, and HMCS *Skeena*. These worthies patrolled the western end of the English Channel until the latter part of June without much action. Their next patrol in July—named Operation Dredger—was meant to roll up German armed trawlers that were escorting U-Boats to and from Brest.

Operation Kinetic followed where EG 12 attacked a German convoy in Audierne Bay the night of August 10. In the mist of this furious gun action, and after several trawlers had been sunk or beached—including the lead ship—HMCS *Skeena* dashed out of the smoke and darkness to find *Qu'Appelle* right in front of her bows. While *Skeena* went full astern on both turbines, she was unable to prevent a collision and the two Canadian destroyers crashed into each other with *Qu'Appelle's* steering being knocked out. While it took some time to recover control, the remainder of *Qu'Appelle's* damage was light and *Qu'Appelle* put into Plymouth for repairs between

---

[23] (English, Amazon to Ivanhoe: British Standard Destroyers of the 1930s, 1993) p. 85

August 12th and September 5, 1944.

By then EG 12 had been rolled into EG 11 and *Qu'Appelle* returned to become senior officer once more[24]. EG 11 at that time consisted of HMCS *Assiniboine*, HMCS *Chaudière*, HMCS *Ottawa (II)*, and HMCS *Restigouche*, but soon after *Ottawa* and *Restigouche* would be replaced by HMCS *Skeena* and HMCS *St. Laurent*. At that point EG 11 was assigned to Iceland to protect against a possible U-Boat breakout from Norwegian waters to the Atlantic. It was during these operations that the group took shelter in Reykjavik Harbour from a storm the night of October 24, and *Skeena* was blown aground and wrecked after dragging her anchors.

Qu'Appelle, *Chaudière*, and *St. Laurent* would return to Canada for refit; *Qu'Appelle* arriving in Halifax on December 5, 1944. The war in Europe was over by the time she reemerged in April of 1945, and so she was assigned troop ferrying duty to repatriate Canadian servicemen back to Canada from the UK. After four trips to Greenock and back she was assigned training duties as a tender to the Torpedo School at HMCS *Stadacona*.

Paid off into reserve in May of 1946, *Qu'Appelle* was sold in 1947 to German & Milne of Montreal to be broken up in Sydney Nova Scotia in 1948.[25]

---

[24] Notwithstanding her change of command; previously under the command of Commander J.D. Birch, she was now the command of Commander J.D. Prentice

[25] (MacPherson & Barrie, Ships of Canada's Naval Forces: 1910-2002, 2004) p. 53

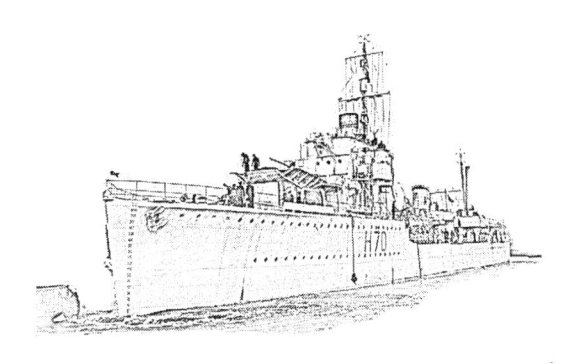

HMCS Saskatchewan (River–class (F))

Length:	329'	Laid Down:	25-07-1933
Beam:	33' 3"	Launched:	29-08-1934
Draft:	10' 10"	Commissioned:	31-05-1943
Displacement:	1405 tons	Paid Off:	28-01-1946

Armament: 2 x 4.7" LA guns, four 21" torpedo tubes, 6 x 20mm Oerlikon AA guns, Hedgehog ASW mortar

HMS *Fortune*, like her sister *Foxhound* was built by John Brown & Co. Ltd. at Clydebank in 1934. Both of these destroyers would end up in Canadian service less than a decade later.

She commissioned into the Royal Navy in May of 1935 and joined the 6th Destroyer Flotilla in the Home Fleet. She saw service with the Mediterranean Fleet in 1937 and Non-Intervention patrols in the Bay of Biscay during the Spanish Civil war. In April of 1939, with the arrival of the Tribal-class Destroyers and the soon-to-be-completed J- and K-Class destroyers, the 6th Flotilla was re-designated the 8th Flotilla, while continuing its fleet duties until the outbreak of war.

Fortune participated with the 8th Flotilla in sinking two of the first U-Boats to be lost in the war. She took part in sinking U-27 with depth charges and gunfire in September of 1939—rescuing her crew—and later in March of 1940 while escorting the battlecruisers of the Home Fleet north of the Shetland Islands, she sank U-44 by depth charges alone. There were no survivors. After this the 8th Flotilla would take part in the

Norwegian Campaign.

On May 8, 1940 she and HMS *Fearless* escorted the cruisers HMS *Berwick* and HMS *Glasgow* which were carrying the 2nd Battalion Royal Marines for the Allies' occupation of Iceland.

In July, *Fortune*, along with three other destroyers, was sent at high speed to find and escort home the submarine HMS *Shark* which had been damaged by German aircraft and was unable to dive. The three destroyers came under heavy air attack while on their hunt for the British submarine, but *Shark* had already surrendered after a brief struggle. While her crew was to become prisoners-of-war, *Shark* herself would sink while under tow by German minesweepers in the North Sea.

In August of 1940, while briefly assigned to the 4th Destroyer Flotilla, *Fortune* stood by the armed merchant cruiser HMS *Transylvania*, which had been torpedoed by U-56 off the Irish coast, and was able to rescue her survivors. *Fortune* was then transferred to Force H in Gibraltar and participated in the unsuccessful attack on Dakar September 24, 1940, during which she sank the French submarine *Ajax* which had been attempting to attack the British fleet. All 76 of the crew were rescued by *Fortune*.

The destroyer spent the next five months assigned to escort duties between Freetown and Gibraltar, followed by three more months assigned to Force H in Gibraltar. She took part in two aircraft-supply operations to Malta: Operation Winch with HMS *Ark Royal* in early April of 1941 and one with HMS *Argus* in late April.

In May, while returning to Gibraltar in company with sisters HMS *Fearless* and HMS *Fury* and with her destroyer leader HMS *Faulknor*, some 20 miles off Bougaroni, Algeria, the flotilla was attacked by aircraft. A near miss on *Fortune's* starboard side near frame 141—caused by a 250-pound bomb exploding 20-feet beneath the surface of the water—stopped all turbine-driven machinery and made a 12-foot hole in the hull between frames 142 and 143. Flooding forward and aft of this caused *Fortune* to list to starboard.

Reducing her speed and sealing the after magazines and

shell rooms, her crew cleared away the wreckage and proceeded onwards at 12 knots. Soon after it was found that the magazine and shell room hatches needed to be opened again to avoid a build-up of pressure that could rupture the deck. Eight tons of equipment was removed from the upper deck within 20 minutes of the explosion and another 1,500 pounds of davits, depth charge throwers and towing cables were also jettisoned. The destroyer's shafts were bent and neither of the aft 4.7-inch guns could be used due to the risk of further damaging the aft structure and the flooding of the magazines.[26]

Fortune was sent home for repairs at Chatham and once these were complete in November she was sent back to Gibraltar. Apparently the repairs didn't see everything entirely set right; as late as April 1944 her steering was quirky—answering helm quickly to starboard but slowly to port.[27]

In Gibraltar she was limited to local patrol duties due to remaining defects and a green crew, both of which had been resolved by February of 1942. On February 9 she joined a convoy to Malta and from there escorted the transport HMS *Breconshire* to Alexandria, Egypt, where they arrived on the 17th. *Fortune* then left to join the 2nd Destroyer Flotilla at Trincomalee, Sri Lanka, arriving in early March and spending the next three months on escort duty with the Eastern Fleet. In April she rescued 88 survivors of MV *Glenshiel* which had been torpedoed 300 miles east of Addu Atoll.

In June of 1942, *Fortune* was detached back to the Mediterranean to join the destroyers HMS *Hotspur* and HMS *Griffin* (which would become HMCS *Ottawa (II)* less than a year later.) in the unsuccessful Operation Vigorous. This had intended to supply Malta but in the face of Axis air and sea

---

[26] (English, Amazon to Ivanhoe: British Standard Destroyers of the 1930s, 1993) p. 84

[27] (Easton, 1966) p. 235

opposition had to turn back to Alexandria June 16 after a four-day struggle. *Fortune* returned to the Eastern Fleet for the remainder of 1942.

In early 1943 she sailed to London for refit, arriving in February. After completing this time in dock she emerged the end of May to be commissioned as HMCS *Saskatchewan*. She was officially gifted to Canada in June 15th.[28]

Upon commissioning she was assigned to Escort Group C-3 as senior officer. She would spend the next year on escort duties in the North Atlantic, with little of note happening other than a minor collision with the destroyer USS *Kendrick* in the River Foyle in January 1944. In March of that year she joined Escort Group 12 to take up patrol of the English Channel during and after the Normandy Invasion in June of 1944. In July, while undertaking Operation Dredger with HMCS *Qu'Appelle*, HMCS *Restigouche*, and HMCS *Skeena*, she sank one armed trawler and damaged two others off the coast of Brest, suffering four wounded and one killed.

EG 12 was posted to Londonderry at the end of July and *Saskatchewan* would sail independently for Halifax, arriving August 6. Later that month she would go to Shelbourne, Nova Scotia for refit, which was initially completed by November, but further work was needed so she again entered dock, this time in St. John's, Newfoundland until January 1945. She returned to British waters in the middle of that month and then spent the remainder of the war first with Escort Group 14 and then EG 11. She was in Plymouth when the war in Europe ended. The end of May, 1945 she left Greenock for Canada, bringing Canadian personnel home after the end of hostilities. Once back in Canada she ran similar 'trooping' runs between St. John's, Newfoundland and Quebec City. After five round trips she arrived back in St. John's in September, to

---

[28] (English, Amazon to Ivanhoe: British Standard Destroyers of the 1930s, 1993) p. 84

be declared surplus to requirements and paid off in Sydney, Nova Scotia January 28, 1946. She was sold later that year to International Iron & Metal Company, Hamilton for scrap.[29] This would spell the end of the good *Fortune*.[30]

HMCS Ottawa (II) (River–class (G))

Length:	323'	Laid Down:	20-09-1934
Beam:	33'	Launched:	15-08-1935
Draft:	10' 7"	Commissioned:	20-03-1943
Displacement:	1350 tons	Paid Off:	31-10-1945

Armament: 2 x 4.7" LA guns, four 21" torpedo tubes, 6 x 20mm Oerlikon AA guns, Hedgehog ASW mortar

Originally built as HMS *Griffin* by Vickers-Armstrong Ltd. at Barrow-in-Furness, she was completed in March of 1936 and commissioned into the Royal Navy on June 6th. Upon commissioning she left for the Mediterranean to join her sisters in the 1st Destroyer Flotilla. While in the Mediterranean she took part in the search for the *Kronprins Olav* which had been drifting with her propeller shaft broken and no radio. This search was started when four people from the ship were picked up by the naval auxiliary RFA *Olynthus* and taken to Malta. *Griffin* and her sister HMS *Greyhound* and the net-layer HMS *Protector* went in search of *Kronprins Olav*, and having been found by *Griffin*, the ship was safely returned to Malta.

HMS *Griffin* acted as an escort for the P&O liner *Strathnaver*

---

[29] (MacPherson & Butterley, River Class Destroyers of the Royal Canadian Navy, 2008) p. 91

[30] I feel I must apologize for this pun, but it was too good to leave out — Author

and the cruiser HMS *Arethusa* in the Eastern Mediterranean during the Munich Crisis of 1938. In February of 1939 she was in a collision with the target destroyer HMS *Shikari* where she was holed above the waterline near her stern. The damage was reasonably minor and repairs were completed within days. She was in Alexandria, Egypt when war was declared.

In November *Griffin* arrived in Plymouth and a week after arrival joined the rest of the 1st flotilla in Harwich, where she remained based until April 1940. Soon after arrival she took part in rescuing the crew of sister HMS *Gipsy* after she had struck a mine off Harwich November 21st. Later in the month she was holed while in the harbour and was taken in hand at Harland and Wolff's East India Docks for repair. These were completed in early December. The remainder of her time in Harwich was quiet and *Griffin* was transferred to the Home Fleet for service in Norwegian waters in April of 1940. On the 24th of that month she captured a German trawler in the North Sea which had been transporting U-Boat supplies. She later participated in the evacuation of Namsos, Norway.

Having been transferred to the 13th Destroyer Flotilla at Gibraltar, she served with Force H between August and November of 1940. On October 20th, in company with her sister HMS *Gallant* and fellow destroyer HMS *Hotspur*, she sank the Italian submarine *Lafole* near Gibraltar. In November she was amongst the reinforcements to the Mediterranean Fleet and was transferred to the 14th Destroyer Flotilla until December of 1941. During this time she deployed to the Red Sea to take part in the final capture of Italian Forces in East Africa; this occurring in February and March of 1941.

January 7, 1941 she came to the aid of her sister HMS *Gallant* which had been mined off Pantellaria, picking up survivors and wounded after *Gallant* was lost. She participated in the Battle of Matapan before taking part in the disastrous campaigns for Greece and Crete. During these she avoided receiving any combat damage and was able to evacuate over 700 troops from Suda Bay. She completed four months' duties without incident on the Tobruk run between July and

November of 1941, and in December joined the 2nd Destroyer Flotilla while continuing to serve in the Mediterranean until February of 1942.

At that point the 2nd Destroyer Flotilla was sent east as reinforcement to the Eastern Fleet based in Kilindini, Kenya. *Griffin* was assigned to escort duties between East Africa and South Africa until September, but was borrowed by the Mediterranean Fleet for the failed Operation Vigorous convoy attempt to Malta in June. Unlike many others she saw no damage or casualties during this time.[31]

By September 1942 *Griffin* was in serious need of refit and returned to the UK in October to Thornycroft's Southampton (Woolston) shipyard to begin work.[32] She would be in dockyard hands from November 1942 to the end of March 1943. While there she was converted to escort destroyer configuration. March 1, 1943 she was officially handed over to the RCN as a replacement for the original HMCS *Ottawa* which had been lost the previous September. She was commissioned into the RCN at the Thornycroft yard on March 20 as HMCS *Griffin*, but despite objections from her Commanding Officer Commander H.F. Pullen, RCN she would be renamed *HMCS Ottawa (II)* on April 10, both to commemorate the lost destroyer and to conform with the River-class nomenclature. The newly named *Ottawa* worked-up at Tobermory before joining Escort Group C-5 as senior officer. She crossed the Atlantic with fifteen convoys of the ON-, HX-, ONS- and SC-series before being assigned to EG-11 in May of 1944 as Senior Officer.

---

[31] (English, Amazon to Ivanhoe: British Standard Destroyers of the 1930s, 1993) p. 100

[32] This is the same shipyard where HMS *Decoy* (later HMCS *Kootenay*) was built. *Griffin's* G-class sister HMS *Glowworm* was built in the Woolston yard in 1935. *Glowworm* won fame—and a VC for her Commanding Officer—by bravely attacking and ramming the German cruiser *Admiral Hipper* in 1939, after being badly mauled by gunfire.

With her sisters, River-class destroyers HMCS *Chaudière*, HMCS *Gatineau*, HMCS *Kootenay* and HMCS *St. Laurent*, she took part in patrolling the English Channel to protect against U-boat attacks on Allied shipping leading up to and after the Normandy Landings. [33]

July 6, 1944 *Ottawa* and *Kootenay* were detached to assist HMS *Stattice* which had an ASDIC contact off Beachy Head. The English Channel was well known as a difficult place to hunt submarines; oftentimes a good ASDIC contact turned out to be an old wreck sitting on the bottom. Worse still, sometimes enemy U-boats would hide amongst the old wrecks on the bottom. Any hunt would need to be a hunt to exhaustion.

Once *Ottawa* and *Kootenay* reached *Stattice*, they began a box search around *Stattice's* last ASDIC contact. With no further results, and unsure that it was an actual contact *Stattice* decided it was a 'non-sub', and not being under the command authority of the Canadian vessels, departed the scene. The Canadian Senior Officer in *Ottawa* was not deterred so easily, and *Ottawa's* echo sounder seemed to show a bottomed U-boat. Kootenay maintained a plot while *Ottawa* gained a solid contact two hours and twenty-three minutes into the hunt. Attacks were made with both depth charges and hedgehog for two more hours with inconclusive results. Some oil was seen as was some debris and *Ottawa* registered an explosion, but none of that was enough to confirm a kill. By this time it was noon, and both Canadian COs felt they had localized the U-boat using *Kootenay's* careful plot—it was simply bottomed. One of the challenges of a hunt to exhaustion was the limited number of depth charges carried by the destroyers—and after weeks of dropping charges on bottomed shipwrecks, supplies aboard the two Canadian ships were running low.

---

[33] (MacPherson & Butterley, River Class Destroyers of the Royal Canadian Navy, 2008) p. 81

At this point Lieutenant R.W. Timbrel—working from the idea that if you knew where the U-boat was and it wasn't moving, you could lower a depth charge over the side on a wire with a grapnel attached and once it was hooked to the sub it was detonated electrically—set up such a depth charge and grapnel system. Lt. Timbrel was a rare Canadian officer who had taken the long anti-submarine specialist course in the UK and was well versed in unorthodox tactics—and bravery. He had won a DSC while evacuating British Tommies from Dunkirk, and was a survivor of HMCS *Margaree's* fatal encounter with MV *Port Fairy*.

The towed charge brought up additional debris, and throughout the next several hours this tactic, as well as shallow-dropped depth charges and additional hedgehog attacks, brought additional debris to the surface—including a tin of German butter—but nothing was deemed conclusive— yet. *Ottawa* would in fact depart to hunt another nearby contact, leaving *Kootenay* (and *Stattice* who had returned) to finish the U-boat off. The next morning *Kootenay's* final attack brought up a locker door, a German codebook and some other papers. This was definitive enough—it was adjudged that the U-boat had been destroyed. Analysis afterward indicated that they had sunk U-678.[34]

Ottawa and *Kootenay* would again take part in a similar attack along with *Chaudière* off LaRochelle in the Bay of Biscay, which would end in the destruction of U-621. Two days later, west of Brest, the three hunters caught and sank U-984. During this time *Ottawa* was commanded by Commander J.D. Prentice, DSO, RCN.[35] Cmdr. Prentice had made his name—and earned his DSO—while in command of HMCS *Chambly*, when he and HMCS *Moosejaw* shared one of the RCN's first U-Boat kills, U-501 in September of 1941. It was clear that when it

---

[34] (McKee & Darlington, The Canadian Naval Chronicle 1939-1945, 1998) p 166

[35] (MacPherson & Barrie, Ships of Canada's Naval Forces: 1910-2002, 2004) p. 53

came to anti-submarine tactics, Cmdr. Prentice knew his stuff.

September 25, 1944 *Ottawa* and *Restigouche* departed Londonderry bound for Canada, and after arriving in October, *Ottawa* went into a long refit in St. John, New Brunswick. Returning to sea the end of February 1945, *Ottawa* was assigned to Northwest Atlantic Command and would remain in Canadian waters. Less than a month later, while conducting an anti-submarine sweep off Halifax she collided with HMCS *Stratford*, with both vessels receiving extensive damage to their bows. *Ottawa* would be under repair until the end of April, and early in May the war in Europe ended. *Ottawa* then became a troop ferry making a series of runs between Halifax, St. John's, Newfoundland and Quebec City as well as four round trips to Greenock. The second Canadian destroyer to be named *Ottawa* was paid off at Sydney, Nova Scotia on the first of November 1945. She sold for scrap the following August, going to International Iron & Metal Co of Hamilton, Ontario.[36]

---

[36] (MacPherson & Butterley, River Class Destroyers of the Royal Canadian Navy, 2008) p. 80

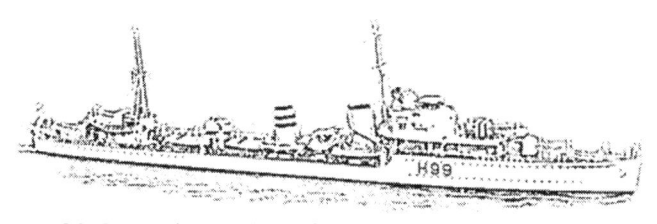

HMCS Chaudière (River-class (H))

Length:	323	Laid Down:	28-02-1935
Beam:	33'	Launched:	10-03-1936
Draft:	9' 11"	Commissioned:	15-11-1943
Displacement:	1340 tons	Paid Off:	17-08-1945

Armament: 2 x 4.7" LA guns, four 21" torpedo tubes, 2 x 6pdr AA guns, Hedgehog ASW Mortar

This vessel was laid down as HMS *Hero* by Builder Vickers-Armstrong Ltd. at its High Walker Yard at Newcastle-on-Tyne. She was designed with a modified bridge structure[37] to test out the new location for the helmsman, which was required for the soon-to-be-constructed Tribal-class (as they had taller forward gun mountings). This different bridge structure set her apart from most of her sisters in the H-class—although the next flotilla of I-class destroyers would have similar forward superstructure; as would succeeding classes.

Hero was the first of the H-Class to be completed, being commissioned into the Royal Navy on October 23, 1936. She would undergo a series of trials to test the new bridge layout. All concerned praised it as being simpler and more efficient than earlier ships. She was assigned to the 2nd Destroyer Flotilla of the Mediterranean Fleet, to take up normal fleet destroyer duties with detachments to the Spanish coast for Non-Intervention patrol during the Spanish Civil War. *Hero* returned to England for a refit in June of 1939.

She returned to service with the Mediterranean Fleet the

---

[37] (Friedman, British Destroyers: From Earliest Days to the Second World War, 2009) p. 224. HMS *Hereward* also had the modified bridge structure, but she carried an experimental Twin 4.7-inch gun mount in B position as well.

end of July of 1939 and was in Malta when war was declared. She remained in the Mediterranean for the next month until it was felt that Italy's neutrality was secure. She left Gibraltar in October for service in the South Atlantic based out of Freetown. She was based in Pernambuco, Brazil in December and took part in a surface raider hunting group until January of 1940, when she returned to Gibraltar on her way to Portsmouth for refit. *Hero* refitted between February and March of 1940. Afterwards she rejoined the 2nd Flotilla for service in Norwegian waters.

Hero found action quickly. She took part in Operation Wilfred—the mining of Vest Fjord—between April 5th and 8th and then on April 10th depth charged and sank U-50 off Muckle Flugga. Two of her sisters, HMS *Hardy* and HMS *Hunter* were sunk during the First Battle of Narvik on April 9th. On April 13th *Hero* was part of the destroyer escort for the battleship HMS *Warspite* along with HMS *Icarus*, HMS *Foxhound* (the future HMCS *Qu'Appelle*), HMS *Kimberly*, HMS *Forester*, and Tribal-class destroyers HMS *Bedouin*, HMS *Punjabi*, HMS *Eskimo* and HMS *Cossack* (Commanded by future Admiral of the Fleet P.L. Vian) during the Second Battle of Narvik. Eight German destroyers were sunk during the battle. *Hero* remained in Norwegian waters for another month before she was sent as reinforcement to the newly reformed 2nd Destroyer Flotilla in the Mediterranean. Once there she took part in the action off Cape Spada when HMAS *Sydney* sank the Italian cruiser *Bartolomeo Colleoni*. At the end of August, while transiting the Mediterranean with HMS *Mohawk* (a Tribal-class destroyer) and sister H-class destroyer HMS *Hostile*, *Hostile* was mined off Cap Bon and broke her back. *Mohawk* picked up *Hostile's* survivors while *Hero* fired two torpedoes into her stricken sister to scuttle her. She joined the convoy Operation Hats during its successful transit to Malta while under air attack.

After refitting at Malta in November of 1940 she took part in the action off Cape Spartivento on the 27th of that month. Afterwards she joined the 13th Destroyer Flotilla as part of Force H in Gibraltar. When the German cruiser *Admiral*

Hipper attacked the troop convoy WS 5A and scattered it, *Hero* was amongst those sent to round up and protect the scattered ships.

New Year's Day 1941 saw *Hero* at sea with the 13th Flotilla, where they intercepted a Vichy French convoy on its way to Oran and diverted it to Gibraltar. Five days later *Hero* joined HMS *Jaguar* and sisters HMS *Hereward* and HMS *Hasty* to escort part of the Operation Excess convoy and return to the Mediterranean Fleet. On the 20th of January she was part of the escort for cruisers HMS *Orion* and HMS *Bonaventure* for their abortive mission to shell Tobruk. She came through the Greek and Crete disasters without damage or casualty, and in May of 1941 participated in Operation Tiger's successful resupply of Malta. On the night of May 23rd 1941, *Hero* and HMS *Decoy* (who would be HMCS *Kootenay* in less than two years) evacuated the Greek King and his court from Crete to Alexandria, Egypt. The next day the two future River-class destroyers carried 600 special service troops to Suda Bay and returned unharmed.

In June *Hero* was off the Syrian coast and in July she took up the first of her many stores runs to Tobruk. She would be on this hazardous duty for three months, broken only by her part in a diversionary operation with HMS *Queen Elizabeth*, meant to distract from the passage of convoy WS 11 during Operation Halberd in September.

In late October, while en-route to Tobruk with the minelayer HMS *Latona* and the E-class destroyers HMS *Encounter* and HMS *Express* (anther future Canadian) the four ships were subjected to a series of serious air attacks from midafternoon onwards. At around 8:10 p.m. *Latona* was struck by a bomb and set alight. Forty-minutes later *Hero* was alongside the disabled minelayer having secured herself to *Latona's* bow. While securing alongside three bombs fell 10 feet from her outboard side, one abreast her number three boiler, one abreast her 3-inch AA gun mount, and one just clear of the stern. The ship whipped violently with each explosion but initial damage reports indicated there was nothing seriously harmed and *Hero* completed evacuating *Latona's* crew.

On further inspection *Hero's* starboard side had been crushed inwards from frame 87 to frame 122, between 4-feet and thirteen-feet from the upper deck and rivets in her hull plating sprung—notwithstanding that the H-class had been built using welding extensively.[38] Her fighting efficiency was of course impaired by this as was her maneuverability, and her maximum speed reduced from 35 knots to 29 knots. She would return to Alexandria for repairs and afterward was on escort duties in the Eastern Mediterranean.

In February of 1942 she joined HMS *Sikh*, HMS *Zulu*, HMS *Legion*, HMS *Lance*, HMS *Lively*, and sisters HMS *Havock* and HMS *Hasty* to form the 22nd Destroyer Flotilla. By September of that year she was the only survivor of the original members of that flotilla. British destroyers were paying a stiff price in the Eastern Mediterranean in 1942. *Hero* would take part in the Second Battle of Sirte in March of that year, escorting convoy MW 10. The end of May she and HMS *Eridge* and HMS *Hurworth* tracked and killed U-568 off Sollum northeast of Tobruk, taking fifteen hours to do so; 42 survivors from the U-Boat were rescued.

The end of June U-732 torpedoed and sank the submarine depot ship HMS *Medway* while it was on passage from Alexandria to Haifa. *Hero* and HMS *Zulu* picked up 105 survivors.

Having not seen a proper refit in nearly 18 months, with only repairs done to make right what combat had made wrong, *Hero* was in dire need of dockyard time. Unfortunately, it was out of the question at that point, considering the losses and operational tempo for destroyers in the Eastern Mediterranean. So *Hero* soldiered on, escorting convoys between Cyprus and

---

[38] (Friedman, British Destroyers: From Earliest Days to the Second World War, 2009) p. 224

Alexandria and other Levant ports until the end of 1942. In August she rescued 1,100 survivors of the troop transport *Princess Marguerite* which had been torpedoed while on passage from Alexandria to Cyprus, and in October in company with four other destroyers and a Vickers Wellesley bomber from 42 Squadron RAF, successfully hunted and sank U-559 60 miles northeast of Port Said.

Finally a full refit could be put off no more and on December 12, 1942 HMS *Hero* sailed for England. She was in refit at Portsmouth from April to November of 1943 and at the same time was converted to escort destroyer configuration. On November 15th she was officially transferred to the Royal Canadian Navy as a gift and commissioned as HMCS *Chaudière* the same day.[39]

She sailed for Scapa Flow for work-ups and joined Escort Group C-2 in Londonderry in mid-February 1944. By early March, as part of a support group assisting convoy HX 208, she was part of a 32-hour hunt for U-744 before driving it to the surface where it surrendered. HMCS *Chilliwack* and HMCS *St. Catharines* both sent over boarding parties, but the rough water smashed them against the submarine's casing and capsized them. *Chaudière* sent her own boats into the water to rescue both boarding parties and the German survivors. When it proved impractical to take U-744 in tow, HMS *Icarus* sank the submarine with a torpedo.

In late April *Chaudière* was assigned to Escort Group 11 alongside four other River-class destroyers, HMCS *Gatineau*, HMCS *Kootenay*, HMCS *Ottawa (II)*, and HMCS *St. Laurent*. In their previous lives *Chaudière* and *Kootenay* had worked together quite successfully in evacuating the King of Greece and landing troops in Suda Bay in 1941; it may have felt like a family reunion.

---

[39] (English, Amazon to Ivanhoe: British Standard Destroyers of the 1930s, 1993) p. 108

EG 11's stated purpose was to protect English Channel shipping from the predations of Bay of Biscay-based U-Boats before, during, and after the Normandy Invasion. The one-time Suda Bay duo proved they still had chops when *Chaudière* and *Kootenay*—with an assist from HMCS *Ottawa (II)* sank U-621 on August 18 and U-984 on August 20.

EG 11 move to Iceland in October to patrol the Iceland-UK Gap, to keep bottled-up any U-boats that had fled the Biscay ports to Norwegian waters in an attempt to break out into the Atlantic. By this time HMCS *Ottawa (II)* and HMCS *Restigouche* had been replaced by HMCS *Skeena* and HMCS *St. Laurent*. On October 24 foul North Atlantic weather drove EG 11 to find shelter in Reykjavik Harbour and that night, at the height of the gale *Skeena* dragged her anchors and piled up on the rocks, with the loss of 15 crewmen. The remainder of the group retuned to Londonderry in early November, and *Chaudière* along with *Qu'Appelle* and *St. Laurent* were ordered back to Canada for refit. Having left her comrade HMCS *Kootenay* behind—*Kootenay* had withdrawn to Plymouth with a defective feed pump—*Chaudière* joined the other two as escorts on the west-bound convoy ON 267.

Arriving in Halifax the 19th of January 1945, *Chaudière* put into Sydney, Nova Scotia for her refit. Due to her lengthy time in combat and the various indignities done to her by bombs and guns—and in all likelihood because she had gone nearly two years in the Mediterranean without a refit—*Chaudière* was ascertained to be the River-class destroyer most worn out by this stage in the war. For that reason, and with the war in Europe winding down, there was little urgency in completing her refit. When VE day came she was still in the dockyard—work having been stopped in April. EG 11 was disbanded on June 6, and *Chaudière* declared surplus to requirements a week later. She finally paid off in Sydney on August 17 and sold to Dominion Steel Company for scrap.[40]

---

[40] (MacPherson & Butterley, River Class Destroyers of the Royal Canadian Navy,

TIN CAN CANUCKS

Ex-HMCS *Chaudière*, ex-HMS *Hero*, perhaps the most successful River-class destroyer and certainly one of the most successful destroyers of the war—with no less than six U-boat kills to her credit—went to the cutters torch in 1950. She was the last of the River-class destroyers.[41]

Ultimately, for all the hard work of convoy escort that the Canadian destroyers were involved in, the Royal Canadian Navy's top brass were looking to the future with an eye on a true Blue-water capable fleet. For this the RCN needed fleet destroyers, and those were the Tribals.[42]

2008) p. 102

[41] (English, Amazon to Ivanhoe: British Standard Destroyers of the 1930s, 1993) p. 109

[42] (Whitby, 1992)

5

TRIBES OF ALL TYPES
ARE CRUSADERS A TRIBE?

The British Tribal class of 1935 was one of several 'super-destroyer' designs evolved by various navies in the 1930s. Originating from a light-cruiser design[1], the Tribal class proved to be big, bold and beautiful, giving the Royal Navy an added anti-surface punch when war descended. Canada would build eight of these ships—four in England during the war, and four at home, completed shortly after the end of hostilities. They were expensive, in both initial purchase and upkeep, but few would want a lesser destroyer at their backs when facing hostile surface units. Canadian experience made them better anti-submarine platforms than they were designed to be, and Canada is the home of the last of them—HMCS *Haida* still lies alongside in Hamilton, a reminder, and a tribute to her sisters and the men who served aboard during and after the Second World War.

Although not of the Tribal-class, the last four destroyers in this section belong here, as they are named for 'Tribes', or are

---

[1] (Friedman, British Destroyers: From Earliest Days to the Second World War, 2009) p 25

sisters to those so named. They are late-war emergency types, built by the British to be cheaper and easier to manufacture, while still sending ships to sea with the most up-to-date equipment necessary. Post war, many British emergency types were converted to Type 15 or Type 16 frigates—anti-submarine and escort platforms rather than surface combat vessels—but few lasted more than a decade in this guise before going to the breakers.

The Canadian ships saw similar conversion to destroyer escorts at the end of hostilities (some later than others), but lasted longer, with both *Crusader* and *Sioux* as well as three of the British-built and three of the Canadian-built Tribals[2] seeing combat off Korea.

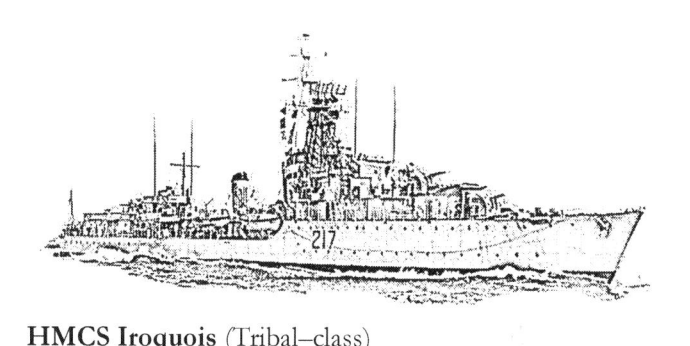

HMCS Iroquois (Tribal–class)

Length:	377'	Laid Down:	19-09-1940
Beam:	37' 6"	Launched:	23-09-1941
Draft:	11' 2"	Commissioned:	30-11-1942
Displacement:	1927 tons	Paid Off:	24-10-1962

Armament: 6 x 4.7" LA guns, 2 x 4" HA guns, four 21" torpedo tubes, 4 x 2pdr , 1 x 12pdr 6 x 20mm Oerlikon AA guns

One of the first two Tribal-class destroyers ordered by the RCN, the vessel that was launched and commissioned as

---

[2] These would be *Iroquois*, *Huron* and *Haida* as well as *Nootka(II)*, *Cayuga* and *Athabaskan (II)*.

HMCS *Iroquois* was originally laid down as HMCS *Athabaskan*. The two ships were under construction at Vickers Armstrong Ltd.'s High Walker yard during the infamous Luftwaffe Blitz of 1940/41, and it was during one of these raids in April of 1941 that the vessel laid down as HMCS *Iroquois* was struck by German bombs and severely damaged—her launching would be delayed months until the damage could be made good and construction resumed. As the ship on the slip beside her was undamaged it was decided to swap names of the ships to allow for HMCS *Iroquois* to be launched by the scheduled date. Thus, HMCS *Athabaskan* became HMCS *Iroquois* when launched in September of 1941.[3]

Upon commissioning fourteen months later, HMCS *Iroquois* joined the Home Fleet's 3rd Destroyer Flotilla, but the discovery of structural flaws when she suffered weather damage during work-up at Scapa Flow delayed her full operational readiness until repairs were completed in January of 1943. In March she suffered more weather damage while undertaking a trip to Canada, necessitating dry-docking in Halifax for repairs. It was concluded that extra stiffening in the Canadian Tribals was vital. By April of 1943 she was back in British waters, but once more suffered weather damage, and was back in dockyard hands at Plymouth until early June.

Once back in service *Iroquois* joined the escort of several convoys to Gibraltar throughout June, and in the first part of July she was assigned to escort the troopships SS *Duchess of York*, *California*, and MV *Port Fairy* along with the destroyer HMS *Douglas* and the frigate HMS *Moyola*. Two days after sailing, three German Fw 200 Condor long range bombers found the convoy 300 miles off Vigo. A high-level bombing attack struck both *Duchess of York* and *California*, both of which caught fire. *Iroquois* was able to stave off another bombing attack focused on *Port Fairy*, and was able to rescue 628 men

---

[3] (Burrow & Beaudoin, 1987) p. 6

from *Duchess of York*. By the early morning of July 12 the two stricken transports has slipped beneath the waves, and *Iroquois* escorted *Port Fairy* into Casablanca.[4]

At Casablanca *Iroquois* took aboard six German prisoners-of-war—an officer and five other crew from the sunken U-506. On the return voyage to Plymouth it was discovered that the officer's jacket had a badge removed by a member of *Iroquois'* crew. As this violated the Geneva Convention on prisoners-of-war, the destroyer's Commanding Officer Commander W.B.L. Holmes, RCN stopped all shore leave until the badge was returned.[5] This didn't go over well with the crew, and when *Iroquois* was ordered to sea on the 19th of July all ratings below the rank of Leading Seaman refused to leave their mess or return to duty.[6] The CO suffered a heart attack, and was taken ashore. Although the second in command, Lieutenant Commander E.T.G. Madgwick commanded the ship temporarily as Acting Commanding Officer, formal command was passed to Commander J.C. Hibbard, DSC, RCN the end of July.[7]

While on passage through the Irish Sea to rejoin the Home Fleet, *Iroquois* collided with the trawler *Kingston Beryl*. She underwent repairs at Troon and arrived back at Scapa Flow on August 26, 1943. There she underwent trials and workups and then undertook patrols around the Orkneys.

In the winter of 1943/44 she worked as an escort with the

---

[4] (English, Afridi to Nizam: British FleetDestroyers 1937 - 43, 2001) p. 55. MV *Port Fairy* was the same ship that sank HMCS *Margaree* in 1940 when that destroyer cut across the merchantman's bow during a convoy operation.

[5] (Madgwick, 2003) p. 83

[6] (Audette, 1982) p. 236 Apparently one officer aboard Iroquois described the incident as "a locking of the forward lower mess doors."

[7] (MacPherson & Barrie, Ships of Canada's Naval Forces: 1910-2002, 2004) p. 62

Russian convoys, as part of Operation Holder in October of 1943 and Operation Gearbox III—the relief of Spitsbergen. She returned to join the 10th DF at Plymouth, but was almost immediately detached to take part in Operation Post Horn with sisters HMCS *Athabaskan* and HMCS *Haida*.

While 250 miles off the French coast in February of 1944 she was able to avoid a U-boat's torpedoes, thanks to the keen ears of the ASDIC operator who heard them approaching off the starboard bow. After this she would refit in Halifax until returning to Liverpool in June of 1944. Her new lattice foremast was fitted with Type 293 radar at this time, after which she went to Scapa Flow to work-up before returning to Plymouth to rejoin the 10th DF.

In August of that year she joined the destroyer HMS *Ursa* as escort for the cruiser HMS *Mauritius* on a patrol off Les Sables. During the subsequent night action the cruiser and destroyers attacked and damaged the German torpedo boat T-24, set fire to a small tanker which later grounded, and later set alight a pair of merchant ships and a pair of minesweepers which also went aground off Ile d'Yeu. Later in the month the three ships again undertook night patrol, this time destroying two more merchant ships and a trawler in Anderne Bay.

September of 1944 saw *Iroquois* escorting the French cruiser *Jean D'Arc* into Cherbourg and afterward as far as the Azores. She was then escort for *Queen Mary* which was carrying Churchill to the Ottawa Conference. Upon return to Plymouth she underwent a boiler cleaning, after which she returned to her patrols in the Bay of Biscay. Throughout the remainder of the winter she would act as escort for capital ships and troop transports in British waters, including assignment to the Home Fleet in October to November 1944 and March to April 1945. She took part in intercepting and damaging a merchant convoy and its escort off Jossingfiord the night of April 3rd, 1944. She was in company with the destroyers HMS *Onslow*, HMS *Zealous*, and HMS *Zest* at the time.

Iroquois then joined her sisters HMCS *Haida* and HMCS

Huron in escorting Russian convoys to and from Kola. During one of these trips she and *Huron* were narrowly missed by torpedoes from U-427. VE day found *Iroquois* at Scapa Flow, and subsequently she took part in the liberation of Norway and Denmark, returning to Canada to be refitted for deployment to the Pacific against Japan. She was still in dockyard hands in Halifax when the Japanese surrendered, and at that point the tropicalization refit was suspended and *Iroquois* was used as a depot ship until 1947 when she underwent a long refit which completed in June of 1949. She undertook cadet training duties for a short time before re-entering reserve in September of 1949. It wasn't until October 1951, after completing an escort destroyer conversion lasting 16 months that she returned to service. Trials were run off Norfolk, Virginia, as were exercises with her new 3-inch gun.

She served in Korean waters between June and November of 1952, during which time, while undertaking shore bombardment (targeting an already damaged train), she was struck by a shell on her B gun mount. The damage was minimal and her fighting capabilities unaffected, although 3 men were killed and 10 others injured. After a return to Halifax she was once more in Korean waters by mid-1953 and took part in the evacuation of Chodo, which was being returned to North Korea. Another trip home to Halifax via the Mediterranean completed a circumnavigation of the globe. Arriving in February of 1954 she refitted and then sailed again for Korea, finally arriving home with sister *Huron* on March of 1955.

In July of that year she suffered a boiler room fire in her aft boiler room while in Argentia, Newfoundland, and suffered weather damage off Bermuda in August. She returned to Halifax for repairs before being deployed to Western Atlantic exercises. She then entered dockyard hands in October for another refit, but suffered more weather damage while on post-refit trials the following February.

By March she was at sea again undertaking NATO exercises, seeing active service until once more entering dry-dock for a year-long refit in October 1957. She saw little active service after completing the refit however, as within a few months her propellers and propeller shafts needed replacement. After this she served until October of 1962 when she was paid off and entered operational reserve. Towed to Sydney, she remained there on the disposal list until sold for scrap and broken up at Bilbao, Spain in 1966.[8] First of the British-built Canadian Tribals to be commissioned, she was the last to go to the breakers (excepting her sister HMCS *Haida* which is still extant).

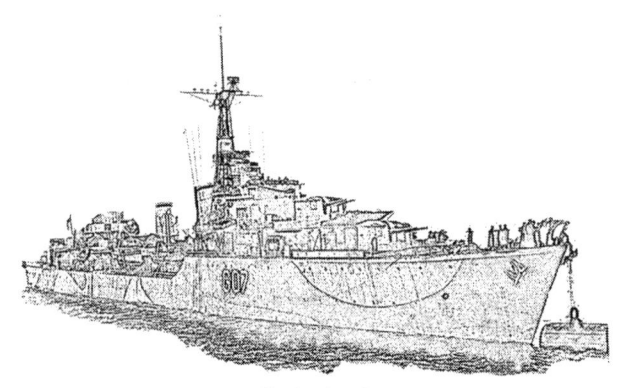

HMCS Athabaskan (Tribal–class)

Length:	377'	Laid Down:	31-10-1940
Beam:	37' 6"	Launched:	18-11-1941
Draft:	11' 2"	Commissioned:	03-02-1943
Displacement:	1927 tons	Lost:	29-04-1944

Armament: 6 x 4.7" LA guns, 2 x 4" HA guns, four 21" torpedo tubes, 4 x 2pdr, 1 x 12pdr 6 x 20mm Oerlikon AA guns

The first HMCS *Athabaskan* was built by Vickers Armstrong Ltd. at its High Walker Yard in Newcastle-on-Tyne. The ship that one day would to be known as 'Ashcan' to her crew, was laid down as HMCS *Iroquois* in October 1940 having

---

[8] (English, Afridi to Nizam: British FleetDestroyers 1937 - 43, 2001) p. 57

been officially ordered April 5th of that year. When the ship originally laid down as HMCS *Iroquois* was severely damaged by Luftwaffe bombs in April of 1940, it was decided to swap names of the two Canadian Tribals to be able to still meet the launch deadline for HMCS *Iroquois*. For this reason, HMCS *Athabaskan* (ex-*Iroquois*) would be delayed in completion, as much of the previous construction work had been destroyed or damaged by the German Bombs.[9]

Upon commissioning she sailed to Scapa Flow to work-up, and undertake Clyde escort duty in late February 1943. She suffered hull damage while berthing alongside the oiler *Danmark* and was under repair at Greenock for much of the following month.

Assigned to the Home Fleet, she left Scapa Flow on March 29th to patrol for German blockade runners passing through the Iceland to Faeroe Island passage. Dirty weather caused hull strain and damage was serious enough to see her in dockyard hands for five weeks. Having left South Shields following the completion of repairs in June, *Athabaskan* sailed as part of Operation Gearbox III—the relief of the Spitsbergen garrison.

Mid-month she collided with the boom defense vessel HMS *Bargate* while at Scapa Flow, which required another month's repair at Devonport.

Throughout July and August of 1940 she was based our of Plymouth and took part in anti-submarine patrols throughout the Bay of Biscay. In July of 1943 she picked up five survivors from U-558 who had been adrift for three days. In late August she was struck by a glider bomb while off the Spanish coast. She had been in company with the destroyer HMS *Grenville*, the sloop HMS *Egret* and frigates HMS *Jed* and HMS *Rother* when they were attacked by 16 Do 217s carrying one Hs 293 radio-

---

[9] (Burrow & Beaudoin, 1987) p. 6

controlled missile each.[10] *Egret* was struck squarely and exploded—taking 200 officers and men with her—while *Athabaskan* suffered two near misses before being hit on her portside aft of her B gun mount and forward of her wheelhouse. The glider bomb penetrated both sides of her hull; exiting the starboard side before exploding. *Athabaskan* had flooding in her forward boiler room, forward magazines and torpedo mess. She had suffered significant damage but with minimal casualties—one man was killed, one lost overboard, three were fatally injured and another 12 wounded.[11] It took her 75 minutes to get underway again, but she made Plymouth under escort—still able to make 15 knots.

Upon reaching Devonport she lay under repair until early November. She returned to Scapa Flow early enough the next month to join convoy JW 55A as an escort. This convoy was part of the series to supply Russia with war materials. Such convoys were renowned for their danger—the high latitude at that time of year meant almost no daylight; good for avoiding U-boats, but it made for hazardous sailing conditions in the ice-filled northern waters.

By February of 1944 she had been reassigned to Plymouth, there to join the 10th Destroyer Flotilla. She took part in the action against German destroyers and torpedo boats off Ushant the night of 25th April 1944. Force 26 (as this task force was known) consisted of *Athabaskan*, fellow Tribal-class Destroyers, HMS *Ashanti*, HMCS *Haida*, HMCS *Huron*, and the cruiser HMS *Black Prince*. In a running gun battle between the four Tribals and the three destroyers of the German 4th Torpedo Boat Flotilla (TBF), the *Elbing*-Class destroyer T-29 was sunk and her sister T-27 took a serious shell hit to her forward engine room requiring her to retire. T-24, the third *Elbing*, also disengaged after taking a hit that disabled her radio.

---

[10] (English, Afridi to Nizam: British FleetDestroyers 1937 - 43, 2001) p. 48

[11] (Burrow & Beaudoin, 1987) p. 44

The victorious Tribals returned to Plymouth, Black Prince having signaled "Force 26 will wear battle ensigns on entering harbour."[12]

Three days later fate conspired against *Athabaskan* when she was patrolling the Brittany coast north of Ile de Bas with HMCS *Haida*. After being made aware of several radar contacts *Haida* fired star shell and illuminated a pair of *Elbing*-class destroyers. T-24 and T-27—having escaped the two Canadian Tribals days before—turned away and fired a spread of torpedoes. *Athabaskan* was struck in her gearing room and sunk by a torpedo from T-24. Although her sister *Haida* was able to rescue 44 of her crew, her commanding officer Lieutenant Commander J.H. Stubbs and 128 men lost their lives, with another 83 taken prisoner after the threat of German U-boats drove *Haida* off.[13]

The reasonably healthy Canadian prisoners-of-war were taken to Bremen by rail, and eventually went to the Marlag und Milag Nord camps for captured allied naval and merchant seamen where they would be detained until the end of the war.[14] The seriously injured were sent to Front-Stalag 133A—and army hospital in Orleans. The men from this group who survived were liberated by the US Army during its encirclement of Paris in August of 1944.

---

[12] (Gough, 2001) p. 67

[13] (MacPherson & Barrie, Ships of Canada's Naval Forces: 1910-2002, 2004) p. 59

[14] (Burrow & Beaudoin, 1987) p. 143; One of these POWs, J.A. 'Dunn' Lantier had served as a Lieutenant aboard *Athabaskan* for her entire career. He would later return to the RCN after repatriation and in 1952 now-Commander Lantier became the Commanding Officer of one of *Athabaskan's* sisters, HMCS *Haida*. Under Lantier's command *Haida* joined the 'Trainbuster's Club' while in Korean waters in 1953. (Burrow & Beaudoin, 1987) p. 15

HMCS Huron (Tribal–class)

Length:	377'	Laid Down:	15-07-1941
Beam:	37' 6"	Launched:	25-06-1942
Draft:	11' 2"	Commissioned:	19-07-1943
Displacement:	1927 tons	Paid Off:	30-04-1963

Armament: 6 x 4.7" LA guns, 2 x 4" HA guns, four 21" torpedo tubes, 4 x 2pdr, 1 x 12pdr 6 x 20mm Oerlikon AA guns

HMCS *Huron* was built by Vickers Armstrong Ltd. at Newcastle-on-Tyne as part of the second batch of Canadian Tribals ordered from British yards. Working up was delayed by the need to escort HMS *Onslow* from Scrabster to Scapa Flow on 12 August 1942; *Onslow* was transporting King George VI on a visit to the Home Fleet. *Huron* was also detailed to salvage a Fleet Air Arm Blackburn Skua that had ditched off Orkney during this time. She finally completed working up in early September and joined the 3rd Destroyer Flotilla based with the Home Fleet. She left Scapa Flow on October 1st with sister HMCS *Iroquois* and the O-class destroyer HMS *Onslaught* to delivery machinery and equipment to Murmansk, returning with Russian diplomats back to Scapa Flow on October 11. She was damaged going alongside an oiler in the anchorage and repairs—done at Leith—lasted until mid-November.

From the time she left the dockyard in November to February of 1944 *Huron* took up escort duties with Russian convoys sailing to arctic waters. After six such convoy operations she was posted to the 10th DF in Plymouth and was tasked with convoy and patrol operations leading up to the Normandy Invasion on June 6th.[15]

On one such patrol, she was part of Force 26 with sisters HMCS *Athabaskan*, HMCS *Haida,* and fellow-Tribal HMS *Ashanti* (lead by the cruiser HMS *Black Prince*) off Ushant, on the night of April 26th, when the destroyers intercepted and engaged three German destroyers of the *Elbing*-class. One destroyer, T-29 was sunk and two others escaped after being damaged. During the melee *Ashanti* collided with *Huron*, striking the Canadian destroyer amidships. *Huron* suffered hull damage and the bulkhead between her boiler rooms was buckled. She also had her port cutter and its davits smashed, had damage to her guard rails and stanchions, as well as damage to her torpedo davits. Damage to *Ashanti* was even more significant—her bow being split from the stem 19 feet back.[16] Repairs to *Huron* were completed by early May.

Huron played a significant role in the D-Day landings and post D-Day naval actions. On the night of June 8th she took part in the destruction of the German destroyers ZH-1 and Z-32, and was with HMS *Eskimo* on the night of June 27th when she engaged German trawlers in the Gulf of St. Malo. *Huron* would also stand by and tow *Eskimo* to Plymouth after the destroyer collided with HMS *Javelin* on July 1st.

Mid-august saw *Huron* heading home to Halifax for a refit, and this being completed by mid-November she underwent trials in Canadian waters, returning to Cardiff the end of November. There she was fitted with new radar and fire control equipment, with further trials occupying her time until late January of 1945. After working-up in February she undertook escort duties with Western Approaches Command based out of Plymouth until the end of March, when she was assigned back to the Home Fleet in Scapa Flow. There she

---

[15] (English, Afridi to Nizam: British FleetDestroyers 1937 - 43, 2001) p. 54

[16] (Burrow & Beaudoin, 1987) p. 83

sailed with two more Russian Convoys—JW60 and RA66.

The end of the war in Europe found *Huron* operating in Norwegian waters until returning to St. John's, Newfoundland the first week of June 1945 to refit for service in the Pacific. This refit was suspended with the Japanese surrender and *Huron* was decommissioned and placed in reserve March of 1946, remaining there until 1950. While in reserve she underwent a refit in 1949/50 and upon completion of this work she undertook work-ups in Bermuda joining the Canadian Special Service Squadron in June of 1950. The squadron undertook a European cruise, returning home to Halifax in late November.[17]

Huron underwent another refit in preparation for a Korean War deployment. Leaving Halifax on 22 January 1951 she stopped at Pearl Harbor, Kwanjalein and Guam—where she had repair work done—arriving in Sasebo, Japan in mid-March. The Tribal spent six-months on station undertaking escort, carrier screening and shore bombardment tasks before turning east towards Halifax, after stopping in Esquimalt via the Aleutian Islands.

In Halifax *Huron* underwent conversion to an anti-submarine destroyer, at which time she was fitted with two twin 4-inch AA mounts in place of her forward twin 4.7-in guns, a pair of 3-inch guns, four torpedo tubes, and a pair of Squid ASW mortars. Conversion work was followed by trials and work-ups which were delayed in completion due to damage sustained while berthing in Bermuda. Ready for duty once more in April of 1953, *Huron* sailed for Korea but suffered from an unintentional grounding off Tang-do on the night of July 13th. She was refloated quickly, but had to put into Sasebo for repairs to her bow. These took until October 6th and after trials she undertook Armistice patrol duties in Korean waters. During this time she was part of an abortive

---

[17] (Madgwick, 2003) p.143

search for a missing Lockheed P2V Neptune A/S aircraft in January of 1954. She departed Sasebo in early February and sailed for Halifax via the Mediterranean, arriving by mid-March to put in for a refit until July.

Huron returned to Korean waters between October 1954 and late-March 1955, once more returning to Halifax via the Mediterranean at the completion of this tour.

Much of the next several years was taken up with NATO exercises and ongoing maintenance struggles. She suffered hull damage at Southampton in October of 1956 which was repaired in Halifax, followed by more repairs in 1958 after brushing against the Type 15 frigate HMS *Troubridge* in Bermuda. These latter repairs included work on her sonar and on her mis-aligned port propeller shaft.

While undertaking exercises off Golfe Juan in the south of France in November 1958, *Huron* collided with the French destroyer *Maille-Breze*, glancing off the Frenchman's hull near her engine room. *Huron* came away with a crumpled bow and *Maille-Breze* with serious damage to her superstructure. *Huron* required a tow to Tulon for repairs. A full bow replacement was required, and this wasn't completed until mid-December. While on passage to Canada she suffered damage to the new bow and had to be escorted into Halifax by the destroyer HMCS *Saguenay (II)* and the frigate HMCS *Buckingham*.

After a short refit in early 1959, *Huron* acted as escort for HMY *Britannia* during the latter's visit to Canada the end of July. Later that year she suffered a galley fire, the repairs of which took until January of 1960. She underwent another refit at Lauzon, Quebec from April to September of 1960, but a refit scheduled for 1962 was canceled as not economical.

HMCS *Huron* was decommissioned in Halifax April 30th 1963, and was towed to Sydney, Nova Scotia to be placed in operational reserve. She was placed on the disposal list in 1964 and was sold to Marine Salvage Ltd. of Port Colborne, Ontario, who then resold her to an Italian shipbreaker. She was finally broken up at La Spezia in August of 1965.[18]

HMCS Haida (Tribal–class)

Length:	377'	Laid Down:	29-09-1941
Beam:	37' 6"	Launched:	25-08-1942
Draft:	11' 2"	Commissioned:	30-08-1943
Displacement:	1927 tons	Paid Off:	11-10-1963

Armament: 6 x 4.7" LA guns, 2 x 4" HA guns, four 21" torpedo tubes, 4 x 2pdr , 1 x 12pdr 6 x 20mm Oerlikon AA guns

The last of the British-built Canadian Tribals commissioned, HMCS *Haida* was built by Vickers Armstrong Ltd. at Newcastle-on-Tyne. Upon commissioning, she—like her sisters—sailed to Scapa Flow for working-up. Surviving typically foul weather during her working-up period over September and October of 1943, once judged 'efficient' she joined the Home Fleet's 3rd Destroyer Flotilla. She formed part of the escort for the battleship HMS *Anson*, carrier USS *Ranger*, and cruiser HMS *Norfolk* during the relief of the Spitzbergen garrison and passage of minesweepers to Russia in mid-October. The following two months consisted of further Russian convoy escort work and another relief of Spitzbergen before returning to Scapa Flow.

In January of 1944 she was transferred to the 10th DF in Plymouth. She went into dockyard hands in Devonport for alteration prior to deployment to pre-invasion exercises and destroyer sweeps. In February she was detached to the Home

---

[18] (English, Afridi to Nizam: British FleetDestroyers 1937 - 43, 2001) p. 55

Fleet to take part in Operation Post Horn, a strike against coastal traffic along the Norwegian coast. After more channel patrol duties she was to take part in the action off Ile de Bas on the night of April 28th when her sister *Athabaskan* was torpedoed and sunk by the German destroyer T-27. With dawn about to break, and unable to stay longer than 15 minutes for fear of becoming a tempting U-boat or aircraft target herself, *Haida* was forced to abandon *Athabaskan* survivors in the water, having rescued only 44 of the most seriously wounded. When forced to depart, *Haida* also left her motorboat and its crew at the site of the sinking—the boat ended up making it across the channel before being towed into Penzance several days later. She had been able to drive T-27 ashore however, and the *Elbing*-class destroyer was finished off by a Motor Torpedo Boat attack in early May.

After D-Day, *Haida* was part of the June 8th night action off Ushant—which included Tribals HMS *Ashanti*, HMS *Tartar*, and HMCS *Huron*—that sank the German destroyers ZH-1 and Z-32. She also took part in the sinking of U-971 off Land's End late in June, this time in company with Tribal-class destroyer HMS *Eskimo*. In mid-July she was again with *Tartar* and the Polish destroyer ORP *Blyskawica* (who had also been with the Tribals on June 8th off Ushant) when the trio sank the German submarine chasers UJ-1420 and UJ-1421 off Lorient. In early August, while in action off Belle Isle, a shell struck her aft 'Y' Gun mount, destroying the mounting, killing two and wounding eight of her crew. *Haida* returned to Devonport for repair, spending the remainder of August receiving a new 'Y' mount. In late September, after having supported the Free French resistance along the French coast, she departed British waters for Halifax and a refit in Canada.

After completing the refit, trials and working-up, she arrived in Plymouth the first part of January 1945 to rejoin the Home Fleet in March, having undertaken additional working-up in Scapa Flow. Her first mission back with the Home Fleet required her to cover the operations of escort carriers whose aircraft were tasked with minelaying along the Norwegian coast followed by an airstrike on Trondheim in late March. She followed this up with another stint with the Russian convoys—being very nearly torpedoed by a U-boat while on return passage. She and sister *Huron* escorted the cruiser HMS *Berwick* to Trondheim on May 17th, 1945 and tarried there for a week during victory celebrations. The first week of June 1945, the surviving British-built Canadian Tribals departed Greenock and set sail for Halifax, carrying several returning RCN passengers with them. *Haida* immediately went into dry-dock for tropicalization so she could serve in the Pacific against the Japanese, but the surrender of that island nation saw her refit terminated, at which point she was decommissioned and laid up in reserve.

After a year in reserve she was brought forward for a refit which included fitting a lattice foremast and upgrades to her AA weaponry. The refit was delayed when a fire broke out, but *Haida* was once again commissioned into the RCN in May of 1947. Between May of 1947 and December of 1949 *Haida* served on Canada's East Coast and during this time she rescued two aircrew who had ditched at sea in August of 1948, as well as fifteen crew members of a downed American Boeing B-17 that had ditched off Bermuda in November of 1949. Between December 1949 and July of 1950 she acted as a depot ship for the Senior Officer Reserve Ships in Halifax. That July she stood by her half-sister, the Canadian-built Tribal HMCS *Micmac* after *Micmac's* collision with SS *Yarmouth County*.

Under the command of Lieutenant Commander E.T.G. Madgwick, RCN HMCS *Haida* acted as plane guard for HMCS *Magnificent* in 1949. [19]

Between July 1950 and March 1952 *Haida* underwent extensive conversion and modernization, eventually emerging from the dockyard as a destroyer escort. Her twin 4.7-inch mountings had been replaced by two twin 4-inch mounts and a

---

[19] (Madgwick, 2003) p. 105

pair of twin 3-inch/50 AA guns. Additional 40mm single and 20mm single mounts rounded out her AA armament. She was fitted to carry twin Squid anti-submarine mortars and four torpedoes. Her electronics were upgraded with improved radar and radio systems fitted. After re-commissioning on March 15th, 1952 she undertook a shakedown cruise to Europe, which was followed by a deployment to Korean waters, arriving in Sasebo, Japan in mid-November for operations off the Korean coast. She spent six months being utilized for shore bombardment—including targeting rail lines and locomotives, which earned her entry into the 'Trainbuster's Club'—before being rotated back to Canada in late July 1953. She re-deployed to Korea in December for another tour, returning to Halifax via the Indian Ocean in November 1954.

Haida would spend the rest of her active career undertaking exercises and training cruises, interspersed with refits and hull repairs as she got longer in the tooth. In January 1958 she needed hull repairs, and in December of that year her steering gear failed, and it was found that her forward magazine bulkhead needed shoring up. She refitted in Halifax again between April 1959 and January of 1960, but ongoing hull repairs were required in July of 1960, 1961, and March of 1962. She was finally paid off on 11 October 1963 and placed in operational reserve.[20] When she went on the disposal list, she was purchased not by a shipbreaker, but instead by a group who would see her refurbished and put on display as a museum ship. Originally displayed on the Toronto waterfront, HMCS *Haida* eventually moved to Hamilton, Ontario where she resides to this day.

HMCS *Haida* (the last Canadian ship to carry the name) stands as a monument to the RCN's Second World War destroyers and the men who crewed them. She is the last of

---

[20] (English, Afridi to Nizam: British FleetDestroyers 1937 - 43, 2001) p. 54

her kind, having outlived all her Canadian sisters and half-sisters, as well as all the remaining Tribal-class destroyers of the Royal Navy or any other Commonwealth navy. She is a sleek, predator-like throw-back to the time of the Big Gun Destroyers and a memory from a time when the Tribals prowled the ocean in search of prey.

HMCS Micmac (Tribal–class)

Length:	377'	Laid Down:	20-05-1942
Beam:	37' 6"	Launched:	18-09-1943
Draft:	11' 2"	Commissioned:	12-09-1945
Displacement:	1927 tons	Paid Off:	31-03-1964

Armament: 6 x 4.7" LA guns, 2 x 4" HA guns, four 21" torpedo tubes, 4 x 2pdr, 1 x 12pdr 6 x 20mm Oerlikon AA guns

One of the first pair of Canadian-built Tribals to be laid down by Halifax Shipyard Ltd. in the spring of 1942, of her sisters and half-sisters, *Micmac* alone never fired a shot in anger; her entire career was spent as a training ship. With a construction time of almost five years—it had been 39 months between laying down the destroyer and her commissioning—she was estimated to have cost some $8.5 million to construct and arm. This was nearly three times the average cost of British-built Tribals.[21]

---

[21] (Chappelle, 1995)

A month after her commissioning, *Micmac* carried the former commander of the First Canadian Army in Europe, General H.D.G. Crerar on an inspection tour of the Maritime provinces; Crerar would retire from the Canadian Army the following year. *Micmac* received minor damage just before Christmas when HMCS *Algonquin* collided with her while berthing alongside. Repairs were completed in Halifax in January and she sailed for Bermuda to undertake two months of new entry training—*Micmac* was, at the time, the only operational destroyer on the East coast. In mid-February she assisted the landing craft LCI-164, towing her into Bermuda. Later in the year she was assigned as escort for SS *Aquitania* which was carrying Canada's new Governor General Field Marshal Earl Alexander of Tunis, and later still in that year she escorted SS *Mauretania* which was transporting Field Marshal Montgomery to Canada.[22]

After another year of training duties, she entered refit in Halifax in late March of 1947. Completing the refit in July, she put to sea for full power trials off Sambro Head on the 16th. She entered a fog bank while on her return to Halifax and with visibility poor she collided with the freighter SS *Yarmouth County*.[23] The freighter suffered only minor damage and no injuries, but *Micmac's* damage was much more severe, with extensive port-side damage above the waterline, including the destruction of her 'A' position gun mount. She lost 40 feet of her bow and her keel was broken underneath 'B' gun mount. Five men were killed, five more and a civilian dockyard worker were missing and presumed lost and another 15 sustained various injuries. Her half-sister HMCS *Haida* stood by to offer her assistance.

Micmac was paid off into reserve for repairs and reconstruction, emerging as an escort destroyer over two years

---

[22] (English, Afridi to Nizam: British FleetDestroyers 1937 - 43, 2001) p. 57

[23] (Montreal Gazette, 1947)

later. A Squid anti-submarine replaced her 'A' gun mount, while a quadruple 40mm Bofors AA mount replaced her 4.7-inch twin mount in 'B' position. This was a necessary reduction in weight of armament forward as the keel damage had not been fully repaired and her compromised structural integrity would not allow for heavier armament forward without significant risk to the safety of the ship, should that armament be fired. Like the other Tribals rebuilt as destroyer escorts, she had her twin 4.7-inch 'Y' gun mounting replaced by a twin 4-inch mounting and she retained the twin 4-inch mount she had in X position. She re-commissioned mid-November of 1949 and departed for Bermuda on January 9th 1950 for working up and to act as plane guard for the carrier HMCS *Magnificent*. In this latter role she rescued a Fairy Firefly observer on February 25th and pulled a Firefly pilot from the water on June 7th. Later that fall she and 'Maggie' formed part of the Canadian Special Service Squadron along with half-sister HMCS *Huron*. The squadron was at sea until returning to Halifax in late November. Minor hull repairs were completed during January of the following year, and while on her winter cruise to the Caribbean in April, she rendered assistance to the passenger vessel *Gilbert Jr.* which had run out of fuel. *Micmac* towed her into Willemstad on April 4th.

Between May and August of 1951, *Micmac* was at Halifax Dockyard undergoing a refit, and on completion of trials and working up she sailed for the Mediterranean to act once more as plane guard for HMCS *Magnificent*. On October 24th she undertook a rescue three days out of Halifax, where she recovered the pilot of a ditched Hawker Sea Fury.

Later that November she was in Charlottetown, PEI to escort the cruiser HMCS *Ontario* from that Island port to another one in Newfoundland; H.R.H. Princess Elizabeth and the Duke of Edinburgh were aboard and were on their way on a visit to Canada's newest province beginning in St. John's and arriving on the 8th.

On the last day of November 1951 *Micmac* paid off to complete her partial destroyer escort conversion. On completion she carried her full complement of twin 4-inch guns (including one twin mount each in A and B positions), with her Squid anti-submarine mortar relocated to her quarterdeck (and another added), a pair of 3-inch/50 AA guns on her aft superstructure, and four torpedo tubes. While the quadruple Bofors mount had been removed, she had several single mounts added to increase her AA firepower.

She re-commissioned on August 14, 1953 but in October of that year a leak between her number five and number six fuel tanks was discovered and repaired. In 1954 she needed eight days of dockyard time to repair damage from a small electrical fire that occurred in early April.

Micmac subsequently participated in several training cruises and in the summer of 1954 visited Britain. On return she escorted HMY *Britannia* to Québec City, arriving in August.

Once more in refit between May and September of 1956, she sailed to join fellow Canadian Tribals HMCS *Huron* and HMCS *Iroquois* on a European cruise, visiting Britain, France, and Portugal over the course of two months.[24] Her subsequent service in late 1956 and 1957 was disrupted by several mechanical issues: a failure of her steering gear during full power trials in December of 1956, condenser problems while in Puerto Rico the next year, and a damaged propeller after striking a coral reef in Bermuda. This last incident required the removal of the propeller to have it hammered back into shape before replacing it.

In 1959 she was one of the Royal Yacht's escorts during the opening of the St. Lawrence Seaway, but late that year she suffered damage when undertaking a jackstay transfer between herself and sister Tribal, HMCS *Cayuga*. In February of 1961 she was on fisheries protection duties off Newfoundland. She put into St John's for a refit, but delays from equipment preservation efforts, a fire, and labour disputes meant she

---

[24] (Madgwick, 2003) p. 149

didn't make Halifax until just before Christmas 1961.

While working-up she experience a variety of mechanical issues, including the breakdown of her steering gear again, blocked condensers (again), and pump failures. She returned to Halifax in March to address these issues with additional repairs. In 1962 and again in 1963 she undertook European cruises, but persistent mechanical problems brought her home to Halifax in December of 1963, where she was officially paid off the end of March 1964 and declared surplus to requirements. On the disposal list with sisters HMCS *Cayuga* and HMCS *Nootka*, all three were sold to Marine Salvage Ltd. of Port Colborne, Ontario, with *Micmac* being resold to Shipbreaking Industries of Faslane, Scotland where she was broken up on October 14th, 1964.[25]

HMCS Nootka (Tribal–class)

Length:	377'	Laid Down:	20-05-1942
Beam:	37' 6"	Launched:	26-04-1944
Draft:	11' 2"	Commissioned:	07-08-1946
Displacement:	1927 tons	Paid Off:	06-02-1964

Armament: 6 x 4.7" LA guns, 2 x 4" HA guns, four 21" torpedo tubes, 4 x 2pdr, 1 x 12pdr 6 x 20mm Oerlikon AA guns

The second HMCS *Nootka*[26] was laid down by Halifax

---

[25] (English, Afridi to Nizam: British FleetDestroyers 1937 - 43, 2001) p. 58

[26] The first HMCS *Nootka* was a *Fundy*-class minesweeper commissioned the end

Shipyard Ltd. the same day as her sister *Micmac*, but she would be launched nearly seven mothers after and commissioned almost a year after her sister. Overall, from being laid down to commissioning *Nootka* took 51 months to complete—this was the longest building time of any of the Canadian-built Tribal-class destroyers. She was off Halifax on August 9th, 1946 undertaking her sea trials prior to acceptance.[27]

Shortly after commissioning she and her sister *Micmac* were assigned to escort the liner SS *Mauritania* aboard which was Field Marshal Montgomery on passage to Halifax. In October she was assigned as plane guard to the carrier HMCS *Warrior* during exercises in the Atlantic. After this she escorted *Warrior* to Panama, from where the carrier would continue on to Esquimalt. *Nootka* would arrive back in Halifax on November 28th.

1947 consisted mainly of training for *Nootka*. She undertook a training cruise to the Caribbean with *Warrior* and *Micmac* in April and May, a series of exercises with the corvette HMCS *Portage*, and the scuttling of the captured U-boat U-190[28] off Halifax on October 21st.

The sink exercise was to involve an attack by surface vessels with firing guns and torpedoes, while at the same time naval fighters would attack the submarine with rockets. Finally, it was intended that the *Algerine*-class minesweeper HMCS *New Liskeard* would use its Hedgehog anti-submarine

---

of 1938. She was renamed HMCS *Nanoose* in April 1943 to allow one of the first pair of Canadian Tribals to be christened *HMCS Nootka (II)*.

[27] (Montreal Gazette, 1946)

[28] U-190—a Type IXC U-boat—surrendered to the RCN on 12 May 1945 and was commissioned by the Canadian Navy for testing and evaluation. She was paid off from Canadian service on July 24th 1947. Prior to her surrender she had sunk the Bangor-class minesweeper HMCS *Esquimalt* on April 16th 1945. See (MacPherson & Barrie, Ships of Canada's Naval Forces: 1910-2002, 2004) p. 186

spigot-mortar to finish off the ex-U-boat. In the event, things didn't go as planned—*Nootka* and her sister HMCS *Haida* had to break off their first attack run when *New Liskeard* fouled the range. The second 30-knot run was interrupted by a 'Check Fire' signal accidentally triggered on *Nootka's* bridge. Finally, when the destroyers were in position to open fire, the aircraft had already engaged U-190 with rockets and the submarine was beginning to sink. It has been in dispute ever since whether she was sunk by the aircraft or the surface vessels.[29]

HMCS *Nootka* was in dry-dock in Halifax by the end of the year for a refit that would last into January of 1948. Later in that year, having participated in exercises in the Caribbean and off the East coast, she joined *Haida* once more to escort the carrier HMCS *Magnificent* on a cruise of Hudson Bay as well as Labrador.

1949 saw further exercises and in June *Nootka* and *Haida* were required to assist *Magnificent* after the carrier ran aground. On April 15th *Nootka* was back in Halifax to undergo her conversion to destroyer escort configuration. Once her trials and working-up were completed in late-November 1950, *Nootka* sailed for Korean waters. She needed to put into Balboa, Panama for repairs to weather damage received in passage, but eventually arrived in Sasebo, Japan in mid-January 1951, after which she relieved her sister HMCS *Cayuga* as Senior Officer's ship for the Canadian forces in the Korean theater.[30] She took part in shore bombardment, 'Train Busting' and patrols off Inchon, as well as screening Allied carriers off the west coast of Korea.

The night of May 13th *Nootka's* crew undertook a cutting-out operation using the ship's motorboat. The targets—two junks and four sampans—were just off the mouth of the Yalu River, but unfortunately the captured craft foundered on the

---

[29] (McKee & Darlington, The Canadian Naval Chronicle 1939-1945, 1998) p. 223

[30] (Thorgrimsson & Russell, 1965) p. 44

way back to Inchon. Their crews were handed over to shore authorities upon reaching Inchon on May 23rd.

After this *Nootka* undertook shore bombardment of the Korean east coast, targeting railways and gun emplacements near Wosan. These operations continued until she was relieved by HMCS *Sioux* in early June. *Nootka* underwent a short period in dockyard hands in Kure, returning to the Korean west coast to supervise all junk traffic and daylight screening of Allied carriers, until she departed Korean waters in late July 1951, bound to the Aleutian Islands and Esquimalt. Once at the Vancouver Island naval base she underwent minor hull repairs before departing for Halifax. Upon arrival she went into dry-dock for a three month refit, but after completion it was found that there were still issues with the portside condenser discharge and additional repairs delayed her departure for Korea until the end of December.

Nootka was back at Sasebo by mid-February 1952, and once again took up patrol and shore bombardment duties. Between March 27th and April 10th she provided support to guerrilla groups based on nearby islands. Things got interesting the night of April 17th when *Nootka* found herself under fire from both sides during a nighttime exchange of fire between emplacements on the island of Kirindo and the mainland. She relieved the Australian Tribal HMAS *Warramunga* on the east coast of Korea on May 28th. While undertaking shore bombardment two days later, shore emplacements off Chongjin landed several near-misses around the Canadian destroyer.

In early June HMS *Constance* relieved *Nootka* and she and her crew spent two weeks at Hong Kong for R&R before returning to her duties on the west coast of Korea. Apart from her patrol and shore bombardment work, she salvaged the South Korean sub-chaser *Bak Dusan* on the last day of July. The Korean vessel had run aground off the mainland near Yongpyong-ni. The night of September 25th a radar echo disclosed the presence of a small craft nearby. This oar-propelled junk was fitted to carry delayed action mines. In the engagement that followed, one North Korean was killed and five more captured. It was the only seizure of a North Korean vessel during the war. *Nootka* departed Korea in early November bound for Sasebo; making her way home via Singapore, Suez, Malta, and Gibraltar, before reaching Halifax on December 17th. She was only the second Canadian vessel to have circumnavigated the globe at that point—the first being the cruiser HMCS *Quebec*.

The destroyer was out of commission for conversion until December 15th, 1954. During this dockyard period she received a new lattice foremast and a 3-inch/50 AA mount. While in Bermuda in May the next, year she ran into a breakwater at Ireland Island Dockyard and suffered extensive damage forward. She set out for Saint John, New Brunswick in the company of her sister HMCS *Iroquois* and the *Prestonian*-class frigate HMCS *Toronto*. All three were limited to *Nootka's* maximum speed of 6 or 7 knots due to the need to reduce stresses on the destroyer's fore end. *Nootka* would be under repair from May 24th, 1955 to September 6th.

Her last years were overshadowed by ongoing hull and machinery repairs necessitated by the pounding the vessel received in her Atlantic service. By this time she was undertaking exercises and cruises in American and European waters. In December of 1955 fuel tank leaks caused contamination of her bunker oil with seawater, bringing her to a dead stop in the Bermuda Narrows. In April 1956 she was in company with frigates HMCS *Outremont* and *Buckingham*, the trio searching for a missing RCN F2H-3 Banshee fighter jet and its pilot off the coast of Nova Scotia. She underwent a refit between September 1956 and February 1957 which added a funnel cap, and another refit in April 1958 when she received replacement 4-inch mounts.

Fellow Tribal-class destroyers HMCS *Huron* and HMCS *Haida* joined *Nootka* in rendering assistance to Nova Scotia fishermen throughout March of 1961; and on the night of

November 15th Nootka stood by the fishing boat *Harvey And Sisters* when the latter found itself in difficulty off Cape Sable.[31]

In 1962, during the Cuban Missile Crisis, *Nootka* took part in the massive RCN deployment under the guise of a training exercise to ensure Canadian warships weren't caught in port should hostilities erupt. Assigned a patrol area off the northern tip of Cuba, *Nootka* return to port once it was clear that the crisis was past.[32]

She undertook a Great Lakes tour with her sister HMCS *Haida* between June and September of 1963—travelling some 17,000 miles—before joining exercises in Bermuda. This would be her last deployment, as she arrived back in Halifax in December of 1963 and paid off in February of 1964 before transfer to Crown Assets Corporation for disposal. She, along with HMCS *Micmac* and HMCS *Cayuga* was sold to Marine Salvage Ltd. of Port Colbourne, Ontario before going to Shipbreaking Industries. Towed from Halifax, she was scrapped at Faslane, Scotland in late September 1964.[33]

---

[31] (English, Afridi to Nizam: British FleetDestroyers 1937 - 43, 2001) p. 58

[32] Per former crewman Robin Cox via (Proc, 2014)

[33] (MacPherson & Barrie, Ships of Canada's Naval Forces: 1910-2002, 2004) p. 241

HMCS Cayuga (Tribal–class)

Length:	377'	Laid Down:	07-10-1943
Beam:	37' 6"	Launched:	28-07-1945
Draft:	11' 2"	Commissioned:	20-10-1947
Displacement:	1927 tons	Paid Off:	27-02-1964

Armament: 6 x 4.7" LA guns, 2 x 4" HA guns, four 21" torpedo tubes, 4 x 2pdr, 1 x 12pdr 6 x 20mm Oerlikon AA guns

Built by Halifax Shipyard Ltd., HMCS *Cayuga* was the second-last Canadian-Built Tribal to complete. A skeleton crew commissioned her and it wasn't until her fire control equipment was fully installed that she received her full crew complement. After trials and working-up she departed Halifax for Esquimalt. During passage she made several stops to show the flag, but among the defects that began to appear, the worst was the failure of her port low-pressure steam turbine which reduced her to a top speed of only 8 knots.[34]

Upon reaching Esquimalt she entered dockyard hands for repairs between March 22nd and May 18th 1948. Her officers and crew took part in relief efforts during the Fraser Valley floods that occurred in late May and early June. She was back in dry-dock for a month in the fall, and then undertook training exercises with sister HMCS *Athabaskan* for the remainder of 1948. She paid off for refit the end of that year, being re-commissioned mid-September of 1949, having had

---

[34] (English, Afridi to Nizam: British FleetDestroyers 1937 - 43, 2001) p. 51

her 'X' position gun mount removed and replaced with a pair of Squid anti-submarine mortars along with the required fire control and sonar equipment. Trials and work-ups uncovered additional defects and *Cayuga* wasn't considered effective until January of 1950.

Between February 14th and 23rd she was part of search efforts looking for American airmen who had bailed out of a damaged Convair B-36 bomber off the Canadian West coast. The bomber—which was carrying a Mark IV atomic bomb—was to have crashed at sea as the pilot intended, but instead went down in the coastal mountains of British Columbia. Three of the crew were pulled from the water by the fish packer *Cape Perry* on the 15th while another group was found ashore. *Cayuga* stood offshore while a mountain rescue team tracked and recovered the bomber's radio operator who was almost dead from exposure. On the morning of the 16th *Cayuga's* crew recovered another American crewman along with evidence that another two had survived bailing out. In all, twelve of the crew were rescued.[35]

Cayuga followed this with a cruise, as she prepared to join sister HMCS *Athabaskan (II)* on a European cruise with the Canadian Special Service Squadron. Upon the outbreak of the Korean War, the cruise was terminated and *Cayuga* and *Athabaskan* joined HMCS *Sioux* in escorting the cruiser HMCS *Ontario* from Esquimalt to Korean waters on July 5th. *Cayuga* undertook patrol and shore bombardment operations until she was sidelined by condenser problems, which necessitate repairs in Sasebo in late September 1950. After a shore leave in Hong Kong in November, she returned to her duties off the coast of Korea. Thanks to the sharp lookout being kept by her sonar operators, *Cayuga* was able to avoid entering an enemy

---

[35] (Leach, 2008) p. 120; The Mark IV bomb aboard the stricken aircraft was the 'production' version of the Fat-Man bomb dropped on Nagasaki. The nuclear weapon was unarmed at the time of the incident and was dropped over the ocean and explosively scuttled before the bomber crashed.

minefield off Chodo. She took part in the evacuation of Chinnampo and the Inchon landings. After completing maintenance at Sasebo in January 1951, she joined sister HMCS *Nootka* in patrol and shore bombardment duties until she was detached in mid-March to return home. *Cayuga* made Esquimalt on April 7 and went into refit until May 25th. After work-ups she sailed for Korea once more, stopping in Pearl Harbor for exercises and arriving at Sasebo on July 25th.

Cayuga provided gunfire support, carrier screening, interception and inspection of inshore small craft, and supported guerrillas and raiders until January of 1952. She then made Hong Kong to spend a month undergoing repairs and R&R for her crew. She returned to her station on February 12th and had a reasonably quiet remainder of her Korean War deployment.

She departed for Esquimalt the first of June, arriving two weeks later. She was de-stored and paid off in preparation to her conversion to a destroyer escort. This completed the end of March 1953, and *Cayuga* emerged having had her steel lattice foremast replaced with an aluminum one, and with two twin 4-inch mounts (one each in A and B positions), a twin 3-inch/50 AA mount in X position, and a pair of Squid anti-submarine mortar in Y position. Four 40mm Bofors single mounts and four torpedo tubes rounded out her armament. All told, her full-load displacement was now 2745 tons.

She completed trials, work-ups and a shakedown cruise in November—this having been delayed when during trials she struck a jetty in March, necessitating repairs—this being followed by a low-pressure steam turbine failure which put her in dock from May 23rd to June 28th.

Cayuga returned to Korean waters on November 25th to police the Armistice, and was on patrol and undertaking exercises along the Korean coast until mid-December of 1954. She then went into an eight-week refit, emerging in late February to take up training duties along the Canadian west coast with sister HMCS *Athabaskan*. These occupied the two Tribals—which were part of the 2nd Canadian Escort

Squadron—for the next four years.

In September 1958 *Cayuga* experienced a serious boiler room fire in which two men were badly burned. In January 1959 she and 'Athabee' were transferred to the 3rd Canadian Escort Squadron on the east coast, where they operated in the North Atlantic and European waters. She and HMCS *Micmac* had a minor collision during a jackstay transfer off Bermuda in late November 1959; *Cayuga* suffered only minor damage but *Micmac* had several of her transverse frames distorted.

February 27th of 1964 saw *Cayuga* paid off for disposal. She and her sisters HMCS *Micmac* and *Nootka* were sold to Marine Salvage Ltd. of Port Colbourne, Ontario, after which they were resold to Shipbreaking Industries for £132,000. HMCS *Cayuga* arrived in Faslane, Scotland under tow by the tug *Rotesand* for breaking-up the last day of September, 1964.[36]

---

[36] (English, Afridi to Nizam: British FleetDestroyers 1937 - 43, 2001) p. 52

HMCS Athabaskan (II) (Tribal–class)

Length:	377'	Laid Down:	15-05-1943
Beam:	37' 6"	Launched:	04-05-1946
Draft:	11' 2"	Commissioned:	20-01-1948
Displacement:	1927 tons	Paid Off:	21-04-1966

Armament: 6 x 4.7" LA guns, 2 x 4" HA guns, four 21" torpedo tubes, 4 x 2pdr, 1 x 12pdr 6 x 20mm Oerlikon AA guns

Built by Halifax Shipyard Ltd., and later nicknamed 'Athabee' by her crew, the second *Athabaskan* was the last of the Canadian-built Tribals to complete, and the last Canadian Tribal to commission, entering the RCN in 1948—three years after the end of the war she had been designed to fight. After commissioning, she took her time on trials and work-ups before departing for her west coast station on May 15th 1948. Due to an outbreak of poliomyelitis[37] *Athabaskan* was quarantined upon her arrival in Esquimalt on June 29th. This outbreak had resulted in the death of one crewman while on passage from Halifax.

Once the quarantine was lifted, *Athabaskan* and her sister

---

[37] (English, Afridi to Nizam: British FleetDestroyers 1937 - 43, 2001) p. 50. This illness is more commonly known as Polio and is caused by the poliovirus, which is generally transferred by contaminated water.

HMCS *Cayuga* undertook a series of exercises and showed the flag along Canadian and American west coasts. While in Esquimalt harbor in November of 1948 she was bumped by a fire tender, which caused some buckled hull plates. She undertook a winter Caribbean cruise between January and May of 1949, after which she made further port calls in California and Alaska. Between mid-September 1949 and mid-March 1950 *Athabaskan* was in dockyard hands to be refitted for a training role. This saw the replacement of her 4.7-inch twin gun mounting in Y position replaced with a pair of Squid anti-submarine mortars. She also had her Action Information Center enlarged, and a pair of depth-charge throwers removed—although she retained her aft depth charge rail. The intention was to have *Athabaskan* join the Canadian Special Service Squadron on a cruise of European waters, but the outbreak of the Korean War saw the termination of the cruise on June 25th.

Athabaskan and *Cayuga* were joined by HMCS *Sioux* and the trio escorted the cruiser HMCS *Ontario* from Esquimalt on their deployment to Korean waters. After making calls at Pearl Harbor, Kwajalein and Guam, the Canadian ships arrived at Sasebo, Japan on July 30th. *Athabaskan's* deployment saw her undertake various duties including cruiser escort, interdiction of small costal transport craft, and gunfire support, including acting in support of the Inchon landings. She grounded on December 4th while covering the Chinnampo evacuation, the damage causing subsequent engine issues.

After a period of maintenance and R&R in Hong Kong, she undertook inshore patrol and screening of the *Colossus*-class carrier HMS *Theseus* for much of February and March, before taking up station on the Korean east coast. She departed the war zone on May 2nd, bound for refit in Esquimalt.

Upon completion of the refit she sailed from Esquimalt on October 29th for her third tour in Korean waters. Taking up her assigned roles of screening and patrolling the first week of November, save for a brief respite in Hong Kong in May of 1953, she remained in Korean waters until the ceasefire on

June 27th 1953. *Athabaskan* remained on station until the peace was established; rescuing the crew of a downed helicopter and a Vought Corsair fighter in August and standing by to assist the stranded tanker *Tongshu* in October.

Athabaskan arrived back in Canada for conversion to an anti-submarine destroyer escort on December 11th, 1953 staying in dockyard hands until October 1954. Like other Canadian Tribals she emerged armed with a pair of twin 4-inch gun mounts forward and a twin 3-inch/50 mounting aft alongside a pair of Squid anti-submarine mortars and four torpedo tubes. Her anti-aircraft fit included four 40mm Bofors single mounts. She also received a lattice foremast to support her new radar and radio antennas. While on trials in December of 1954 she responded to a call for assistance by the oceanographic survey vessel *Cedarwood* which was in danger of foundering.

The first of October 1955 she grounded on Spanish Bank off Vancouver and had to be towed off by the tug *Glendon*— luckily she suffered only minor damage to her sonar dome.

Between 1955 and 1958 she undertook patrol duties off the Canadian west coast, including an unsuccessful submarine hunt off the British Columbia coast in June of 1957.

In January of 1959 *Athabaskan* and *Cayuga* departed Esquimalt to join their fellow Tribal-class destroyers in forming an all-Tribal east coast squadron. Arriving in Halifax on the 16th of February, the two destroyers swapped crews with east coast *St. Laurent*-class destroyers HMCS *Saguenay* and HMCS *St. Laurent*—the crew of *Athabaskan* assigned to *Saguenay* for the return voyage to Esquimalt where *Saguenay* and *St. Laurent* would then be stationed. In May of that year *Athabaskan* was one of the escorts for HMY *Britannia* which was carrying Queen Elizabeth II to Canada for the opening of the St. Lawrence Seaway. [38]

---

[38] (English, Afridi to Nizam: British FleetDestroyers 1937 - 43, 2001) p. 50

On September 29th 1962 *Athabaskan* responded to a request for help from a ditched Lockheed Super Constellation airliner, rescuing 48 people, but later that year her tour of European ports was cut short by the Cuban Missile Crisis in October. The crisis saw the deployment of twenty-two anti-submarine surface vessels, two submarines, the carrier *Bonaventure*, all of 'Bonnie's air wing as well as shore-based Grumman Trackers and Canadair Argus patrol aircraft. Supported by the RCN's auxiliaries and commanded by Vice Admiral K.L. Dyer the Canadian deployment on 'Cubex' allowed for anti-submarine coverage of the majority of the Canadian and US east coasts, while the USN's blockade of Cuba drew American vessels away from their own coasts. [39]

In March of 1964 *Athabaskan* undertook the rescue of 18 survivors from the stern of the Liberian-flagged tanker *Amphailos* which had foundered in the mid-Atlantic.

Athabaskan was then paid off into reserve and used as a source of spares and equipment before finally being placed on the disposal list. She departed Halifax under tow in July of 1969, bound for La Spezia, Italy to be broken up.[40] She was the last of the Canadian Tribals to commission, and the last to be taken out of active service. With her demolition, only her half-sister HMCS *Haida* remained—and by 1969 *Haida* was a museum ship on the Toronto waterfront.

By 1938, with war imminent, the Royal Navy recognized the need for large numbers of destroyers for wartime deployments, and due to their complexity the most recent designs—the Tribals and the J-, K-, N-, L- and M-classes—were not suitable as they were too expensive, and their weaponry took too long to construct and procure. The Admiralty took the machinery of the J-class, and using a new

---

[39] (German, 1990) p. 272

[40] (English, Afridi to Nizam: British FleetDestroyers 1937 - 43, 2001) p. 51

hull design and lighter weapons fit, put the O- and P-class 'Intermediate Type' destroyers into production upon the outbreak of war in 1939.[41]

Additional flotillas of the Q- through Z-class 'Emergency Type' destroyers were also ordered—these used the larger J-class hull design initially, to save time and effort as the molds, jigs and toolings existed. Over time, however, modifications to the hull shape were made to provide a more seaworthy ship. The Q- and R-classes were ordered in 1940, while the U-, V- and Z-classes were ordered to the modified hull form between mid-1941 and early 1942. Some of the other modifications included reduction in the use of aluminum, which was eliminated wherever possible; the hull was stiffened to reduce stresses; the R-class was outfitted for tropical service; and the V-class introduced a gangway between the forecastle and the after superstructure.[42]

The final flotillas of the British war emergency program were the Ca-, Ch-, Co- and Cr-classes—the last of which HMCS *Crusader* and HMCS *Crescent* belonged. These, and the preceding Z-class had their 4.7-inch main armament replaced with newer 4.5-inch single gun mounts at the design stage. This weaponry change would begin the implementation of the 4.5-inch caliber as the standard for all future Royal Navy destroyers.[43]

---

[41] (Raven & Roberts, Ensign 6: War Built Destroyers O to Z Classes, 1976) p. 2

[42] (Friedman, British Destroyers and Frigates: The Second World War and After, 2008) p. 89; as the middle of British destroyers was taken up by the boilers and turbines, the only access fore and aft was along the weather deck; the gangway provided safer, if not as exposed, travel between the ends of the ship.

[43] Up to and including the most recent Type 45 *Daring*-class. The prototype destroyer 4.5-inch single and twin mounts were first trialed at sea aboard HMS *Savage* in 1943.

HMCS Sioux (V–class)

Length:	362' 9"	Laid Down:	08-10-1942
Beam:	35' 8"	Launched:	02-09-1943
Draft:	11' 6"	Commissioned:	07-02-1944
Displacement:	1710 tons	Paid Off:	01-04-1970
Armament:	4 x 4.7" LA guns, eight 21" torpedo tubes, 4 x 40mm, 4 x 20mm AA guns		

HMCS *Sioux* was not—despite her name—a member of the famous Tribal-class. Instead she was one of the War Emergency Destroyers—designed to be quick and inexpensive to produce in numbers to fill the most pressing needs for destroyers in the Royal (and Dominion) navies. As a member of the V-class, she was to have become HMS *Vixen*, but was transferred to the RCN on December 28th, 1943—before her commissioning. Built by J. Samuel White & Co. at their Cowes, Isle of Wight yard, She was completed in 17 months and 6 days—a construction time beaten only by her sister HMCS *Algonquin* (ex-HMS *Valentine*) amongst her class[44]. Upon commissioning she undertook work-ups at Scapa Flow before being assigned to the Home Fleet's 26th Destroyer Flotilla, and took part in escorting airstrikes against the German Battleship *Tirpitz* in Norway and German shipping

---

[44] (Raven & Roberts, Ensign 6: War Built Destroyers O to Z Classes, 1976) p. 3; this as compared to the Canadian built HMCS *Nootka's* construction time of 51 months or the British-built Canadian Tribal HMCS *Iroquois* which took 25 months to build and commission.

along the coast of that country.[45] She would remain with the 26th Flotilla for the remainder of her wartime career.

She undertook operations along the Normandy coast, including operating with Force 'E' of Juno Beach on D-Day in support of her countrymen's advance inland. On the night of November 10th and 11th, *Sioux* and the Polish Hunt-class destroyer *Krakowiak* undertook to intercept the German 4th MTB Flotilla—based out of Boulogne—while it was laying mines off Le Havre. In July she rotated back to Scapa Flow from where she took part in escorting four Russian convoys. From March 20th to April 5th, 1944 she escorted the convoy JW58/RA58; from September 15th to October 5th she was an escort for JW60/RA60; from December 30th to January 1st, 1945 she was again on escort duty with JW63/RA63; from February 3rd to the 13th she escorted JW64/RA64; and from March 12th to 30th, 1945 she was an escort with convoy JW65/RA65. On the return leg of the penultimate of these convoys—RW64—bound to English waters from Polyarnoe, *Sioux* with her half-sisters HMS *Zambesi* and HMS *Zest* took part in the evacuation of 500 inhabitants of the Norwegian island of Soroy, who had been left by the Germans without food or a means of leaving the island.[46]

In addition to her escort work during the unsuccessful airstrike against *Tirpiz* in Kaafjord from the 20th to 22nd, 1944, *Sioux* also escorted the strike against the airfield at Gossen on August 10th, 1944, an attack on the Bardinfoss airfield on April 21st and attacks on the Bodo area from October 26th to 28th, 1944. She was also involved in attacks on a German convoy of Mosjoen, north of Namsos on November 27th, before taking part in Operation Urban—an anti-shipping and mining operation between December 7th and 14th, 1944.

HMCS *Sioux* sailed for Canada on April 6th, 1945 for refit in

---

[45] (MacPherson & Barrie, Ships of Canada's Naval Forces: 1910-2002, 2004) p. 64

[46] (English, Obdurate to Daring: British Fleet Destroyers 1941 - 45, 2008) p. 94

Halifax, which took until November 1945 to complete. With the war having been concluded while she was in dock, *Sioux* was transferred to the Pacific Ocean. She arrived in Esquimalt before the end of the year and on February 27th, 1946 she was paid off into reserve.

While in reserve she underwent conversion to a destroyer escort and was recommissioned into the RCN's Pacific Division on January 18th 1950. This conversion saw her two aft 4.5-inch gun mounts removed to be replaced by a pair of Squid anti-submarine mortars. It also saw the destroyer fitted with bunks as opposed to having the crew sling hammocks—a first for the Canadian Navy.

Sioux was in dockyard hands when the Pacific Division's three destroyers were ordered to Korean waters on the declaration of war. She and the Tribal-class destroyers HMCS *Cayuga* and HMCS *Athabaskan* departed Esquimalt on July 5th, 1950 arriving in Sasebo, Japan on July 30th. She and *Athabaskan* were assigned to Task Force 96.5, escorting convoys to Pusan. In August she was posted to the Korean west coast where she undertook the bombardment of Popusompu on August 20th. Ten days later she and the British light cruiser HMS *Kenya* bombarded the Korean Island of Te bu Somu. The following month she provided naval support for the landings at Inchon, being tasked with escorting the Logistics Support Group and enforcing the naval blockade, and remaining on blockade duty until her departure for Sasebo at the end of October. Leaving Sasebo on November 5th, she sailed for Hong Kong ending up passing through Typhoon Clara and suffering storm damage which required repairs upon her arrival. Returning from Hong Kong, *Sioux* took up patrol duties off Inchon and the mouth of the Yalu River.

On December 3rd, 1950 *Sioux* and her Task Group were dispatched to cover the Chinnampo withdrawal with naval gunfire support and by escorting the transports into the harbor. Forced to sail the mine-swept channel at night, *Sioux* ran aground. While getting herself free she fouled her starboard screw, forcing her to retire for the night. The next day she was back in action with the Australian destroyer HMAS *Warramunga*, once again providing a covering force for the withdrawal.

For the remainder of her first Korean War tour she was attached to the screening force for the British carrier HMS *Theseus*, as well as additional naval support for the allied forces withdrawing from Inchon. She was relieved by the Canadian Tribal-class destroyer HMCS *Nootka* and departed the Far East on January 15th, 1951 bound for Esquimalt.[47]

In all, *Sioux* would complete three full tours of Korean waters from 1950 to 1955, being the last Canadian warship to depart the Korean littoral zone when she finally sailed for home in Esquimalt in January of 1955.

She would spend two years operating from that west coast port as a training vessel before being assigned to the east coast for similar deployments out of Halifax. She was paid off in Halifax on October 30th, 1963 and stripped of all usable equipment and placed on the disposal list while alongside at Sydney, Nova Scotia. Sold to an Italian shipbreaker on June 30th 1965, she was towed to La Spezia for breaking.[48]

---

[47] (Thorgrimsson & Russell, 1965) p. 31

[48] (MacPherson & Barrie, Ships of Canada's Naval Forces: 1910-2002, 2004) p. 64

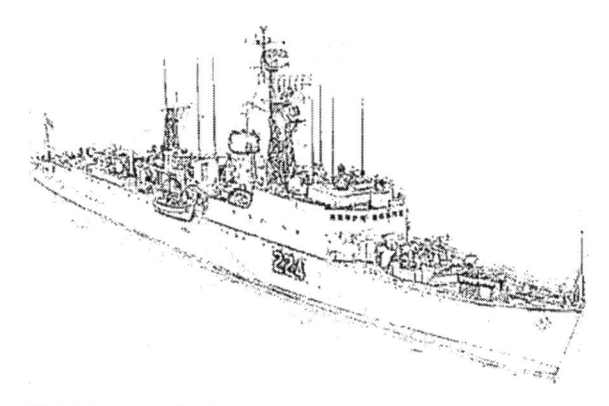

HMCS Algonquin (V–class)

Length:	362' 9"	Laid Down:	08-10-1942
Beam:	35' 8"	Launched:	02-09-1943
Draft:	11' 6"	Commissioned:	07-02-1944
Displacement:	1710 tons	Paid Off:	01-04-1970
Armament:	4 x 4.7" LA guns, eight 21" torpedo tubes, 4 x 40mm, 4 x 20mm AA guns		

Like her sister HMCS *Sioux*, *Algonquin* was one of the War Emergency destroyers of the V-class. She was to be HMS *Valentine*, but was commissioned into the RCN instead. Construction was by John Brown & Co. Ltd. on the Clyde. A perfect example of the War Emergency destroyers, she was built in 15 months and 20 days—the fastest construction time in her class.[49] After commissioning she was assigned to the Home Fleet's 26th Destroyer flotilla and sailed from Scapa Flow on March 31st, 1944 on her first escort mission on the passage to Northern Russia with convoy JW58, before being assigned to take part in Operation Tungsten—as part of the

---

[49] (Raven & Roberts, Ensign 6: War Built Destroyers O to Z Classes, 1976) p. 3; In fact, of the O to Z-classes of War Emergency Destroyers, *Algonquin* was the second fastest construction time overall—only HMS *Onslow* (also built by John Brown & Co. Ltd. at their Clydebank yard) had a shorter construction time of 15 months and 8 days. *Onslow* was completed in October of 1941. She survived the war and was sold to Pakistan in 1949.

carrier escort for an attack on *Tirpitz* in Altafjord, Norway. This successful attack saw the German battleship put out of action for three months.

Following this, the Canadian destroyer took part in escorting the Royal Navy carriers HMS *Searcher* and HMS *Furious* on an anti-shipping strike off Kristiansund on May 8th, 1944. The end of that month she departed Scapa Flow, bound for the Normandy beaches. There she would serve with a support group off Juno Beach. When the beachhead was established and secured, *Algonquin* carried General H.D.G. Crerar—General Officer Commanding First Canadian Army—and his command staff and landed them on Juno Beach. By the end of June, *Algonquin* was assigned back to the Home Fleet and based out of Scapa Flow.

The remainder of the war in Europe saw the destroyer assigned to carrier escort duties on several occasions. On August 10th, 1944 she was part of the escort for the carries HMS *Indefatigable*, HMS *Trumpeter* and HMS *Nabob*—the last was crewed by RCN officers and ratings (although the flight crews were Royal Navy Fleet Air Arm). On this occasion the three carries were part of a strike against the airfield at Gossen. Later that same month she took part in another attack on *Tirpitz*—this time unsuccessful. Not all escort missions ended well, sadly; on August 22nd, *Algonquin* stood by *Nabob* after the carrier had been torpedoed by U-354. The Canadian destroyer was able to take off over 200 of the badly damaged carrier's crew.[50]

The Canadian destroyer survived harsh winter weather once more from September 15th and October 5th, to escort the Northern Russian convoy JW60/RW60 past the Arctic Circle from September 15th and October 5th, 1944. She subsequently took part in Operation Athletic—a carrier attack against enemy

---

[50] Although seriously damaged and listing significantly, HMS *Nabob* made it home and eventually survived the war to be converted into a merchantman.

shipping in the Bodo area of Norway—between October 26th and 28th. This was followed by the successful destruction of the German convoy KS357 off Listerjord on the night of November 12th/13th, before she returned to the Russian convoys as an escort for JW63/RW63 to Kola Bay, Russia and back during the first twenty-one days of 1945. Upon completion of these duties, *Algonquin* was detailed to return to Halifax for a refit in February of 1945.

After six months in dockyard hands undergoing tropical conversion, *Algonquin* emerged in August and departed Halifax on the 12th of that month, bound for service with the British Pacific Fleet via the Mediterranean. On VJ day she received recall orders and departed Alexandria on November 3rd, 1945, sailing for Esquimalt, British Columbia. Upon her arrival on February 6th, 1946 she was immediately paid off into reserve, where she would remain for the next five years.

In January of 1951 she was towed from reserve across to the Yarrows Ltd. shipyard to undergo a destroyer escort conversion and modernization. Her revised fit saw changes to her superstructure, with a new enclosed bridge and lattice mast, as well as a complete revision to her armament which now consisted of a 3-inch/50 twin mount forward of the bridge, a 4-inch Twin anti-aircraft mount aft, two single Bofors boffin mounts, and a pair of Limbo anti-submarine mortars right aft. In this guise she approximated the Type-15 frigate conversion the Royal Navy had undertaken with some of its war emergency destroyers. She recommissioned in February 25th, 1953.[51]

Not selected for service in the Korean conflict, *Algonquin* was assigned to Halifax as Senior Officer of the 1st Canadian Escort Squadron, departing Esquimalt for this post in August of 1953. She spent the next dozen years as a training ship both in the waters off Halifax, and off Bermuda and in the

---

[51] (MacPherson & Barrie, Ships of Canada's Naval Forces: 1910-2002, 2004) p. 63

Caribbean.

She was sent back to reserve in Halifax in June of 1965, and two years later she and half-sister HMCS *Crescent* made passage to Esquimalt where they immediately entered reserve, and there *Algonquin* was finally paid off on April 1st, 1970.

Ultimately, the two destroyers were sold to Chi Shun Hai Steel Co. of Taiwan and in May of 1971 *Algonquin* and *Crescent* were towed to Formosa to be broken up.[52]

HMCS Crusader (Cr–class)

Length:	362' 9"	Laid Down:	15-11-1943
Beam:	35' 8"	Launched:	05-10-1944
Draft:	11' 6"	Commissioned:	15-11-1945
Displacement:	1730 tons	Paid Off:	15-01-1960
Armament:	4 x 4.5" LA guns, four 21" torpedo tubes, 4 x 40mm, 4 x 20mm AA guns		

Some may dispute that the Crusaders were a tribe, but the first destroyer named HMS *Crusader* belonged to the pre-WW1 Tribal class, and so she is presented here. The previous HMS *Crusader* was also a Canadian vessel—being renamed HMCS *Ottawa* when commissioned in the RCN in 1938. She was lost in a U-boat attack while escorting a convoy in 1942. This *Crusader* was laid down by John Brown & Co. Ltd. as a member of the 14th Emergency Destroyer Flotilla—the Cr-class.

In January of 1945 the Royal Navy made arrangements to loan the RCN a flotilla of destroyers for use in the Pacific as

---

[52] (English, Obdurate to Daring: British Fleet Destroyers 1941 - 45, 2008) p. 90

part of the British Pacific Fleet's campaign against Japan. The eight vessels of the Cr-class of destroyers would be transferred to Canada—much as the C-class of the 1930s had been prior to the war. With the end of the war in August, only *Crusader* and her sister *Crescent* underwent the transfer of commands—an arrangement made permanent in September of 1951.

Once *Crusader* had commissioned into the RCN, she proceeded to Portland where she underwent work-ups until December 15th, 1945. Departing for Esquimalt that day she visited Ponta Delgada, Jamaica, between New Year's Eve 1945 and January 4th, before arriving at her new home on Vancouver Island on January 21st, 1946. Upon arrival she immediately entered into Reserve to remain there for the next four years.

Between January and May of 1951 she underwent refit, after which she undertook training duties for the remainder of the year. She was in refit once more in March of the following year, and after completions sailed from Esquimalt on May 25th bound for Korean waters. She joined the Canadian Tribal-class destroyer HMCS *Iroquois* in operations with the American aircraft carrier USS *Bataan*, beginning her tour in June of 1952.

The evening of August 14th and 15th she and the New Zealand frigate HMNZS *Rotoiti* provided gunfire support for an attack on Ongjin. Later that year, in September and October she patrolled the Korean east coast off of Songjin. In January of 1953 she joined the escort force for the British fleet carrier HMS *Glory*, before returning to east coast patrols in late January until early February and later again in mid-April before departing for home. *Crusader* arrived in Esquimalt on Canada Day 1953, where she entered dockyard hands for a refit until September 11th. She undertook another Korean tour from November 1953 to August 1954.[53]

Crusader was in refit in Esquimalt from November 1954 to February 1955, after which she transferred to Canada's East

---

[53] (English, Obdurate to Daring: British Fleet Destroyers 1941 - 45, 2008) p. 144

Coast to undertake flagship duties for Canadian Flag Officer Atlantic, which included operations in the West Indies between January and June of 1957.

In September of that year she joined a search and rescue operation for the German ship *Pamir*, which was sunk in a hurricane 600 miles west of the Azores. Only six of *Pamir*'s crew survived the vessel's loss. The following August *Crusader* was once again tasked with a search and rescue operation—this time in concert with the Hunt-class destroyer HMS *Brocklesby* —for a Royal Dutch Airlines Super Constellation. The aircraft had gone missing 130 miles North West of Ireland. No survivors were recovered.

Once again in dockyard hands for refit between November of 1958 and February of 1959, she emerged with a partial conversion to an Anti-Submarine escort. This saw her fitted with an experimental version of the Canadian Variable Depth Sonar outfit in place of her Y-position gun mount, which in a more refined form would be part of her sister *Crescent*'s A/S escort conversion the following year.[54] After reentering fleet service she joined the 3rd Canadian Escort Squadron, with whom she served for the next year before being paid off on January 15th, 1960.

Crusader was placed in dockyard hands at Point Edward Naval base in Sydney, Nova Scotia in April of 1960. It was intended that she would be refitted once more, but this was cancelled and she was placed on the disposal list in October of 1962. On the 30th of that month she became the property of Crown Assets Disposal Corporation. She was ultimately sold to Metal Processors Ltd. in August of 1963 to be scrapped.[55]

---

[54] (Milner, Canada's Navy: The First Century, 1999) p. 207

[55] (MacPherson & Barrie, Ships of Canada's Naval Forces: 1910-2002, 2004) p. 242

HMCS Crescent (Cr–class)

Length:	362' 9"	Laid Down:	16-09-1943
Beam:	35' 8"	Launched:	20-07-1944
Draft:	11' 6"	Commissioned:	10-09-1945
Displacement:	1730 tons	Paid Off:	01-04-1970

Armament: 4 x 4.7" LA guns, eight 21" torpedo tubes, 4 x 40mm, 4 x 20mm AA guns

A fellow Cr-Class War Emergency Destroyer HMCS *Crescent*, like her sister, perpetuated the name of a destroyer previously provided to Canada. The previous HMS *Crescent* became HMCS *Fraser* in 1937, and was lost in a collision off France in 1940.

Also like her sister, she was loaned to the RCN by the British—the intent being that Canada would receive all eight ships of the 14th Emergency Destroyer Flotilla for use in the Pacific War; but with Japan's surrender only *Crescent* and *Crusader* were transferred. HMCS *Crescent* was made a permanent member of the Royal Canadian Navy in September of 1951.

After commissioning and working up in England in September of 1945, *Crescent* sailed for Esquimalt, British Columbia, arriving in November. From this Vancouver Island Naval Base she would operate in a training capacity for the next five years. These years weren't necessarily dull however.

Deployed to Shanghai in January 1949 to protect British interests during the Chinese Civil War as a guard ship on the Yangtze, she became an unwitting witness of the *Amethyst* Incident: HMS *Amethyst* having been sent to take up similar duties, when the British frigate came under fire from Chinese communist forces. The damaged *Amethyst* found herself aground on the Yangtze, surrounded by Communist forces for some ten weeks before she slipped away after dark on July 30th.

Meanwhile, *Crescent* found herself in her own awkward situation earlier that year, in March. While in Nanjing, China on March 20th, eighty-three of *Crescent*'s junior ranks locked themselves in their mess and refused work until their grievances had been heard by the commanding officer. Lieutenant Commander D.W. Groos handled the situation delicately, entering the messdecks to speak with the aggrieved crew—the term 'mutiny' was avoided—and was able to diffuse the situation and get the crew back to work.

Similar cases of disobedience aboard the destroyer HMCS *Athabaskan(II)* and the carrier HMCS *Magnificent*—also handled with great sensitivity by the respective ship's commanding officers—which occurred around the same timeframe prompted the Navy to look into issues around morale; setting up a committee headed by Rear Admiral E.R. Mainguy, RCN to report on causes and resolutions on this issue.

In looking back at the results of the Mainguy report, and more specifically the effects the events of March 15, 1949 had on the officers and crew of HMCS *Crescent*, one historian notes:

> "It seems that the gravity of what had transpired worked in combination with the continuing absence from home port to bring the crew together, not unlike squabbling children being locked in a room and not allowed to come out until things are settled."[56]

Apparently this led to a noticeable increase in ship morale and resulted in a happier ship to serve in during the final three months of the cruise.

Crescent was posted to Halifax in December of 1950 and

---

[56] (Gimblett, "Too Many Chiefs and Not Enough Seamen:" The Lower-Deck Complement of a PostwarCanadian Navy Destroyer –, 1999)

undertook training duties on the east coast until the end of 1952. In January 1953 she headed west once more, going to dock upon arrival in Esquimalt, for conversion into an anti-submarine escort. This consisted of having her superstructure razed, with the forecastle being extended aft with a new superstructure with enclosed bridge, wheelhouse, and operations room, and the replacement of all her existing armament. She now carried a twin 4-inch HA/LA mount on her forecastle, a twin 3-inch/50 mount aft, with a pair of single Bofors Boffin mounts and a Limbo anti-submarine mortar right aft. Her half-sister HMCS *Algonquin* had completed a similar transformation shortly before.[57]

Upon completing her conversion she joined the 2nd Canadian Escort Squadron as the Senior Officer's ship, and served as a training vessel and on operational deployments including a tour of Pacific Rim ports in 1958. Once more assigned to Atlantic waters in March of 1959, *Crescent* would be based out of Halifax for the next six years.

HMCS *Crescent* was placed in reserve in Halifax in January of 1965, only being recommissioned in two years' time to sail for Esquimalt where she was paid off. Placed on the disposal list on April 1st, 1970 she was sold to Taiwanese Chi Shun Hua Steel Company for scrapping. She departed Esquimalt under tow on April 21st, 1971 in company with half-sister, ex-HMCS *Algonquin*, on their final voyage bound for the breakers.[58]

The end of the war saw the end of one type of ASW and the dawn of another: the high-speed 'elecktroboot' Type XXI U-boats that Donitz had placed so much hope in, would become the basis for the Soviet Union's next generation of attack submarines. They would be fast, very quiet, and deadly should war break out between the Soviet Union and the West.

---

[57] (MacPherson & Barrie, Ships of Canada's Naval Forces: 1910-2002, 2004) p. 242

[58] (English, Obdurate to Daring: British Fleet Destroyers 1941 - 45, 2008) p. 142

The advent of the atomic bomb also changed how ships would be fought at sea—the days of open bridges were now gone, and destroyers would have to become weapons fought from operation rooms deep inside their bowels.

The speed of the latest generation of submarines, and the need to field as many ASW platforms as possible—especially the fast hunter-killer groups—demanded that late-war destroyers (many of which had barely seen combat) be reconstructed to serve in such roles while the next generation of destroyer was built and deployed.

The British called such full conversions Type-15 frigates[59] while less extensive conversions became known as Type-16 frigates. The Canadian Navy used no specific design designation, but made similar modifications (both extensive and minimal) to *Algonquin, Sioux, Crusader* and *Crescent*.

---

[59] (Friedman, British Destroyers and Frigates: The Second World War and After, 2008) p 219. During the war dedicated ASW vessels were known as corvettes or frigates depending on size—destroyers were both faster and well-armed enough to engage surface units unlike ASW vessels. Post-war submarine threats required speed and armament however, and so dedicated ASW destroyers in the RN became known as frigates as well. Canada's terminology was different—the RCN's 'Cadillac' destroyers would have been called frigates in the RN or Destroyer Escorts in the USN at the time.

6

THE EARLY CADILLIACS
CANADA SETS A NEW STANDARD

The war over, the Royal Canadian Navy found itself the owner of a vast and obsolete fleet of ocean escort vessels—many of which were so heavily worn from their battles with the U-Boats and the North Atlantic, that there was little to do with them but sell them for scrap.

One thing had been made clear however: Canada was a leading expert in anti-submarine warfare, and although the yearning for a blue-water navy with cruisers and carriers would ensure the presence of heavier units in the new RCN fleet, the destroyer—most specifically the anti-submarine destroyer—was the Canadian Navy's legacy from the war.

Fresh from the lessons of the Battle of the Atlantic, the Canadian navy sought to employ what they had learned of surface, and more importantly sub-surface, warfare by designing and developing a new generation of destroyer/escort that would meet the challenges of the next war—which many feared may come sooner rather than later.

These ships, dubbed the 'Cadillacs'[1] for their crew amenities no less than their combat capabilities, would set the standard for Canadian, and NATO, destroyers for decades to come. The equipment and techniques developed and tested at sea aboard these hardy little ships are still in use in today's Navy—proving again that Canadian Naval ingenuity, resourcefulness and courage is second to none. In fact, as early as November 1956 the US Navy considered the *St. Laurent* (and presumably her sisters) "Potentially as effective as any ASW ship in existence".[2]

The power plant of the Cadillacs was a next-generation integrated steam turbine plant known as Y100, which was jointly developed by the Admiralty and Yarrow. This same power plant would be used by the Royal Navy in its *Leander*-class frigates; contemporaries of the Cadillacs. Major weaknesses of this power plant were its complex cruising turbines and gearbox—it was the latter which would spell trouble for HMCS *Kootenay*. Overall however, it was a highly successful propulsion system which evolved out of late-war demands and set the standard for British post-war destroyer machinery.

The Y100 emerged from the Royal Navy's need for an anti-submarine escort vessel of some 2,000 tons with a power plant generating 30,000 shp on two shafts. War experience showed that destroyers spent 80% of their lives at less than 20% of their installed power. The efficiency of new destroyers would be paramount—to extend their range while on patrol or convoy escort duties; and so the Admiralty determined it

---

[1] In this they were similar to the original HMCS *Saguenay* and *Skeena*—when first built in the 1930s that pair were known as the 'Rolls-Royce destroyers'. (Barnaby, 1964) p. 96

[2] (Friedman, British Destroyers and Frigates: The Second World War and After, 2008) p 213

needed a power plant that produced 15,000 shp per shaft on a weight of only 660 tons. In comparison, this would be a 33% reduction in the weight and volume of the wartime *Dido*-class Anti-aircraft light cruisers machinery, which produced 15,000 shp per shaft.

The Yarrow Admiralty Research Department (YARD) developed the specification and initial design work in early 1949, shortly before the RCN decided to fit this power plant to its new generation of destroyers. While the majority of the Cadillac machinery was constructed in Canada, the first set for the prototype HMCS *St. Laurent* would be built in Britain—and had to be shipped to Montreal prior to the St. Lawrence river's freeze-up the winter of 1951.

Three British firms tendered for the turbine design and manufacturing contract. The Admiralty accepted the English Electric Company's proposal and a prototype design and manufacturing contract was let. The final power plant saw several features new to British destroyer steam machinery. These included a tighter integration of the boilers (supplied by Babcock and Wilcox and operating at 550 lb./sq.in. and 850°F) turbines and condensers—the condensers being integrated directly into the low pressure turbine casing.

Beyond the increased efficiency bought by the higher steam temperature and pressures, the system was designed with an additional cruise turbine which would be used in series with the main turbines while cruising—this way getting more power out of the steam and thus increasing efficiency further. While cruise turbines were nothing new (the argument for and against had raged it seemed, since the first turbine destroyer HMS *Viper* was put into service), one of the main drawbacks was the time it took to switch from cruise to full power (as the cruise turbine had to be disengaged). In the Y100 machinery this challenge had been surmounted with the design and construction of the Napier Automatic Clutch. This allowed the cruise and ahead turbines to be controlled by a single ahead throttle wheel—once the plant reached 30% power the Napier clutch would disengage the cruise turbine automatically and allow the ahead turbine set to take over propulsion entirely.

These innovations were expected to provide the increased range demanded by the British Admiralty for these next generation anti-submarine vessels—but like many cutting-edge technologies they weren't entirely successful. The Automatic clutch and cruise turbine assembly was fraught with difficulties in service. The Napier clutch especially, as a flaw in its design caused it to 'shuttle' at certain power levels—a situation where it would move from being engaged to disengaged and back, never truly being in- or out-of-line. Beyond the difficulty this would cause for a vessel under way (namely causing the cruise turbine to overheat), it also caused excessive wear on the clutch itself. Ultimately the Canadian vessels would have the problematic clutch and cruise turbine removed.[3]

Less well known was a design flaw in the reduction gears which transmitted the power from the turbines to the propellers. Because of the high rotational speed of efficient steam turbines and the necessity for a slower rotating propeller to transmit more power to the water (and in anti-submarine work, reduce cavitation), most marine steam plants after World War One use a set of reduction gears to transmit the power between the two ends of the drive train—allowing the turbines and the propellers to rotate at their own optimum speeds.

In the Y100, the gearbox bearing shells had a design flaw which allowed them to be installed backwards—a position in which they were unable to conduct the cooling and lubricating oil to the fast turning gears. In this circumstance—as the tragedy of HMCS *Kootenay*'s accident would show—the gearbox could get hot enough to cause the oil to burn—and explode. Aboard *Kootenay*, nine men died due to the explosion and fire, another fifty-three were injured.

---

[3] The RN would develop a replacement clutch, called the Synchro-Self-Shifting (SSS) clutch, but for Canada, removal of the Cruise turbines (or never installing them in later classes of Cadillacs) proved simpler and less costly. (McClearn, Y100 Machinery, 2010)

Yet the Y100 was undoubtedly a success—it would power four classes of Canadian destroyers as well as numerous British designed and built vessels that would serve with a variety of navies. In some ways it represented a quantum leap in power plant design—at least for the British and Canadians. Its flaws—the Napier automatic clutch, cruise turbine and gearbox bearing shells—were resolved as they appeared, or they were worked around. Its successor would be the gas turbine—and in that, Canadian destroyers would lead the way again.

Powered by the Y100 steam plant, this generation of Royal Canadian Destroyers would represent the transitionary period between the Navy's previous British-influenced procurement policy to the later more American-influenced ships, sensors, weapons and equipment. In this manner they were highly representative of the Canada that they would serve so ably over the next four decades.

HMCS St. Laurent (II) (*St. Laurent*–class)

Length:	366'	Laid Down:	24-11-1950
Beam:	42'	Launched:	30-11-1951
Draft:	13' 2"	Commissioned:	29-10-1955
Displacement:	2263 tons	Paid Off:	14-06-1974
Armament:	4 x 3"/50 HA/LA guns, 2 x Limbo ASW mortar, homing torpedoes		

The second HMCS *St. Laurent*, the lead ship of her class, was built by Canadian Vickers Ltd. of Montreal. Unique among the class, her machinery was constructed by Yarrows & Co. of Scotstoun, Glasgow and shipped to Canada for installation in the prototype.

She arrived in Halifax in early November of 1955 and in mid-February 1956 she made her way to Key West, Florida, where she would undergo a three-month evaluation at the United States Trials Center. Easily surpassing all expectations, she sailed for Washington D.C., there to showcase the new Canadian standard anti-submarine destroyer to interested Americans. In May she made a similar trip to the UK for the purpose of showing off to the Admiralty. While she was widely considered the best of a new breed of anti-submarine destroyer, it did surprise some that Canada was able to produce such a superb vessel.

While in British waters she took part in escorting HMY *Britannia* to Sweden. Aboard the yacht, and on a state visit to that country were Queen Elizabeth II, Prince Phillip, and the Earl of Mountbatten. On her return to England she stopped in the Port of London, and while securing, received an unexpected visit from the Lords of the Admiralty—one of whom, upon completing a tour of the ship apparently wondered "Why couldn't the RN come up with a ship like this?" [4]

In February of 1960, *St. Laurent* and sisters HMCS *Ottawa* and HMCS *Saguenay* sailed from Esquimalt for an operational cruise around the Pacific, which was to last nearly three months. In addition to tactical and anti-submarine exercises they made port calls to Long Beach, California; Pearl Harbor; Yokosuka and Okinawa in Japan; and Hong Kong. After spending a week in that last port undertaking self-maintenance, *St. Laurent* and her sisters departed on March 28th bound for Esquimalt via Okinawa, Kobe, and the Aleutian Islands.

In March of 1961 the three sisters once again departed Esquimalt to undertake exercises with the USN's Carrier Division 17 off Hawaii, returning home the next month.

Prior to her conversion to a destroyer helicopter escort

---

[4] (Barrie & Macpherson, 1996) p. 36

(DDH) in 1962, she was test fitted with the new Variable Depth Sonar (VDS). Her conversion was done at Burrard Dry Dock in Vancouver and she re-commissioned on October 4th 1963, proceeding to the east coast afterwards. She was part of the Canadian 'mobilization' during the Cuban Missile Crisis, where she took part in tracking a Cuban-bound Soviet task force as it passed through Canadian waters.

St. Laurent was the first of her class to be paid off, this occurring on June 14th 1974. She remained alongside near the Bedford Magazine in Halifax as a source of spares for her sisters. In June 1979 the cannibalization had nearly stripped her bare and it was decided to put her on the disposal list. Sold by Crown Assets Corporation for $76,250 to Dartmouth Salvage Ltd., who stripped her of the most easily salvaged scrap and resold her gutted hull to Consolidated Andy of Brownsville Texas for a reported $87,000. The next few months saw her hulk prepared for towing to Texas.

On January 8th, 1980 the ex-HMCS *St. Laurent (II)* left Halifax under tow by the Norwegian tug *Odin Salvatore*. On the 12th the two vessels ran into the fringe of a tropical hurricane and the former destroyer began taking on water. *Odin Salvatore* cast off her tow and began circling the sinking hulk. Going down by the stern, the former *St. Laurent*'s bows rose out of the water and she eventually capsized and disappeared at 11:05 a.m. some 250 miles south of Nantucket in 2,000 fathoms of water.[5]

The first of the Cadillacs was gone.

---

[5] (Lynch, Twilight of the St Laurents, 1990)

HMCS Assiniboine (II) (*St. Laurent*–class)

Length:	366'	Laid Down:	19-05-1952
Beam:	42'	Launched:	12-02-1954
Draft:	13' 2"	Commissioned:	16-08-1956
Displacement:	2263 tons	Paid Off:	14-12-1988

Armament: 4 x 3"/50 HA/LA guns, 2 x Limbo ASW mortar, homing torpedoes

When Marine Industries Ltd. of Sorel, Quebec delivered HMCS *Assiniboine* to the Royal Canadian Navy, it was the first post-war warship built by that yard for the RCN which subsequently commissioned her the 16th of August 1956. Her arrival in Halifax on the 25th saw her assigned to the 3rd Canadian Escort Squadron.[6] She, her squadron-mates and ships from the 1st Canadian Escort Squadron undertook a goodwill tour of North Europe ports in October and returned to Halifax in mid-November.

With sister HMCS *Margaree*, *Assiniboine* took part in an International Naval Review at Hampton Roads, Virginia in

---

[6] Wartime RCN ships built by Marine industries' Sorel yard included Flower-class corvettes *Arrowhead, Bittersweet, Dunvegan, Fennel, Sherbrooke, Sorel, Calgary, Fredericton, Kitchener, La Malbaie*, and *Regina*; as well as *Bangor*-class minesweepers *Brockville, Esquimalt, Transcona*, and *Trois-Rivières*. They would later build the hydrofoil HMCS *Bras d'Or* in 1968 with their last ship for the Canadian Navy being the frigate HMCS *Calgary* which was commissioned in 1995.

June of 1957.

She was transferred to Esquimalt in January of 1959 where she became part of the 2nd Canadian Escort Squadron. She hosted Queen Elizabeth II and Prince Phillip in mid-July when they travelled from Vancouver to Nanaimo, British Columbia.

In 1962 she underwent conversion to a destroyer helicopter escort (DHH) which saw her after end remodeled to include a 78 x 40 foot flight deck and hangar. Forward accommodation spaces were revised, providing larger and better equipped recreation spaces and messdecks.[7]

The single stack was split in two, each of which was outboard of the helicopter hangar. To make room for the flight deck, the aft 3-inch/50 mount and the Limbo anti-submarine mortars were removed. *Assiniboine* was the first of her class to undergo conversion; much of the work was done by the Victoria Machinery Depot Company of Victoria, British Columbia. The remainder of the work was undertaken by HMC Dockyard Esquimalt. This comprehensive modernization took nearly 2.5 million man-hours in labor to complete, for a final cost of $24 million.

June 28, 1963 she re-commissioned and departed for Halifax in September. There she had the 'Beartrap' rapid helicopter haul down equipment installed and became the trials vessel for this system. In that capacity she spent two years chasing storms around the North Atlantic, purposely hunting for poor weather in which she could trial the 'Beartrap' system. Ultimately the trials were successful and the 'Beartrap' became a common fitting on all future Canadian destroyers and frigates.[8]

In January 1975 she rendered assistance to the freighter

---

[7] (Lynch, Twilight of the St Laurents, 1990) p. 187

[8] Known in other navies as a Helicopter Hauldown and Rapid Securing Device (HHRSD) the 'Beartrap' was developed by the RCN's Experimental Squadron VX-10 in conjunction with Fairey Aviation in the 1960s.

Barma, rescuing her crew after the freighter began to take on water some 185 miles off Boston.

Assiniboine was selected for the Destroyer Life Extension Refit (DELEX) which she undertook entering dock at the Canadian Vickers yard in Montreal on April 23rd, 1979. She returned to service in mid-November.

In June of 1981, *Assiniboine* was leading four other NATO Standing Naval Force Atlantic (STANAVFORLANT) vessels out of Halifax harbor when she grounded on Point Pleasant Shoal in heavy fog. It took several tugboats to get her free. Her participation in a NATO exercise was thus canceled while she underwent a damage inspection and repairs.[9]

In 1984 she was assigned to escort the Tall Ships Race from Bermuda to Halifax during the early summer. When the British sailing vessel *Marques* sank, *Assiniboine* took up a prominent role in the search for survivors. She would receive the Chief of Defense Staff Unit Commendation for her efforts, becoming only the second ship in the RCN to receive it.

She returned to Halifax in July of 1984 having discovered fractures in her upper deck stringers and plating. She entered dry-dock for repairs on July 17th at Marine Industries Ltd.'s Sorel shipyard—her birthplace—for a ten-month refit. This stretched out to seventeen months due to a strike at the shipyard.[10]

HMCS *Assiniboine* was decommissioned on December 14th, 1988, and taken out of service the following January. After being surveyed post-decommissioning, it was discovered that her steaming plant was in excellent condition; and as she was of similar configuration of the remaining steam-powered destroyers, it was decided to use her as the alongside steam training vessel, replacing HMCS *St.Croix*.[11]

---

[9] (Cleaves, 1981)

[10] (Barrie & Macpherson, 1996) p. 19

[11] (Lynch, Twilight of the St Laurents, 1990) p. 192

She served as a floating classroom for technicians at the Fleet School for 6 years, before being handed over to Crown Assets for disposal. She subsequently sank in the Caribbean Sea while under tow to the breakers.

HMCS Skeena (II) (*St. Laurent*–class)

Length:	366'	Laid Down:	01-06-1951
Beam:	42'	Launched:	19-08-1952
Draft:	13' 2"	Commissioned:	30-03-1957
Displacement:	2263 tons	Paid Off:	01-11-1993
Armament:	4 x 3"/50 HA/LA guns, 2 x Limbo ASW mortar, homing torpedoes		

Built by Burrard Dry Dock Ltd. of Vancouver, HMCS *Skeena* was the third of the *St. Laurent*-class to be built, and one of only two built on the B.C. Coast—the other being HMCS *Fraser*. During a visit to San Diego in the same year she commissioned, her unusually modern design led to rumors that she was nuclear powered and had the ability to operate submerged.[12]

In January of 1958, she and the remainder of the 2nd Canadian Escort Squadron undertook a Pacific exercise with units from the US Navy, and on their completion visited several Far East ports. The squadron returned to Esquimalt on

---

[12] (Barrie & Macpherson, 1996) p. 32

April 2nd of that year.

The following year her ability to operate submerged was tested when—during a severe Pacific storm—she sustained a 57-degree roll before righting herself.

In January of 1962, while in the Strait of Juan de Fuca undertaking gunnery trials, several of *Skeena*'s shells fell onto the American town of Clallam Bay in Washington State. There were no injuries and only minor damage, but *Skeena*'s commanding officer of the time, Commander R.H. Leir, RCN, was court-martialed and found guilty of "committing an act which prejudiced good order and discipline."[13]

On May 26th 1964, *Skeena* departed Esquimalt, bound for Halifax. In July she entered dock at Davie Shipbuilding Ltd. in Lauzon, Quebec, for conversion to a destroyer helicopter escort (DDH). She re-commissioned in August of the next year and joined the 3rd Canadian Destroyer Squadron based out of Halifax.

In company with her near-sister HMCS *Annapolis* and the replenishment ship HMCS *Protecteur*, *Skeena* sailed from Halifax bound for northern Canadian waters. This deployment's primary goal was to provide operational experience in Canada's north, while visiting remote northern communities during Manitoba's Provincial Centenary. The three ships visited Fort Churchill, Rankin Inlet, Chesterfield Inlet, and Wakeham Bay, before returning to Halifax in late September.

In 1972 HMCS *Skeena* was designated the new French Language Unit for the fleet.[14]

Skeena once again joined *Protecteur* as well as her sister HMCS *Fraser* on July 17th, 1976, to provide a naval presence at the Montreal Olympics. Their duties included security and rescue of crews at rowing events, emergency accommodation and support, and provision of security personnel as required.

---

[13] (Spokane Daily Chronicle, 1962)

[14] (MacPherson & Barrie, Ships of Canada's Naval Forces: 1910-2002, 2004) p. 250

The three ships departed for Halifax on August 4th.

Between April 12th and November 20th 1981 *Skeena* was in Montreal once more, but this time she was in dock to undergo her Destroyer Life Extension Project (DELEX) refit. It was hoped that this refit would add 12 years to her life. Like her sisters of the *St. Laurent*-class, *Skeena* was scheduled to undergo a Level One DELEX—this was meant to be a baseline refit that would see the hulls and machinery brought to as-close-to-new as would be possible. No new equipment or armament would be installed. The estimate cost for a *St. Laurent*-class rejuvenation would be $5 million per ship.[15] *Skeena* arrived back in Halifax the end of November and began her trials on January 4th 1982.

May 21st 1985 saw Skeena visiting the port of Leixoes, Portugal as a member of NATO's Standing Naval Force Atlantic (STANAVFORLANT). A Soviet task group—led by the aircraft carrier *Kiev*—passed Gibraltar during the night of May 21-22nd. *Skeena* and the American destroyer USS *Richard E. Byrd* were dispatched to intercept the Soviet ships. The two NATO destroyers caught up to the Soviets the next night and shadowed them for two days while observing Soviet operations.

In June of 1991 *Skeena* took part in the NATO exercise Ocean Safari 91, and following that she undertook a tour of the St. Lawrence and Great Lakes ports to increase both public awareness and recruiting. On August 31st, 1991 she fired her 1,316th anti-submarine mortar round—the last to be fired by a Canadian warship. Having sailed nearly a million nautical miles in her operational life, *Skeena* was decommissioned on November 1st, 1993. During her final sail-past in Halifax she fired a thirty-six gun salute—one for each year of service.

She left Halifax for the last time on July 3rd 1996.[16]

---

[15] (Lynch, Twilight of the St Laurents, 1990) p. 189

[16] (Barrie & Macpherson, 1996) p. 33

HMCS Saguenay (II) (*St. Laurent*–class)

Length:	366'	Laid Down:	04-04-1951
Beam:	42'	Launched:	30-07-1953
Draft:	13' 2"	Commissioned:	15-12-1956
Displacement:	2263 tons	Paid Off:	31-08-1990
Armament:	4 x 3"/50 HA/LA guns, 2 x Limbo ASW mortar, homing torpedoes		

The second HMCS *Saguenay* was built by Halifax Shipyard Ltd. and was the fourth of her class to commission. During a visit to Chicoutimi, Quebec, while on her first deployment in 1957 she was presented the flag of the 'Kingdom of Saguenay.' Special dispensation was made to allow her to fly this flag traditionally on June 11th of each year. Thus *Saguenay* became the only Canadian warship permitted to fly a 'foreign' flag.

Originally assigned to the 3rd Canadian Destroyer Squadron based in Halifax, *Saguenay* was transferred west to Esquimalt in 1959 to join the 2nd Squadron.

In February of the following year, in company with HMCS *Ottawa* and HMCS *St. Laurent*, she left Esquimalt on a two-and-a-half month cruise of the Pacific. The Canadian destroyers undertook various exercises and made calls at several foreign ports from the United States to Japan, including a week's layover in Hong Kong for self-maintenance. They departed the British colony on March 28th for the return trip to Esquimalt, making stops in Okinawa, Kobe, and the Aleutian Islands before arriving the end of April 1960.

The next March the three sisters were once again departing Esquimalt bound for the Hawaiian waters, to undertake maneuvers and exercises with the US Navy's Carrier Division 17—led by USS *Kearsarge*. Canadian and RCN pride was bolstered by *Saguenay's* noteworthy feat of securing four 'kills' over three days during these exercises.[17]

On August 22nd, 1963, *Saguenay* was decommissioned and handed over to dockyard hands at Burrard Drydock Ltd. in Vancouver. There she would undergo an extensive conversion, to emerge as a destroyer helicopter escort (DDH). This work consisted of removing the aft Limbo anti-submarine mortars and their wells and one of the 3-inch/50 twin gun mounts, replacing them with a helicopter pad; and the main stack was split in two to route the machinery's hot gasses around a hangar installed at the forward end of the flight deck. The stern was rebuilt to allow for the installation of a Variable Depth Sonar (VDS).[18]

Additionally, an active roll-damping system was installed— this consisted of two non-retractable hydraulically-controlled fins just forward of the boiler room, which were designed to limit rolling motion in extreme weather to ten degrees. Accommodation space in the forward end of the ship was also revised to provide larger and better-equipped recreation and berthing spaces.[19]

She re-commissioned on May 14th, 1965 and that July departed Esquimalt bound for Halifax, to join the 1st Canadian Destroyer Squadron.

In mid-July 1970, while bound for a courtesy visit to Summerside, PEI, HMCS *Saguenay* ran aground off Port Hood, Nova Scotia—a former coal mining town on western Cape Breton. The night of her grounding three other ships were reported to have been at the scene—HMCS *Chaleur*, HMCS *Thunder* and CCGS *Tupper*—but efforts to pull her off failed. She was refloated on July 16th and sustained no significant

---

[17] (Barrie & Macpherson, 1996) p. 30

[18] (MacPherson & Barrie, Ships of Canada's Naval Forces: 1910-2002, 2004) p. 344

[19] (Lynch, Twilight of the St Laurents, 1990) p. 187

damage from the previous day's grounding.[20] The following spring she was transferred to the 5th Canadian Destroyer Squadron, remaining based out of Halifax.

On October 29th, 1979 she entered dock at Vickers in Montreal for her Destroyer Life Extension (DELEX) refit. Like sister *St. Laurent*-class destroyers, she underwent a structural rejuvenation and work was done to bring her machinery up to as new a standard as possible, but no new armament or equipment was added. Completing the work in late May 1980, *Saguenay* once again returned to service on the East Coast. It was hoped that the DELEX would provide her another twelve years of active service.

Saguenay suffered a gunfire mishap in early April of 1986. She had been off Osborne Head near Halifax with a civilian technical party aboard, undergoing gunnery exercises when one of her 3-inch shells misfired. Several members of her gun crew and one civilian technician were injured, although not seriously. This was followed by a collision in mid-August with the West German submarine U-17. This incident occurred during NATO maneuvers in the Baltic.

There were no injuries, and damage appeared minor on initial inspection, so the vessels continued the exercise. She put into Haugesund, Norway for temporary repairs once the maneuvers were completed, but by November 11th vibrations in her port propeller shaft were bad enough that she had to put into Rosyth, Scotland to have the port screw removed before heading home to Halifax. Upon arrival in early December, she put into dock for permanent repairs to her hulls, shaft, and propeller. It would be March 1987 before she was fully returned to service.[21]

Another collision of a different sort occurred in December of 1989. An American fishing vessel, the *Concordia*—a 114-

---

[20] (Canadian Press, 1970)

[21] (Barrie & Macpherson, 1996) p. 30

foot scallop boat with a crew of eleven, out of Fairhaven, Massachusetts—had strayed across the border into Canadian waters and when confronted by a Canadian patrol aircraft and signaled to stop, refused. Instead, due to a labor dispute with Department of Fisheries' crew, HMCS *Saguenay* was dispatched to intercept her and inspect her catch. Upon catching up with *Concordia* and coming alongside and demanding *Concordia* stop, the American vessel instead made a run for it. During the 'hot-pursuit' *Concordia* apparently purposely collided with the Canadian destroyer three times.

At that point HMCS *Saguenay* requested—and was granted—permission to fire warning shots across *Concordia's* bow. Using her 3-inch twin and small arms she was able to convince the American skipper, William Furey Jr. to heave to. Ultimately his explanation was that his charts indicated he was not in Canadian waters, and that he felt no need to wait for the Canadian destroyer.[22]

After a final four-week deployment to the Great Lakes, *Saguenay* decommissioned on June 26th, 1990 and was laid up alongside at Halifax. Ultimately she was purchased by the South Shore Marine Park Society of Lunenburg, Nova Scotia for $1.00 in November of 1993.

The second HMCS *Saguenay* was to act as an artificial reef and diver's wreck between Cross Island and Sculpin Shoal in Lunenburg Bay, off Lunenburg, Nova Scotia. She was towed out into the bay on June 25th 1994 and at 11:00 a.m. scuttled. It took over 20 minutes for the destroyer's hulk to sink in 90 feet of water, and due to a sand bar she didn't sink as expected—at low tide her mast was considered a navigational hazard. By May 1995 however her wreck had taken on a 70-degree list to starboard, and was expected to eventually settle out of sight.[23]

---

[22] (The Milwaukee Journal, 1989)

[23] (Barrie & Macpherson, 1996) p. 31

HMCS Ottawa (III) (*St. Laurent*–class)

Length:	366'	Laid Down:	08-06-1951
Beam:	42'	Launched:	29-04-1953
Draft:	13' 2"	Commissioned:	10-11-1956
Displacement:	2263 tons	Paid Off:	31-07-1992
Armament:	4 x 3"/50 HA/LA guns, 2 x Limbo ASW mortar, homing torpedoes		

The third *St. Laurent*-class destroyer, HMCS *Ottawa* was built by Canadian Vickers Ltd. in Montreal. Upon commissioning she departed Montreal to join her sisters HMCS *St. Laurent* and HMCS *Assiniboine* with the 3rd Canadian Destroyer Squadron in Halifax, Nova Scotia.

The following year in June 1957 she and *Assiniboine* took part in the International Naval Review at Hampton Roads, Virginia. Following that, in August, *Ottawa* had an experimental flight deck fitted over her Limbo wells and quarterdeck aft. This was to test if ships the size of the *St. Laurent* class could feasibly operate anti-submarine helicopters while at sea. The helicopter in question was a Sikorsky H-34 on loan from the RCAF. During this time *Ottawa* crossed the Atlantic four times, engaged in two major NATO exercises and assisted the carrier HMCS *Bonaventure* in her work-ups off the coast of Northern Ireland. Ultimately this temporary flight deck would be removed after the experiments were completed, but it would eventually be replaced by a permanent structure when *Ottawa* underwent her DDH conversion in 1964.[24]

She was transferred to Esquimalt in 1960, where she joined the 2nd Canadian Escort Squadron. In company with HMCS *Saguenay* and HMCS *St. Laurent* she departed Esquimalt on February 8, 1960 for a two-and-a-half month Pacific cruise. The three destroyers undertook anti-submarine exercises and visited Long Beach, Pearl Harbor, Yokosuka and Okinawa on their way to Hong Kong. There they spent a week in port for self-maintenance, before departing on March 28 bound for Esquimalt. They arrived back at their base on April 29 having sailed via Okinawa, Kobe, and the Aleutians. Later that year, from August 19th to the 22nd *Ottawa* took part in opening the Pacific National Exhibition in Vancouver.

In March of the next year, once again in consort with *Saguenay* and *St. Laurent*, she sailed for the Hawaiian Islands for a three-week operation with the US Navy's Carrier Division 17—based around the American carrier USS *Kearsarge*. The three Canadian destroyers returned to their homeport on April 4th, 1961.[25]

On May 24, 1963 HMCS *Ottawa* entered dry-dock at the Victoria Machinery Depot in Victoria, British Columbia. Here she would undergo a 14-month refit which removed nearly everything aft of the bridge, up to the level of the upper deck—this included the removal of one of her Limbo anti-submarine mortars as weight compensation. Her funnel and uptakes were split in two and routed around a helicopter hangar which was just forward of her new 78'x40' flight deck. Aft of this was fitted a variable depth sonar which operated through a cut-out in her stern.[26] Upon completion HMCS

---

[24] Prior experiments with a similar flight deck aboard the *Prestonian*-class frigate HMCS *Buckingham* in the fall of 1956 had been the first such attempt, and proved to be an overwhelming success.

[25] (Barrie & Macpherson, 1996) p.27

[26] (Lynch, Twilight of the St Laurents, 1990) p. 187

Ottawa was reclassified as a Destroyer Helicopter Escort (DDH). The third of her class to complete this refit, *Ottawa* was recommissioned on October 28th, 1964.

On February 2nd 1965 HMCS *Ottawa*—transferred to the east coast—departed Esquimalt for her new home port of Halifax, Nova Scotia, where she arrived on the 26th of that month. In December 1968 she became the first naval unit to be designated an official French Language Unit within the Navy—French being used as the working language aboard ship.

1976 proved to be a busy year for the destroyer. In July she formed part of the escort for the royal yacht HMY *Britannia* during a Royal visit to Canada, while in September she took part in the NATO exercise Teamwork '76. In all, she had been away from home for 224 days and had sailed 40,151 miles.[27]

The following year, *Ottawa* joined her sister HMCS *Margaree* and the Tribal-class HMCS *Athabaskan* on an official visit to the Soviet Union. After this she spent November and December with the NATO Standing Naval Force Atlantic (STANAVFORLANT) before returning to Halifax in time for Christmas.

Between April 19th and November 26th 1982, *Ottawa* returned to dry-dock at Canadian Vickers Ltd. in Montreal for refit intended to extend her service life. Her DELEX—done at the same shipyard she had been built at over thirty years previously—brought her hull and machinery back to as near new condition as possible, but without new weapons or equipment being fitted.

In June 1985, as part of the Navy's 75th Anniversary celebrations, *Ottawa* took part in the 75th Anniversary Naval Assembly in Bedford Basin. After this she undertook a six-week cruise of the Great Lakes, to further highlight the 75th Anniversary as well as assist in recruiting and spreading

---

[27] (Barrie & Macpherson, 1996) p. 29

awareness of the Navy throughout central Canada. During this cruise nine port visits were made and over 29,000 people toured the ship. At a visit to Midland, Ontario, 7,000 visitors came aboard—from a town with a population of 10,000.

Her remaining years saw participation in additional STANAVFORLANT deployments as well as the NATO exercise Ocean Safari '91 in June of 1991. By that point she had just over a year's worth of service left.

Finally paid off on July 31, 1992, she was sold to Global Shipping of Tampa, Florida for $243,000 in February 1994. In April of that year she was towed out of Halifax by the Russian tug *Sapfir* bound for the breakers in India. In her service life HMCS *Ottawa* had steamed over 600,000 nautical miles and visited ports in some 40 countries.[28]

HMCS Margaree (II) (*St. Laurent*–class)

Length:	366'	Laid Down:	12-09-1951
Beam:	42'	Launched:	29-03-1956
Draft:	13' 2"	Commissioned:	05-10-1957
Displacement:	2263 tons	Paid Off:	02-05-1992
Armament:	4 x 3"/50 HA/LA guns, 2 x Limbo ASW mortar, homing torpedoes		

---

[28] Ibid.

Built by Halifax Shipyard Ltd. and commissioned in Halifax, HMCS *Margaree* was assigned to the 2nd Canadian Escort Squadron based on Vancouver Island when she entered service. Her trip to the Canadian west coast saw her make fueling stops in Havana, Balboa, and San Diego before arriving at Esquimalt on November 27th 1957.

The 2nd Squadron sailed from its base in mid-January of the following year on a cruise of the Pacific, during which time it undertook anti-submarine and convoy escort drills and visited the foreign ports of Long Beach, Pearl Harbor, Yokosuka, Tokyo, Hong Kong, Saigon, and Okinawa, before returning to its home port on April 2nd. Such deployments saw *Margaree* rack up over 70,000 nautical miles and 22 port visits by her second birthday.

Margaree took part in the JETEX '62 exercise in the Pacific in 1962, in company with sisters HMCS *Assiniboine* and HMCS *Ottawa*. This exercise saw the Royal Canadian Navy destroyers working in conjunction with their cousins from the Royal Navy, the Royal Australian Navy, and the Royal New Zealand Navy, as well as units from Fiji and India.

She entered dry-dock at the Victoria Machinery Depot in Victoria, British Columbia on September 24th 1964, for conversion to a Destroyer Helicopter Escort (DDH). Nearly everything aft of the bridge was removed down to the level of the upper deck and a new helicopter hangar and flight deck were added, with the funnel and uptakes being split in half and routed up either side of the hangar. She had one of her Limbo anti-submarine mortars removed and a notch cut in her stern to accommodate a new AN/SQA 502 variable depth sonar. Upon her recommissioning on October 15th 1965, she was assigned to the east coast and based out of Halifax with the 3rd Canadian Destroyer Squadron.

Along with HMCS *Protecteur*, *Margaree* joined the NATO Standing Naval Force Atlantic (STANAVFORLANT) for a five-month deployment in 1973, and she was one of four Canadian ships participating in the 1976 NATO exercise

Teamwork '76. On April 1, 1979 she was 200 nautical miles south of Halifax where the bow of the tanker *Kurdistan* had been towed after breaking in half on March 15th south of the Cabot Strait. She sank the remains with gunfire.[29]

Margaree began her DELEX life-extension refit at Canadian Vickers shipyard in Montreal on May 5th 1980. Amidst labor unrest and a shipyard strike, there were concerns that she wouldn't be completed before becoming ice-bound. She was towed to Halifax-Dartmouth Industries where she was handed over to the Ship Repair Unit, Atlantic—SRU(A)—on December 10th. Her refit was finally completed in the summer of the following year.[30] Once back at sea, she undertook several more deployment to STANAVFORLANT.

On the 12th and 13th of August, 1991 Margaree took part—as the Canadian representative—in a re-enactment of the historic signing of the Atlantic Charter at Argentia, Newfoundland, on the 50th anniversary of that event. Joining *Margaree* was the American frigate USS *Valdez* as the US Navy's representative.

HMCS *Margaree* was paid off on May 2nd 1992 after 35 years of service. During this time she had visited 35 countries under the Canadian flag. Turned over to Crown Assets, on February 3rd 1994, she was sold to the Tampa-based Global Shipping Co. for $193,393. On March 13th 1994 she was towed from Halifax by the Russian tug *Afanasiy Nikitin* on her way to India for breaking.[31]

---

[29] (MacPherson & Barrie, Ships of Canada's Naval Forces: 1910-2002, 2004) p. 247

[30] (Lynch, Twilight of the St Laurents, 1990) p. 189

[31] (Barrie & Macpherson, 1996) p. 26

HMCS Fraser (II) (*St. Laurent*–class)

Length:	366'	Laid Down:	11-12-1951
Beam:	42'	Launched:	19-02-1953
Draft:	13' 2"	Commissioned:	28-06-1957
Displacement:	2263 tons	Paid Off:	05-10-1994
Armament:	4 x 3"/50 HA/LA guns, 2 x Limbo ASW mortar, homing torpedoes		

The second HMCS *Fraser* was laid down at Burrard Dry Dock Ltd. of Vancouver and launched in February of 1953,. However, in an unusual turn of events, she was towed from Burrard in Vancouver more than 80 miles across the Georgian Strait to the Yarrows Ltd. shipyard in Esquimalt on Vancouver Island for completion. Sixth of the *St. Laurent*s to complete, she was commissioned at Yarrows in June 1957.

Fraser spent eight years with the west coast-based 2nd Destroyer Squadron, undertaking patrol and training duties across the Pacific. During this time she made port at Singapore, Hong Kong, Vietnam, Mazatlan, Pearl Harbor, and San Diego.

Not all of her service was patrol or exercises however. In November 1960 she responded to the disabled yacht *Redwitch* and assisted her into San Diego; while in July of 1964 she towed the ship *Yaqui Queen* into Mazatlan, Mexico. In April of 1964 she consigned the ashes of Vice Admiral H.R. Reid to the

TIN CAN CANUCKS

sea; doing the same for Rear-Admiral P. Tisdale in March of the following year.[32]

January 12th 1965 *Fraser* departed Esquimalt to take part in underwater shock tests off the Hawaiian island Kahoolawe—being subjected to her first underwater blast on February 6th, along with several USN vessels before heading home to Esquimalt. She returned for additional testing on April 16th. Such tests were intended to assess how well modern warships could withstand the shock of an underwater detonation of a nuclear device, and if there were any delayed side effects. In both tests *Fraser* passed with flying colors.[33]

On July 2nd *Fraser* entered dry-dock at Canadian Vickers Shipyard in Montreal, for conversion to a Destroyer Helicopter Escort (DDH)—the last of her class so converted. This conversion took some 15 months and saw the removal of one of her Limbo anti-submarine mortars, the repositioning of her stack and uptakes to make room for a hangar, and a 3,000+ square foot flight deck and the installation of a variable depth sonar on her stern. Upon her completion in October 1966 she was recommissioned and assigned to the east coast, being based out of Halifax, Nova Scotia. She landed her first Sea King helicopter on June 15th, and on October was alongside Washington D.C. to demonstrate the Canadian helicopter haul-down system known as 'Beartrap.'

In May of 1969 she took part in Queen Elizabeth's Spithead Review off Portsmouth, as the Canadian representative; and in the summer of the following year she undertook her first Great Lakes cruise, visiting ten cities as far west as Duluth, Minnesota.

HMCS *Fraser* entered Category 'C' reserve in May of 1973,

---

[32] (Barrie & Macpherson, 1996) p. 21

[33] The focus of such concerns were not only how well western warships could weather underwater nuclear attack, but more importantly how well they could survive using nuclear depth charges on Soviet submarines.

but lingered there for less than a year. She was reactivated in March of 1974 and underwent a major refit at Davie Shipyard in Montreal—although some of the refit needed to be completed in Halifax—before she could be certified as completely operational. She rejoined the fleet in the fall of 1974.

While in European waters with the NATO Standing Naval Force Atlantic (STANAVFORLANT), the destroyer took part in the rescue of twelve British seamen on November 28th, 1980. The crewmen had been aboard the fishing vessel *St. Irene* when she met with distress off the coast of Holland. These actions saw *Fraser* awarded with the inaugural Chief of Defense Staff Unit Commendation.

Fraser underwent her Destroyer Life Extension (DELEX) refit at Canadian Vickers Shipyard in Montreal from October 19th, 1981 to May 28th, 1982, after which she was used extensively as a guinea pig for new equipment. In 1986 she was fitted with the ETASS experimental towed array sonar, and spent two years testing and evaluating what would—in its final form—become the CANTASS towed array sonar system used in the new *Halifax*-class Patrol Frigates. In May of 1987 she was fitted with the AN/SQL-25 Nixie torpedo decoy system, and underwent extensive trials on the equipment which was intended to be installed on the *Annapolis*-class destroyers, the post-TRUMP Tribal-class destroyers, and the Patrol Frigates. HMCS *Fraser* also trialed the URN-20A TACAN tactical aircraft beacon, the external fittings being placed on a prominent lattice mast between the funnels—an appearance unique to *Fraser*. She was also the first Canadian naval vessel fitted to operate the passive acoustic HELTAS helicopter, which underwent trials aboard *Fraser* throughout 1988 and 1989 before the helicopter was lost.

October 18th, 1993 saw *Fraser* detailed to take part in enforcing UN Sanctions off Haiti as part of Operation Forward Action. She returned to Halifax in time for Christmas, returning to Haitian waters in January of 1994. On the 10th of that month, while still en route, she suffered a minor boiler fire which injured four crewmen—luckily none seriously—and Fraser was able to continue her deployment. She was relieved by HMCS *Annapolis* on March 25th and arrived back in Halifax on the 30th.

1994 also saw *Fraser* involved with fisheries patrols in Canadian waters. She assisted the Department of Fisheries seize the American fishing vessels *Warrior* and *Alpha Omega II* in late July. These two were reported to have been illegally dragging for scallops in the Grand Banks. On another patrol in September she towed toward Canso, Nova Scotia the disabled sailing vessel *Maja Romm*, before transferring the tow to a coastguard vessel CCGS *Simon Fraser*.

By the fall of 1994 HMCS *Fraser*—having sailed nearly a million miles in service—was the last of her class still in commission. When she was paid off on October 5th, she undertook a final sail-past in Halifax before retiring to replace HMCS *Assiniboine* as a floating classroom alongside CFB Halifax. This she did ably until December 1997, when she was handed over to the Artificial Reef Society of Nova Scotia and towed to Bridgewater to become a museum ship.[34] There she spent twelve years alongside the ARSNS wharf waiting for funding to be secured for such a conversion.

Sadly, with disputes over taxes sapping what little financial wherewithal ARSNS had, the ship's maintenance was neglected and she became an irritant to the Town of Bridgewater and its citizens. In 2009 the Department of National Defense bought *Fraser* back from ARSNS and towed her back to Halifax. She remained there for a little over a year before being sold by DND to Marine Recycling Corporation, which had planned on towing her to Port Colburne, Ontario for scrapping. ARSNS immediately filed a lawsuit against DND for breach of contract and the former destroyer was 'arrested' while alongside in Halifax. The arrest warrant was quashed on September 1st,

---

[34] (Barrie & Macpherson, 1996) p. 23

2010 but plans to tow her from Halifax were interrupted by Hurricane Earl. Finally on September 7th the tug *Tony McKay* towed *Fraser* from Halifax to Port Maitland, Ontario for her date with the scrapper's torch. It was expected at the time that the scrapping process would be completed sometime in 2011.

While she was in Bridgewater, Nova Scotia in, the Historic Sites and Monuments Board of Canada in recognition of the historic significance of the *St. Laurent*-class destroyers, installed the following bronze plaque:

> St. Laurent Class of Canadian Warship
>
> *The pride of the Canadian Navy during the Cold War, these anti-submarine escorts were the first naval vessels conceived and built in Canada. Designed in 1948–1949, they influenced naval construction internationally with their smooth above-water surfaces and distinctive convex deck. They could also be sealed to protect crews against biological and radioactive threats. All seven St. Laurent-class ships were modified du.ing the 1960s to carry helicopters and enhance their anti-submarine capability. Launched in 1953, the HMCS Fraser is the last surviving example of this innovative class of warship.*

Though *Fraser* is now gone, these words still reflect the prestige and pride these ships brought the Canadian Navy, and all Canadians, during their time in service.

The seven ships of the *St. Laurent*-class were the vanguard of the new Canadian destroyer designs, but as the ships were built more slowly than originally expected, it became clear that a design evolution was required to keep the Royal Canadian Navy's destroyers from becoming obsolete, and to keep up with the changing pace of technology and tactics.

In June of 1952 it was announced that an additional $60 million had been added to the 1949 building program. This would allow for the construction of another seven Cadillac destroyers, with tenders let in the fall of that year and contracts in mid-1953.

The successors to the *St. Laurent*-class would be the *Restigouche*-class, and they incorporated several significant improvements, even if the hull, machinery and many other major components remained the same. One key improvement was in the process of how the ships were built—the pre-outfitted modules would be made larger, allowing fewer to be required for delivery to the slipway. This made for easier alignment and assembly, reducing the number of drawings required and the amount of time to complete.

Another improvement was in the main armament. The forward 3"/50 twin gun mount was based on wartime American technology; an improvement in both rate-of-fire and range was bought by replacing it with the British-made 3"/70 twin automatic mount. Unlike the previous mounting which required up to 14 crewmen on deck, the new mounting—being far more automated—had a reduced requirement of only three or four men in the mount proper. The below-decks automation was impressive—referred to as 'the bottling plant' by Canadian sailors for its similarity to such an industrial operation. The 38-ton mount also provided better protection for the guns themselves, which included the added complexity of water-cooled barrels due to the rate of fire.

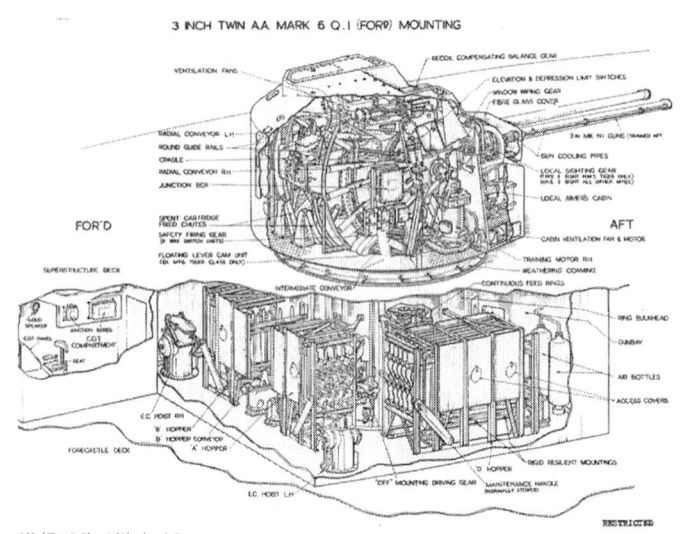

3"/70 Mk 6 Twin Mount
Used aboard RCN Destroyers of the *Restigouche*-class
and some of the *MacKenzie*-class (Official)

With the larger—and taller—gun mount came the need to modify the forward superstructure. The bridge level was raised a full deck and a new breakwater built beneath the gun mount platform. A pair of smoothly faired bridge wing platforms was constructed to assist in resisting and deflecting the gunfire blast. Abaft these was a raised deck for the Mk. 69 Gun Fire Control System. The 3"/50 wasn't completely discarded however—as the new forward gun eliminated the need for the *St. Laurent*-class' Bofors anti-aircraft guns, the new *Restigouche*-class saw these removed. Additionally, the 3"/50 twin mount placed in the aft gun position. Finally the sonar suite saw an update to stay on top of the ever-changing anti-submarine environment.[35]

---

[35] (Lynch, Twilight of the St Laurents, 1990) p. 185

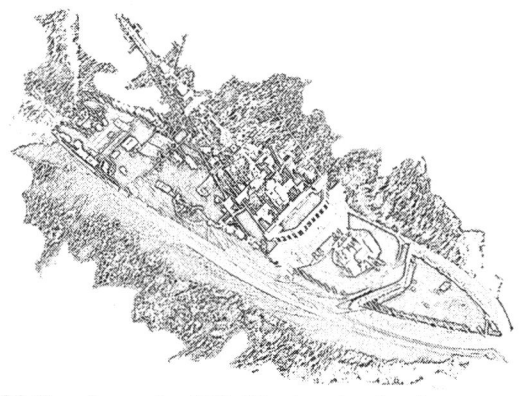

HMCS Restigouche (II) (*Restigouche*–class)

Length:	366'	Laid Down:	15-07-1953
Beam:	42'	Launched:	22-11-1954
Draft:	13' 6"	Commissioned:	07-06-1958
Displacement:	2366 tons	Paid Off:	31-08-1994

Armament: 2 x 3"/70, 2 x 3"/50 HA/LA guns, 2 x Limbo ASW mortar, homing torpedoes

The first of her class, HMCS *Restigouche* was built by Canadian Vickers Ltd. of Montreal. Once completed, she had cost the Canadian taxpayer $23 million to construct.[36] While still in her builders' hands, she was involved in a collision with the freighter *Manchester Port* on November 27th, 1957, while in the St Lawrence River. There was damage to her port-side superstructure and hull, which delayed her commissioning to June of 1958.

In the fall of that year she visited Bermuda and Havana while taking part in CANUS exercises. During anti-submarine drills with an American submarine, she delivered two practice anti-submarine mortar rounds directly on top of her submerged target.[37]

---

[36] Ibid.

[37] (Barrie & Macpherson, 1996) p. 45

When the St. Lawrence Seaway was formally opened in June 1959 *Restigouche* was on hand and subsequently took part in a NATO review in Toronto the following month. After this she carried the Lieutenant Governor of Newfoundland on a tour of some of that province's remote out-ports.

In company with sister HMCS *Columbia* she visited Washington, D.C. in April of 1961. This visit was followed with a port call at Newport, Rhode Island. Both visits were highly successful and allowed the Royal Canadian Navy to show off its newest warships to interested American officials. The two destroyers returned to Halifax in late May.

In 1964 *Restigouche* joined NATO's 'Matchmaker' squadron and took part in the Exercise Magic Lantern off Gibraltar in February. 'Matchmaker' was the forerunner of the NATO Standing Naval Force Atlantic (STANAVFORLANT) task group, which so many Canadian destroyers would be deployed to over the years.

She underwent her Improved Restigouche Escort (IRE) modernization between 1970 and 1972. This update was applied to only four of the *Restigouche*-class, but in doing so it made the good anti-submarine destroyers even better through the integration of their sensors, displays, and weapons. Known as Underwater Combat System 257 (UCS 257) it consisted of the Anti-Submarine Warfare Data System which received data from the variable depth and hull-mounted sonars, processed it via the SMR high-speed computer, and displayed it in real-time for a better overall situational awareness. Additionally, the aft 3"/50 twin gun mount was replaced by an anti-submarine rocket (ASROC) launcher with its magazine in the nearby deckhouse, on which was mounted an illumination rocket launcher. One Limbo anti-submarine mortar was removed and the transom stern notched to allow for a variable depth sonar. Corvus chaff launchers were added aft, and the enclosed foremast was replaced with a lattice one carrying new radar and sensors. Unlike their near-sisters of the *St. Laurent* -class, none of the IRE destroyers was fitted to carry a helicopter.[38]

Emerging from her modernization at Halifax Shipyards, *Restigouche* was recommissioned and redeployed to the west coast in 1973, making Esquimalt on August 2nd.

In August 1984, *Restigouche* was tracking the Soviet spy ship *Semen Chelyushkin* over sixty miles off Cape Flattery. Due to a defect in her portside steam turbine she was running on only a single screw—the propeller on the starboard shaft having been removed to reduce drag. It was estimated that she could still make 25 knots in that condition—enough to continue tracking the Soviet vessel.[39] Finally on December 3rd she entered drydock in Esquimalt for her DELEX life-extension refit.

Unlike the DELEX for *St. Laurent*-class destroyers which saw hull and machinery brought up to near-new condition, *Restigouche* also had older sensor equipment replaced and had new radar, ECM, sonar communications, and gunfire control electronics installed. She emerged from DELEX—which had been completed by the Ship Repair Unit (Pacific)—on November 29th 1985.

When the possibility of deployment to the Persian Gulf during the Gulf War was on the horizon, *Restigouche*—like her sister *Terra Nova*—was fitted with additional, temporary equipment. This included a pair of quadruple Harpoon anti-ship missile launchers mounted behind the aft deckhouse; a 20mm Phalanx CIWS mounted atop her Limbo well; two single 40mm Bofors anti-aircraft mounts on the boat deck amidships; and several shoulder-fired Blowpipe and Javelin missile launchers. Not deployed to the Gulf, she instead saw service with STANAVFORLANT in March, 1991—the first Pacific-based warship to do so.

On February 24th, 1992 she transited the Panama Canal enroute to the Red Sea for a six-month deployment with a

---

[38] (Lynch, Twilight of the St Laurents, 1990) p. 188

[39] (Montreal Gazette, 1984)

multinational force assembled to ensure Iraq wouldn't recommence hostilities. Her temporary armament upgrade was once again installed. She returned home to Esquimalt on August 18th of that year.

Paid off the end of August 1994, she and decommissioned sister HMCS *Kootenay* left Esquimalt under tow bound for Mexico. On her arrival *Restigouche* was sunk as an artificial reef off Acapulco on June 11th, 2001.[40]

HMCS Chaudière (II) (*Restigouche*–class)

Length:	366'	Laid Down:	30-07-1953
Beam:	42'	Launched:	13-11-1957
Draft:	13' 6"	Commissioned:	14-11-1959
Displacement:	2366 tons	Paid Off:	23-05-1974

Armament: 2 x 3"/70, 2 x 3"/50 HA/LA guns, 2 x Limbo ASW mortar, homing torpedoes

The second HMCS *Chaudière* was built by Halifax Shipyard Ltd. Halifax, Nova Scotia. Her construction was not an auspicious one; in September 1958, while fitting-out she

---

[40] (MacPherson & Barrie, Ships of Canada's Naval Forces: 1910-2002, 2004) p. 254

suffered a fire which caused damage extensive enough to require $200,000 worth of repairs. In October two additional incidents occurred. In the first, a visiting engineering officer fell to his death while another man narrowly avoided electrocution. She was the last of her class to enter Canadian service when she was commissioned in mid-November 1959.

She was initially deployed to Halifax with the 5th Canadian Destroyer squadron, and took part in underwater shock tests in 1962 off the Florida Keys. Such tests were to gauge how effective a destroyer would be if a submarine nuclear device detonated nearby—while there was no permanent damage sustained, *Chaudière* was out of service for 11 hours after the blast.

In February of 1964 she took part in the NATO exercise Magic Lantern off Gibraltar, and later that September she returned to the far side of the Atlantic for a cruise of the British Isles. In May of 1965 she was once more in European waters where she visited Portland, England, Copenhagen, Denmark, and Helsinki, Finland.

Chaudière was involved in the search for the missing boat *Puffin* in the North Atlantic in October 1966. She was able to locate the vessel, but the two crewmembers were never found and *Puffin* was returned to the owner's relatives.

Transferred to the west coast, *Chaudière* departed Halifax on October 2nd, 1967, bound for Esquimalt. Initially it had been planned to have her undergo modernization to Improved Restigouche Escort (IRE) status in Esquimalt, but at over $12 million per vessel converted and a freeze on defense spending, *Chaudière* had her IRE cancelled.[41]

In 1970 it was announced that *Chaudière* would be amongst the three older *Restigouche*-class destroyers to have their complement reduced to training level as an additional economy measure.

---

[41] (Barrie & Macpherson, 1996) p. 38

HMCS *Chaudière* was paid off in late May 1974 and was subsequently used as a source of parts for her sisters. This included her entire bow, which was removed to replace that of damaged sister *Kootenay* in 1989. Sold for $1.00 on September 9th, 1992, the former destroyer was sunk as a wreck for sport divers in Sechelt Inlet, British Columbia on December 5th of that year.[42]

HMCS Terra Nova (*Restigouche*–class)

Length:	366'	Laid Down:	14-11-1952
Beam:	42'	Launched:	21-06-1955
Draft:	13' 6"	Commissioned:	06-06-1959
Displacement:	2366 tons	Paid Off:	01-07-1998

Armament: 2 x 3"/70, 2 x 3"/50 HA/LA guns, 2 x Limbo ASW mortar, homing torpedoes

The first—and so far only—Canadian warship to be named *Terra Nova* was built by Victoria Machinery Depot in Victoria, British Columbia and commissioned on June 1959. Like many of her siblings she was named for a river—the Terra Nova River in Newfoundland; this connection is featured on her heraldic badge.[43]

---

[42] (MacPherson & Barrie, Ships of Canada's Naval Forces: 1910-2002, 2004) p. 251

[43] Also on the badge is a penguin which represents the Antarctic voyage of a civilian vessel also named *Terra Nova*.

She was the seventh and last of her class to complete, and on her commissioning was assigned to the east coast. She was on hand at the opening of the St. Lawrence Seaway in July of 1959, and took part in a NATO naval review in Toronto in August. In August of the following year, she and sister HMCS *St. Croix* were part of an assembly of ships from 15 countries gathered off Lisbon to commemorate the 500th anniversary of the death of Henry the Navigator.

In July of 1961 she undertook a twelve-day tour of Newfoundland out-ports where she carried the province's Lieutenant Governor on visits to these remote settlements. She completed the tour, arriving in Corner Brook on July 15th.

Selected for modernization as an Improved Restigouche Escort (IRE), she entered Halifax Dockyard in May 1965 for the first part of the conversion. Returning to service in February of 1966 she undertook extensive tests and trials with her newly-fitted AN/SQS-505 sonar suite over the course of seven months. Upon completion of these she returned to Halifax Dockyard for the remaining portion of her modernization, emerging in the fall of 1968—the first of her class to complete the IRE.[44]

In company with HMCS *Skeena*, *Terra Nova* visited the French islands of St. Pierre and Miquelon in the Gulf of St Lawrence in 1967. The two destroyers then escorted a number of French warships to Montreal for the opening ceremonies of Expo 67.

Posted back to Esquimalt in 1971, *Terra Nova* undertook communications and standby support for the Canadian contingent of ICCS off South Vietnam from January 29th to June 8th, 1973, returning to her home port on June 26th. In May 1983 she undertook a four-day trade visit to China on behalf of the Department of External Affairs.

Terra Nova underwent her DELEX life extension refit

---

[44] (MacPherson & Barrie, Ships of Canada's Naval Forces: 1910-2002, 2004) p. 255

between November 21st, 1983 and November 9th, 1984 at Esquimalt. This work brought her hull and machinery to as-new a condition as possible, while replacing obsolete sensors and adding new radar, communication, sonar and other electronics.

In May 1986 she escorted the Prince and Princess of Wales to Vancouver, and in late 1988 underwent a nine-month refit which would add the NIXIE torpedo decoy system as well as the Canadian Electronic Warfare System (CANEWS). She emerged from refit in June of 1989 and in December she was posted back to the Atlantic fleet—trading crews with the now West Coast-ported HMCS *Annapolis*.

Once in Halifax she was designated for Persian Gulf service, and saw a temporary upgrade made to her weapons systems, with the addition of two quadruple launchers for Harpoon anti-ship missiles mounted abaft the aft deckhouse. A 20mm Phalanx CIWS was mounted on top of the Limbo well and two 40mm single-mount Bofors anti-aircraft guns were mounted on the boat deck amidships. She was also provided a number of shoulder-fired Blowpipe and Javelin missile launchers. In company with the destroyer HMCS *Athabaskan* and the supply ship HMCS *Preserver* she left Halifax for the Gulf in August of 1990, returning on April 7th, 1991.[45]

Later that summer she undertook a five-week tour of the Great Lakes—a thank-you to Canadians for their support during the Gulf War, and a way of increasing the Navy's profile and recruiting. *Terra Nova* stopped in Oshawa, Hamilton, Midland, Goderich, and finally in Toronto, before making Halifax on August 24th.

Terra Nova had returned to her specialty in anti-submarine warfare by February of the following year—the weapons additions having been removed by that point. In October of

---

[45] *Terra Nova* was one of only two (HMCS *Athabaskan* being the other) Canadian destroyers to earn the 'Gulf and Kuwait 1991' battle honor. Uniquely it is the only battle honor earned by a Canadian warship named *Terra Nova*.

1992 she was taken in hand at Port Weller Drydock, St. Catharines, Ontario for a long refit—returning to service a year later.

In late February 1994, while on a drug interdiction patrol, she stopped and boarded the vessel MV *Pacifico*, escorting her back to Halifax. In her hold *Pacifico* carried 5.9 tons of cocaine, with a then-estimated street value of $1.2 billion. In April she relieved the frigate HMCS *Ville de Quebec*, at the time deployed to Operation Forward Action—the blockade of Haitian waters. During her eighty-seven days at sea, she rescued two boats of Haitian refugees on two distinct occasions before returning home; arriving in Halifax on October 19th, 1994. In September she returned to Haiti, only to come home once more on October 19th after the Americans had occupied that island nation.

While on fisheries patrol off Newfoundland on March 10th, 1995, a small hole in the hull was discovered six feet below the waterline near an air-conditioning unit. The crew plugged it and the destroyer remained on patrol until relieved by HMCS *Halifax* on March 13th. Upon arrival in Halifax she entered dry dock for inspection and repair. Overall her hull was found to be in good condition and after permanent repairs she left Halifax Shipyard on March 30th.

The 50th Anniversary of VE-Day had *Terra Nova* attending celebrations at Servermorsk between May 7th and 10th, 1995. On her way there she had made port in St. Johns, Iceland, and Norway. Departing Russian waters she headed south to join the NATO exercise Linked Seas off the coast of Portugal. Once the exercise ended on June 6th she sailed for home, stopping once more in St. Johns and Sydney. Before returning to Halifax she joined Maritime Operations Group One for the MARCOT 1/95 exercise off the south coast of Nova Scotia.

Later in mid-July she sailed for Quebec City where she joined the Great Lakes portion of the visiting 'Tall Ships' and escorted them to Louisbourg, Nova Scotia, with stops in Rimouski, Quebec and Charlottetown, Prince Edward Island. Once at Louisbourg the five sailing ships joined their fifteen-strong Atlantic Squadron brethren in reenacting the siege of Louisbourg. *Terra Nova* had a ringside seat as she was made the official reviewing stand for the reenactment. Afterwards, the destroyer returned home to Halifax, arriving on July 31st, 1995.[46]

HMCS *Terra Nova* was placed in a "state of extended readiness" on 11 July 1997 and finally decommissioned on July 1st, 1998. After being paid off she remained alongside at Halifax awaiting her fate. Not content to languish however, she took on the role of the American destroyer USS *Decatur* in the 2002 film *K-19: The Widowmaker*.[47] Finally, on November 20th, 2009, along with her sister ship HMCS *Gatineau*, *Terra Nova* departed Halifax Harbour by tow and was taken to Pictou, Nova Scotia to be dismantled for salvage.[48]

---

[46] (Barrie & Macpherson, 1996) p. 51

[47] In the same film the former Canadian submarine HMCS *Ojibwa* portrayed the Soviet Whiskey-class submarine S-270.

[48] (MacPherson & Barrie, Ships of Canada's Naval Forces: 1910-2002, 2004) p. 255. *Terra Nova*'s forward 3"/70 twin gun mount survived her scrapping and is currently on display at the Naval Museum of Alberta in Calgary, Alberta. It apparently took several years to remove the hazardous materials (asbestos and lead paint) from the decommissioned mounting, and there was some concern that the weight of the mount could crack the concrete floor of the museum before it was finally placed on display.

HMCS Gatineau (II) (*Restigouche*–class)

Length:	366'	Laid Down:	30-04-1953
Beam:	42'	Launched:	03-06-1957
Draft:	13' 6"	Commissioned:	17-02-1959
Displacement:	2366 tons	Paid Off:	18-02-1974

Armament: 2 x 3"/70, 2 x 3"/50 HA/LA guns, 2 x Limbo ASW mortar, homing torpedoes

Built by Davie Shipbuilding Ltd. of Lauzon Quebec, HMCS *Gatineau* was the first warship built by this shipyard—which had built so many corvettes and other ships during World War Two—to commission into the post-war RCN. To avoid being icebound in Quebec when the St. Lawrence froze over, she was towed from Lauzon by the tug *Foundation Vigilant* to Halifax for completion. She was the third ship of her class to commission, and upon entering service with the RCN she was to be home-ported in Halifax with the rest of her Atlantic-based squadron mates.

In March 1968 *Gatineau* became the first Canadian warship to join the newly formed NATO Standing Naval Force Atlantic (STANAVFORLANT). She would take part in many Canadian, CANUS and NATO exercises during her deployment.

In mid-July 1969 *Gatineau* pulled up stakes and headed west, having been reassigned to the Pacific coast and based out of Esquimalt. She arrived at her new home port on August 14th of that year, and after being de-stored she was turned over to the Ship Repair Unit (Pacific)—SRU(P)—to begin her modernization to Improved Restigouche Escort (IRE) status.

This $3.3 million conversion saw a significant increase in digital and networked data processing, making the IRE one of the best anti-submarine sensor platforms then available. She had her aft 3"/50 twin gun mount removed and replaced by an anti-submarine rocket (ASROC) launcher, the addition of variable depth sonar (VDS), as well as a range of counter measures and electronics upgrades. These changes were also structurally apparent as she carried a taller lattice mast and had a notch in her transom cut for the VDS, once the work was completed.

Returning to service in April of 1971 after completing her trials successfully, she rejoined the 2nd Canadian Destroyer Squadron in Esquimalt. In late August of the next year she—in the company of her near-sister HMCS *Qu'Appelle* and the supply ship HMCS *Provider*—undertook a four-month South Pacific deployment, during which the Canadian ships ran exercises with allied vessels from Australia, New Zealand, and the United States. *Gatineau* and her compatriots made port calls to Hawaii, Tonga, Western Samoa, Fiji, Australia, and New Zealand, putting some 33,000 miles under their keels before returning home.

In September 1981 SRU(P) took *Gatineau* in hand once more for her DELEX refit. Meant to extend the life of the older Canadian destroyers, DELEX included—in addition to bringing the hull and machinery as close to new condition as possible—the replacement of old and out-of-date sensors and the addition of new radar, countermeasure, sonar, and communications electronics. She was the first of the Pacific-based destroyers to undergo such a refit. Once completed in November 1982 she recommissioned and rejoined the fleet.

Gatineau traded duties and home ports with the Tribal-class HMCS *Huron* on April 15th, 1987, once more being based out of Halifax. She left her new home on July 22nd, 1988 for a five-month deployment to STANAVFORLANT. Considering her age at the time (29 years), that she was one of only two ships to complete her tour without mechanical or other problems spoke to the soundness of her design and the hard work of those who ran and maintained her.

She was deployed to STANAVFORLANT again in the fall of 1992 and during this time visited ports in Tallin, Estonia and Varna, Bulgaria. In July of 1993 it was her turn to play host as she welcomed the Russian cruiser *Marshal Ustinov* and two other Russian warships when they made a historic visit to Halifax—the first in fifty years. She carried out drills with the three Russian vessels while escorting them to international waters at the end of their visit—friendly exercises with former Soviet warships was a new experience to be sure.

Along with near-sister HMCS *Fraser* and the supply ship HMCS *Preserver*, *Gatineau* joined the multi-national force enforcing UN sanctions against Haiti in the fall of 1993. She would return home to Halifax on November 23rd.

Departing her home port on February 9th, 1995, *Gatineau* crossed the Atlantic to take part in the NATO exercises Strong Resolve off the coast of Norway. For the purposes of the exercise—which ran from February 20th to March 10th—she took up the role of flagship for the five-ship Canadian contingent. She returned to Halifax on March 24th, but was at sea again on April 10th supporting Department of Fisheries and Canadian Coast Guard vessels off the coast of Newfoundland during the 'Turbot War' with Spain.[49] In June she joined Maritime Operations Group One on Exercise MARCOT 1/95 off the south coast of Nova Scotia.

---

[49] The Turbot War—which the Spanish called 'Guerra del Fletán'—was a fishing dispute between Canada and Spain which erupted after the Canadians stopped the Spanish stern trawler *Estai* in international waters and arrested its crew. Canada claimed that European factory ships were illegally overfishing Greenland halibut (aka Greenland turbot) on the Grand Banks just beyond Canada's 200-mile Economic Exclusion Zone. Things escalated after Spain deployed a pair of patrol boats to the Grand Banks and the Canadian Prime Minister authorized Canadian warships and patrol aircraft to fire on any Spanish vessels which exposed their guns. The EU ultimately negotiated a settlement—although it had to pressure Spain to back down after the initial deal was rejected by the Spanish—and by April 15th, 1995 the situation had been resolved peacefully.

For the remainder of 1995 she underwent work-ups and took part in fleet operations and fishery patrols. One break from the usual was when she attended the Miss Newfoundland Pageant at Harbour Grace, Newfoundland. Early 1996 was similar, with *Gatineau* carrying out two sovereignty patrols of the Maritime provinces during February and March.[50]

HMCS *Gatineau* was paid off on July 1, 1998 and spent the next several years languishing alongside at Halifax. Finally she was sold in October 2009, along with her sister *Restigouche*-class destroyer HMCS *Terra Nova*, for $4,258,529 to Aecon Fabco for scrapping.[51] The sisters were towed to Pictou, Nova Scotia in late 2009 for breaking.

HMCS St. Croix (II) (*Restigouche*–class)

Length:	366'	Laid Down:	15-10-1954
Beam:	42'	Launched:	17-11-1956
Draft:	13' 6"	Commissioned:	04-10-1958
Displacement:	2366 tons	Paid Off:	15-11-1974

Armament: 2 x 3"/70, 2 x 3"/50 HA/LA guns, 2 x Limbo ASW mortar, homing torpedoes

---

[50] (Barrie & Macpherson, 1996) p. 41

[51] (Lambie, 2009)

The second HMCS *St. Croix* was also the second *Restigouche*-class destroyer to commission. Built by Marine Industries Ltd. of Sorel, Quebec, she entered Canadian service in 1958 as a member of the 3rd Canadian Destroyer Squadron. In 1959, after a transfer to the 5th Canadian Destroyer Squadron, she acted as a member of the escort for the Royal Yacht HMY *Britannia* on a Royal visit to Canada.

The following August she and sister destroyer HMCS *Terra Nova* took part in an assembly of ships from 15 countries off the coast of Lisbon, Portugal. The event was to mark the 500th anniversary of the death of Henry the Navigator.

In 1964 *St. Croix* was transferred to the west coast, and save for a short period in early 1966 she would remain stationed there for the rest of her service. In May of 1964 she underwent underwater shock tests off San Francisco. The purpose of such testing was to determine how well modern warships could handle the underwater detonation of a nuclear weapon. No permanent damage was sustained and *St. Croix* recovered her fighting efficiency within 30 minutes.[52] The next day a similar test, but of a more intense nature, was conducted and she didn't fare as well. It was reported that she was "non-operational without dockyard assistance."[53]

In January of 1966, *St. Croix* sailed from Esquimalt in the company of the frigates HMCS *Antigonish* and HMCS *Stettler*; and the submarine HMCS *Grilse (II)* to join the largest Canadian task group ever to sail for South America.[54]

---

[52] By contrast, sister HMCS *Chaudière* was only able to recover her fighting efficiency 11 **hours** after the detonation event, when she underwent similar tests in 1962.

[53] (Barrie & Macpherson, 1996) p. 47

[54] (Snowie, 1987) Also part of the task group under the Command of Commodore J.C. O'Brien, RCN (in the flagship, carrier HMCS *Bonaventure*) was the support ship HMCS *Provider*; the maintenance ship HMCS *Cape Scott* as well as the

In the latter years of the 1960s *St. Croix* had the opportunity to visit her Australian and New Zealand counterparts. In 1967 and again in 1969 she sailed to those two countries, each time via Hawaii and then Fiji.

One of the *Restigouche*-class not selected for IRE modernization due to defense cuts, *St.Croix* began showing her age in the early 1970s, and in 1973 she returned to Halifax. There she was paid off into Category 'C' reserve on November 15th, 1974. Her guns and propellers were removed and her machinery spaces were converted into classrooms. She was then used as a floating school for Canadian Forces Fleet School trainees from 1984 to September 1990.

Finally sold for scrap in 1991 to Jacobson Metal of Chesapeake, Virginia she made the Navy $44,351.76. In early April 1991 she was towed from Halifax bound for the ship breakers.[55]

HMCS Kootenay (II) (*Restigouche*–class)

Length:	366'	Laid Down:	21-08-1952
Beam:	42'	Launched:	15-06-1954
Draft:	13' 6"	Commissioned:	07-03-1959
Displacement:	2366 tons	Paid Off:	18-12-1996

Armament: 2 x 3"/70, 2 x 3"/50 HA/LA guns, 2 x Limbo ASW mortar, homing torpedoes

---

destroyers HMCS *Nipigon*, HMCS *Saguenay*, HMCS *Kootenay*, HMCS *Skeena*, HMCS *Annapolis* and HMCS *Restigouche*. Additionally, the task group was joined by the British submarine HMS *Acheron*.

[55] (MacPherson & Barrie, Ships of Canada's Naval Forces: 1910-2002, 2004) p. 254

HMCS *Kootenay* was the first of her class to hit the water when she was launched from Burrard Dry Dock Ltd.'s Vancouver shipyard on June of 1954. She commissioned and worked-up on the west coast before being posted to Halifax. She and sister HMCS *Columbia* visited Philadelphia for the Canadian Trade Fair in November of 1963, and in February of 1964 *Kootenay* was off Gibraltar to take part in the NATO exercise Magic Lantern. In August of 1967, during Canada's Centennial, she visited Sault Ste. Marie.

HMCS *Kootenay* was to suffer the Canadian Navy's worst peacetime loss of life in October of 1969 when her starboard gearbox exploded, starting an engine room fire which killed nine and injured 53 others.

On October 23rd, she was part of a Task Group which included the aircraft carrier HMCS *Bonaventure* and the destroyers HMCS *Terra Nova*, HMCS *Fraser*, HMCS *St. Laurent*, HMCS *Ottawa*, HMCS *Assiniboine*, HMCS *Margaree*, and HMCS *Saguenay*. The Canadian ships were westbound, out of the English Channel when *Kootenay* and *Saguenay* were detached to conduct routine full power trials. *Saguenay* completed her trials before 0800h and deployed her Sea King Helicopter.

At 0810h—*Kootenay* was now 200 miles west of Plymouth—the order was given for full speed ahead on both engines. Lieutenant A.F. Kennedy, the ship's Engineering Officer returned to the engine room at 0816h, after having completed a brief visit to the boiler room. Also in the Engine Room were Chief ERA CPO1 V.A. Partanen, CPO2 W.A. Boudreau, PO1 John MacKinnon, PO1 E.G. Harman, LS Pierre Bourett, LS T.G. Crabbe, LS G.W. Hutton, AS Allan Bell, and AS M.A. Hardy. Lt. Kennedy was undertaking a routine walk around of the engine room—similar to the one just completed in the boiler room—to ensure equipment was running normally. Unknown to those present, the temperature in the starboard gearbox was climbing rapidly and at 0821h, a sound like a welding torch pierced the air. An instant later the gearbox exploded and the engine room was engulfed in flames.

Lt. Kennedy attempted to close the throttles and report to the bridge but the raging fire forced him to order the compartment evacuated. This was easier said than done as the aft hatch was inaccessible—being near the gearbox—and the circulating fans were blowing flames towards the forward hatch. Meanwhile smoke billowed out of the hatches and filled the ship's main below deck fore-aft passageway (known as Burma Road).

Kennedy, Mackinnon, and Bell were able to make it through the forward hatch, but were badly burned. Bourette made it to the top of the hatch, but died there. The remaining six men in the engine room lost their lives in the inferno below. Two additional crewmen died outside of the engine room due to smoke inhalation; OS Nelson Galloway died that day, and PO John Stringer several days later aboard HMCS *Bonaventure*.[56]

Lt. Kennedy, though badly burned was able to report to the bridge where he indicated that the Emergency steam shut-off valves needed to be closed to stop the flow of steam to the turbines. With a dark, oily smoke filling the ship, it took 40 minutes before the engines could be stopped and the ship finally slowed. During this time power had been lost and it took until 0845h before the rest of the Task Group could be alerted by *Kootenay* as to the disaster. There had been only seven Chemox breathing units aboard ship for fighting the fire, and at one point the ship had only one canister of foam remaining[57]. Firefighting equipment and supplies were delivered by other Task Group members via Sea King, and by 1015h *Kootenay* could report all fires had been put out. Initially

---

[56] (McClearn, 2009)

[57] At the fire's height the ship faced another potential disaster as it was discovered the temperature in the aft 3"/50 ammunition magazine was climbing. Water was sprayed against the bulkhead the magazine shared with the engine room, and the ammunition was relocated away from the heat as quickly as possible. Had the ammunition exploded the ship was sure to have been lost.

towed back to the UK, she would eventually be towed across the Atlantic by the Dutch tug *Elbe*, arriving in Halifax on November 27th.

The root cause of the explosion and fire was later determined to be the improper installation of gearbox bearing journals when the gearbox had been overhauled more than four years before. The journals were designed in such a manner that they could easily be installed backwards, although in that configuration the flow of oil—essential for lubrication and cooling the bearings—was blocked, causing a serious increase in operating temperature. Though the temperature increase caused by the faulty journal installation couldn't ignite the oil on its own, during the full speed trial of October 23rd one of the pinion thrust bearings in the gearbox failed, and the added frictional load drove the temperature up over 900 degrees Celsius—causing ignition of the oil in the gearbox.[58] Subsequent investigations and inquires found that this wasn't an uncommon problem in the gearboxes of the Y100 steam plant used not only in the Cadillacs, but in Royal Navy frigates as well. Future designs for gearbox journal shells would include unique pin arrangements to ensure the proper fitting and alignment of such items.

While *Kootenay* was undergoing repairs, the decision was made to convert her to the Improved Restigouche Escort (IRE) configuration, and when recommissioned on January 7th, 1972 she emerged as—like her sister HMCS *Gatineau*—one of the best anti-submarine platforms in the world. The IRE configuration saw her aft 3"/50 twin gun mount removed and replaced by an anti-submarine rocket (ASROC) launcher. Her transom stern was notched for the addition of variable depth sonar (VDS), and she had a range of counter-measure and electronic upgrades. These last additions required the replacement of her existing mast structure with a taller lattice

---

[58] (Tremblay, 2009)

mast. After trials and workups, *Kootenay* was declared fully operational once more in September of 1972.

Posted to Esquimalt the first of the following year, she departed Halifax on January 23rd, arriving at her new home on Vancouver Island on February 12th. In May of the same year she was deployed to south Pacific waters, to provide support for Canadian Forces personnel serving with the International Commission for Control and Supervision (ICCS) in South Vietnam. With the Canadian withdrawal from ICCS on July 31st of 1975, *Kootenay* returned home, arriving in mid-August.

In the summer of 1978 she was on hand off the B.C. coast to assist the RCMP's seizure of some $28 million worth of marijuana that was being attempted to be smuggled into the country.

Between October 25th, 1982 and October 21st, 1983 *Kootenay* was at Halifax Shipyard undergoing her DELEX life extension refit. This was meant to return her hull and machinery to nearly new condition, replace any obsolete or unsupported equipment, and see the addition of new ECM, radar, sonar, communications, and gunfire control elections. Other additions included a new emergency diesel generator, the addition of lightweight anti-submarine torpedo tubes, Mk 36 Super Rapid Bloom Offboard Countermeasures Chaff and Decoy Launching System (SBROC) emplacements, and an upgraded operations room including the replacement of the older navigation plot with new Canadian Automatic Data Link Plotting System (ADLIPS) stations.

In this refitted form, *Kootenay* took part in the large Pacific Rim exercise known as RIMPAC 86. She departed Esquimalt on May 8th, 1986 in company with sisters HMCS *Restigouche* and HMCS *Terra Nova*, and the supply ship HMCS *Provider*. After the completion of the exercises—which included ships from allied countries all around the Pacific Rim—the four Canadian ships arrived back home on June 21st.

She suffered another major mishap in June of 1989 while undergoing exercises in thick fog off Cape Flattery. While maneuvering without radar or navigation lights, *Kootenay* collided with MV *Nord Pol* some 28 miles offshore. The destroyer emerged from the collision with a rent in her bow that was three feet by sixteen feet long, extending down to just above the waterline. While a later court of enquiry absolved *Kootenay* of any blame[59], the cost of repairs would have been significant were it not for the fact that her sister HMCS *Chaudière* was decommissioned and alongside at Esquimalt.

A section of *Chaudière's* bow was removed and was used as a direct replacement for the damaged section on *Kootenay*—a fine bit of naval vessel surgery. By June 9th, 1989, *Kootenay* was back at sea.

The next summer she joined the destroyers HMCS *Annapolis* and HMCS *Huron* as part of a Canadian Task Group which undertook a three-day visit to Vladivostok, Russia. The Canadian ships were the first foreign warships to visit the port since before World War Two. The visit lasted from June 3rd to June 7th, 1990.

On May 16th, 1994 *Kootenay* once more departed Esquimalt to take part in the semi-annual RIMPAC exercise. Subsequently, on June 21st she left Hawaiian waters to join Operation Forward Action—the naval blockade of Haiti as sanctioned by the UN. She relieved her sister HMCS *Terra Nova* on July 13th and *Kootenay* returned home to Esquimalt on September 15th. Later that fall she conducted a coastal watch patrol of Canadian waters, circumnavigating Vancouver Island as she did so.[60] Throughout the early part of the next year she undertook three more sovereignty patrols in the coastal waters of southern British Columbia.

---

[59] The legal aspects of the collision didn't end there—in January of 1996 (after the ship had been decommissioned) the B.C. Supreme Court awarded the owners of *Nord Pol* $112,000 in compensation, after determining *Kootenay* was 70% at fault for the collision.

[60] (Barrie & Macpherson, 1996) p. 44. The coastal watch was a program at the time organized by the RCMP as a way of encouraging Canadians to report suspicious ships or happenings within Canadian coastal waters.

August 1995 saw *Kootenay*'s last operational deployment: as a part of a series of exercises in south Atlantic waters. Departing Esquimalt on August 18th she joined the east-coast-based destroyer HMCS *Athabaskan* off the coast of South America, where they became the first Canadian ships to take part in the 36th annual series of South American exercises known as UNITAS. After exercises with the Chilean Navy, *Kootenay* headed south for Cape Horn, rounding it on October 16th, while under sail using an ad hoc sailing rig—so it could be said that the ship and her crew had "Sailed around the Horn." Further exercises with the US Navy as well as warships from Argentina, Brazil, and Chile were undertaken before she once more sailed around the Horn bound for Esquimalt. During this passage the crew of *Kootenay* laid a wreath at the location where the British cruiser HMS *Good Hope* had been sunk by a German squadron in the Battle of Coronel during World War One—seventy-one years before. Four Canadian midshipmen had been aboard the *Good Hope* and lost their lives with the rest of the crew—making them the first Canadian Navy casualties of the Great War.

Kootenay was finally paid off after 36 years of service on December 18th, 1995. She had put almost a million miles beneath her keel since commissioning. Stripped of useful equipment, she was towed from Esquimalt on November 6th, 2000, bound for her fate as an artificial reef off Puerto Vallarta, Mexico.[61]

---

[61] (MacPherson & Barrie, Ships of Canada's Naval Forces: 1910-2002, 2004) p. 253

HMCS Columbia (II) (*Restigouche*–class)

Length:	366'	Laid Down:	11-06-1953
Beam:	42'	Launched:	01-11-1956
Draft:	13' 6"	Commissioned:	07-11-1959
Displacement:	2366 tons	Paid Off:	18-02-1974

Armament: 2 x 3"/70, 2 x 3"/50 HA/LA guns, 2 x Limbo ASW mortar, homing torpedoes

Sixth of her class constructed, the second HMCS *Columbia* was built by Burrard Drydock Co. Ltd. in North Vancouver, British Columbia. Commissioned in early November 1959 she was immediately deployed to the east coast for service out of Halifax.

In September of 1960 *Columbia* departed Halifax to represent Canada at the Nigerian Independence celebrations in Lagos, Nigeria. While on that side of the Atlantic she visited several African ports and returned to Halifax on October 25th, having covered some 10,500 miles. [62]

Columbia, in company with destroyers HMCS *Crescent* and HMCS *Algonquin*, left Halifax in March 1967 bound for Esquimalt and service with the Pacific fleet. This assignment to the 2nd Canadian Escort Squadron was part of the reorganization done by Maritime Command (MARCOM) after the Unification of the Canadian Forces.[63]

---

[62] (Barrie & Macpherson, 1996) p. 39

[63] Unification saw the three separate services—RCN, RCAF and the Canadian

Not amongst the *Restigouche*-class selected for IRE modernization due to economy measures, *Columbia* was decommissioned on February 18th, 1974 and made a stationary training ship alongside at Esquimalt. Her propellers were replaced with 'no thrust wheels' allowing her to run her engines full throttle and remain stationary at dockside.[64]

In late-June 1996 she was towed from Esquimalt by the Artificial Reef Society of British Columbia and sunk as a sport diver's wreck off Campbell River, British Columbia.

Army—unified into the Canadian Forces. The RCN became MARCOM but lost its aviation assets to Air Command—along with its distinctive uniforms and much of its traditions. By the dawn of the 21st Century much of what made the Navy distinctive had been recovered, and on August 16th, 2011 MARCOM was once again renamed the Royal Canadian Navy.

[64] (MacPherson & Barrie, Ships of Canada's Naval Forces: 1910-2002, 2004) p. 252

7

THE LATE CADILLIACS
THE LAST OF THE STEAM DESTROYERS

As the 1960s loomed, with its impending retirement of a number of Canadian anti-submarine warships, it was recognized that regardless of how anti-submarine technology evolved in the future, there was a need for platforms to carry sensors and weapons—and Canada was facing a potential shortage.

For this reason an additional six follow-on *Restigouche*-class ships were desirable and the first contract for these six was let in 1950. By mid-1959 all six had been contracted for.

The *Mackenzie*-class—as these repeat *Restigouche*-classes were known—was nearly identical to its previous group of half-sisters; they were just more refined. The ships were made more habitable through changes in design and a reduction of crew complement from 248 to 210. Vinyl-asbestos deck coverings replaced the more flammable linoleum; there were improvements to the air conditioning plants; and the inclusion of on-demand domestic hot-water heaters in place of the previous holding tanks. The NBC pre-wetting system was refined as well, being expanded to cover the entirety of the ship's upper surfaces, while the addition of heated windshield wipers on the bridge windows helped reduce ice buildup during the frigid Canadian winters. Additionally, new propellers were fitted—ones designed to delay cavitation and thus make the destroyers quieter and harder for a submarine to detect.

The *Mackenzie*-class also saw a reversion of weapons of a sort. While the performance of the *Restigouche*-class's 3"/70 twin mount (see Chapter 6) was excellent when it worked; too often it didn't. Maintenance headaches—likely caused by how quickly the mount had been developed by Vickers and put into service by the British—were the bane of the mount's existence. Often time post-fire maintenance would require hours of crawling about the mount's cramped and oil-soaked underbelly in an effort to get the gun to function again. Shear pin failures were an issue—as related to Tony Digiulian:

> This mounting used about 40 shear pins throughout the mount and the ammunition feed system. Two types were provided, pre-scored aluminum pins for peacetime use and un-scored steel pins for wartime use. The aluminum pins were a source of many problems during routine firing missions as the failure of a single pin would cause the mounting to cease fire and shut down. One eyewitness has told me that the only time he ever saw one of the Canadian mountings fire more than a few rounds before jamming was when steel pins were used on a ship emptying her magazines shortly before decommissioning.[1]

Few who served at sea with them would have felt confidence in their abilities or reliability under combat conditions.

It didn't help that major repairs could only be done at the Naval Armament Depot in Dartmouth, Nova Scotia—necessitating the shipment of the west coast gun mounts by rail from Esquimalt. Needless to say, delays for west coast ships

---

[1] (Digiulian, 2012)

were long and frustrating. Further, as the mount was used by so few ships world-wide (the British used less than a handful on their helicopter cruisers; all others were used by Canadian Destroyers), there was a distinct shortage of spares, and the *Restigouche*-class had priority for those. With all that in mind, HMCS *Qu'Appelle* was built with her main armament consisting entirely of the older 3"/50 twin mounts.[2]

Only four of the *Mackenzie*-class were built—despite contracts for the last two being let before 1960. The final pair were delayed, while changes were made to the ship's design to take into account the new developments in operating helicopters from small warships at sea. The very same developments that would see the conversion of the *St. Laurent*-class to DDHs would see the last two *Mackenzie*-class DDE transformed into the *Annapolis*-class DDH.

---

[2] (Lynch, Twilight of the St Laurents, 1990) p. 186. Lynch indicates that the third *Mackenzie*-class destroyer, HMCS *Yukon* gave up her forward 3"/70 later in life to conform with *Qu'Appelle*, but there's no other evidence of that—rather the opposite, as dive photos of the former HMCS *Yukon* now resting at the bottom of Mission Bay in 2013 appear to show the Vickers 3"/70 mount still on the forecastle.

HMCS Mackenzie (*Mackenzie*–class)

Length:	366'	Laid Down:	15-12-1958
Beam:	42'	Launched:	25-05-1961
Draft:	13' 6"	Commissioned:	06-10-1962
Displacement:	2380 tons	Paid Off:	03-08-1993

Armament: 4 x 3"/50 HA/LA guns, 2 x Limbo ASW mortar, homing torpedoes

First of her class, HMCS *Mackenzie*[3] was built by Canadian Vickers Ltd. in Montreal. She commissioned just before the Cuban Missile Crisis of October 1962, and under the command of Commander A.B. German, sped through the equipment trials and work-ups so she could join the 5th Canadian Escort Squadron. By October 25th the squadron was covering Georges Bank off Cape Cod, to allow American Naval forces to concentrate further south.[4] Her first five

---

[3] (Barrie & Macpherson, 1996) p. 53; At the time, the only other ship christened *Mackenzie* in any of Her Majesty's navies was a World War One-vintage trawler of the Royal Navy. She was notable as having salvaged the ketch *Alert* on October 6th, 1917. British wartime artist Francis Dodd produced a series of sketches of life aboard HMT *Mackenzie* in 1918, which are currently in the possession of the Imperial War Museum.

[4] (German, 1990) p 269

months of service were with this squadron based out of Halifax, but March 2nd, 1963 saw her posted to Esquimalt, where she would spend the remainder of her career.

While posted to the Pacific coast *Mackenzie* would belong to either the 4th Canadian Destroyer Squadron, or later in life as part of Training Group Pacific. For most of March 1964 she took part in the Commonwealth exercise JET 64 in the Indian Ocean, and in late February of the next year she and her sister HMCS *Saskatchewan* undertook a three-month cruise of the Far East.

Mackenzie was once more bound for the far side of the Pacific in May of 1970; she and sister HMCS *Yukon*, in company with the supply ship HMCS *Provider* deployed westward to take part in exercises with naval units from Australia, New Zealand, Japan, and the United States. Port visits to all four countries were also made before the trio returned to Vancouver Island.

On June 30, 1973 *Mackenzie* gained a measure of media notice when she intercepted, boarded, and seized the former minesweeper MV *Marysville* in Quatsino Sound off northwestern Vancouver Island. Thirteen men and women were arrested and charged with various offenses, while the ship was impounded in Esquimalt under armed guard. Described by one navy wag as "a floating junk pile," *Marysville* was searched for a suspected thousand pounds of hashish worth at the time over a million dollars.[5]

The summer of 1982 brought her media fame again after it was announced she was tracking the Soviet spy ship *Aavril Sarychev* in waters under Canadian surveillance. The Soviet vessel was thought to be monitoring the North American west coast for new American nuclear ballistic missile submarines. *Mackenzie* came as close as 300 or 400 feet at times while monitoring the Soviet ship which stayed "very meticulous[ly]"

---

[5] (Montreal Gazette, 1973)

in international waters.[6]

In late May of 1986 *Mackenzie* was taken into dockyard hands to begin her DELEX life extension refit. For the *Mackenzie*-class destroyers this consisted of bringing their hulls and machinery to an as-new state as possible, the replacement of sensor equipment that was obsolete or no longer supported, and the addition of Mk 32 ASW lightweight torpedo tubes. *Mackenzie*'s DELEX was done by the Ship Repair Unit (Pacific) which was based out of HMC Dockyard Esquimalt. Once work was competed and she passed her trials, *Mackenzie* was returned to service on January 16th, 1987.[7]

In April of the next year she joined sister HMCS *Yukon* and four other Canadian ships on a tour of the Pacific Rim, during which time they underwent exercises with units of the Japanese, Korean, and American navies. After a visit to Hawaii on June 21st, *Yukon* and *Mackenzie* sailed for home.

Mackenzie joined other Canadian units in taking part in SAMPLOY '89 between May 25th and June 30th, 1989. These exercises were carried out in between visits to ports in the United States, Mexico, Ecuador, and Costa Rica.

August 3rd, 1993 saw the first of the *Mackenzie*-class destroyers paid off. *Mackenzie* had sailed over 845,000 nautical miles and visited nearly a hundred countries during her thirty-year service to the Canadian Navy.

It was announced in March of 1995 that she would be sold to the Artificial Reef Society of British Columbia to be sunk as diver's wreck. Before she was taken over however, she was repainted in US Navy colours and used as the centerpiece set for a submarine interior for the TV episode "End Game"—the seventeenth episode of the second season of the American science fiction television series The X-Files.[8]

---

[6] (Gainsville Sun, 1982)

[7] (Lynch, Twilight of the St Laurents, 1990) p. 189

[8] Film and TV guest appearances weren't uncommon for Canadian destroyers—

After her turn before the camera, *Mackenzie* was handed over to ARSBC who ensured that she was environmentally safe to sink, and who scuttled her near Rum Island off Sidney, British Columbia on September 16th, 1995.[9]

HMCS Saskatchewan (II) (*Mackenzie*–class)

Length:	366'	Laid Down:	29-10-1959
Beam:	42'	Launched:	01-02-1961
Draft:	13' 6"	Commissioned:	16-02-1963
Displacement:	2380 tons	Paid Off:	01-04-1994

Armament: 4 x 3"/50 HA/LA guns, 2 x Limbo ASW mortar, homing torpedoes

HMCS *Saskatchewan* was laid down and launched by Victoria Machinery Depot Ltd. of Victoria, British Columbia, but after being floated she was towed to Yarrows Ltd. in Esquimalt for completion. She was commissioned in Esquimalt on February 16th, 1963—the second of the

---

Mackenzie's half-sister HMCS *Terra Nova* portrayed a USN destroyer in "K-19: The Widowmaker" and HMCS *Huron* appeared in the TV Series "Seven Days" as a new class of American warship in an episode that aired in January 2000.

[9] (Barrie & Macpherson, 1996) p. 53

Mackenzie-class to enter service.

In late April she sailed for the east coast, passing through the Panama Canal on April 30th and reaching Halifax on June 3rd. She was westward bound again in late October, leaving Halifax on October 20th and arriving in Esquimalt November 29th, 1963. Over the course of that single year *Saskatchewan* had transited the Panama Canal twice, crossed the Atlantic four times and taken part in a major NATO exercise.

Additionally, that year she was deployed off Haiti as part of an international force monitoring an insurrection against the sitting president, François Duvalier. On May 15th *Saskatchewan* received orders to proceed to Port-au-Prince with all due haste, arriving off the coast of the island the next day. Planning was undertaken to evacuate Canadian citizens and secure Canadian Government property, should violence erupt. The ship's two Standing Boarding Parties and Demolition Party were enlarged to form a landing organization of seventy-five sailors, with an additional twenty-two assigned to an action and boats crew section. May 16th was spent in preparations, drills, and briefings, should the landing party need to be deployed. Amongst seven American and one British warship, *Saskatchewan* remained on station in the Channel St. Marc, acting as an information conduit to the USN and RN ships. On May 20th other Canadian warships arrived, remaining further out to sea, but departed again on May 22nd. The British and Americans withdrew on May 23rd and *Saskatchewan* received orders to proceed to Kingston, Jamaica on the evening of the 23rd—there had been no need to evacuate Canadians from Haiti at that time.[10]

In the latter part of 1965, *Saskatchewan* was part of an investigation into ways of improving command of warships at sea. In this role she was fitted with an eight-foot square bridge of aluminum and glass fitted atop her existing bridge

---

[10] (Canadian Forces Directorate of History and Heritage)

structure.[11]

On September 8th, 1968 *Saskatchewan* ran aground while approaching Active Pass in the Gulf of Georgia, striking a rock. Her Commanding Officer, Commander N.F. Jackson was court-martialed and found guilty of having "negligently hazarded one of Her Majesty's Canadian Ships." Commander Jackson was a Korean War veteran and served in the RN during World War Two.[12]

In February of 1970 she returned to Maritime Command Atlantic with the crew of *Kootenay*, and relived her half-sister HMCS *Nipigon* as flagship of the NATO Standing Naval Force Atlantic (STANAVFORLANT). Her second-in-command later told the story of a quarterdeck cocktail party rudely interrupted when the ship's NBC prewetting system was inadvertently triggered—understandably dampening the occasion.[13]

Once more back on the west coast by 1973, she would spend the remaining years of her service life based out of Esquimalt with Maritime Command Pacific.

In July 1982, *Saskatchewan*—like HMCS *Mackenzie*—was shadowing the Soviet spy ship *Aavril Sarychev* which was believed to be monitoring the North American west coast for USS *Ohio*; the first in a new class of American Ballistic Missile Submarines. The Soviet vessel remained outside of Canadian territorial waters.[14]

In 1985 *Saskatchewan* underwent her DELEX life extension refit, which was undertaken by Burrard Yarrows Inc. and the

---

[11] (Barrie & Macpherson, 1996) p. 55

[12] (The Spokesman Review, 1968)

[13] (Barrie & Macpherson, 1996) p. 55. At the time the XO position was held by Mike Young. The author also apologizes for that terrible pun.

[14] (Spokane Chronicle, 1982)

Ship Repair Unit (Pacific) in Esquimalt. This consisted mostly of restoring her hull and machinery to as close to new condition as possible, replacing or updating sensor equipment that was obsolete or no longer supported, and adding lightweight ASW torpedo launchers.[15] She went into dockyard hands on May 27th, 1985 and returned to service on June 17th of the next year. In August of 1986 she was one of the Canadian squadron who visited Australia for the 75th anniversary of the Royal Australian Navy.

As *Saskatchewan* grew longer in the tooth, she was retained as part of Training Group Pacific. Her instructional duties would include training up to forty officer cadets at a go in ship-handling, navigation, and marine and combat systems engineering. She underwent a minor refit in 1990, which included in part a new black-water management system meant to make the ship more environmentally friendly and reduce ship-generated pollution in the maritime environment.

HMCS *Saskatchewan* was paid off on April Fool's Day 1994, and was subsequently purchased by the Artificial Reef Society of British Columbia, who sunk her as a sport divers' wreck on July 14th 1997 near Nanaimo, British Columbia.[16]

---

[15] (Lynch, Twilight of the St Laurents, 1990) p. 189

[16] (MacPherson & Barrie, Ships of Canada's Naval Forces: 1910-2002, 2004) p. 25

HMCS Yukon (*Mackenzie*–class)

Length:	366'	Laid Down:	25-10-1959
Beam:	42'	Launched:	27-07-1961
Draft:	13' 6"	Commissioned:	25-05-1963
Displacement:	2380 tons	Paid Off:	03-12-1993

Armament: 4 x 3"/50 HA/LA guns, 2 x Limbo ASW mortar, homing torpedoes

The first Canadian warship to carry the name, HMCS *Yukon* was built by Burrard Dry Dock Ltd. of Vancouver, British Columbia. When she was commissioned she was the third of the *Mackenzie*-class to enter service with the Royal Canadian Navy.

She sailed from the west coast to Halifax on July 27th, 1963 and would operate out of that port for the next 17 months. On January 5th, 1965 she returned to Esquimalt to exchange crews with fellow Cadillac Destroyer HMCS *Ottawa*, which had been ordered to transfer to Halifax.

Yukon, sister ship HMCS *Mackenzie*, and the supply ship HMCS *Provider* left Esquimalt on May 4th 1970, bound for Japan. The pair of *Mackenzie*-class destroyers arrived in Hakodate on May 22nd, while their compatriot *Provider* went instead to Yokosuka. During their deployment they undertook exercises with naval units from Japan, Australia, New Zealand, and the United States. The three Canadian ships also visited the ports of Kobe, Osaka, and Sasebo before returning home to Vancouver Island.[17]

---

[17] (Barrie & Macpherson, 1996) p. 57

After undergoing a mid-life refit in February of 1975, *Yukon* was transferred to Training Group Pacific where she took up the role of instructional vessel for Maritime Surface and Subsurface (MARS) Officers. She underwent her DELEX life extension refit at Barrow Yarrow Inc. in Esquimalt staring May 28th, 1984, and had her hull and machinery repaired to bring her up to as close to as new vessel as practicable. The DELEX also saw replacement of sensor equipment no longer supported or maintained with more up to date equipment, and the addition of a set of lightweight ASW torpedo tubes.[18] *Yukon* returned to service on January 16th, 1985.

The next year, she was one of three Canadian warships to visit Australia in celebration of the Royal Australian Navy's 75th Anniversary.

Paid off on December 3rd 1993, *Yukon* was eventually sold to the San Diego Oceans Foundation. On April 25th, 1999 she was towed from Vancouver, bound for San Diego where it was intended to sink her as a diver's wreck on July 15th. She would sink at the intended site a day early however, due to rough weather.[19]

---

[18] (Lynch, Twilight of the St Laurents, 1990) p. 189

[19] (MacPherson & Barrie, Ships of Canada's Naval Forces: 1910-2002, 2004) p. 259

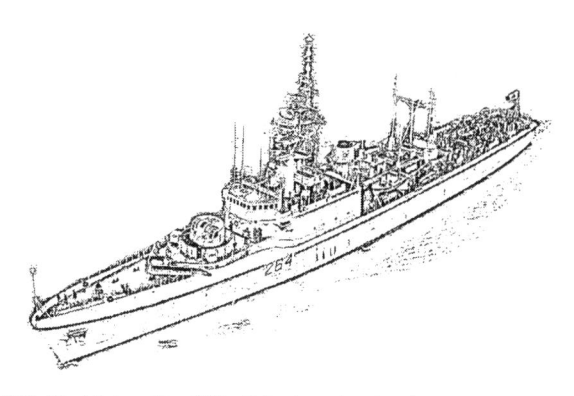

HMCS Qu'Appelle (II) (*Mackenzie*–class)

Length:	366'	Laid Down:	14-01-1960
Beam:	42'	Launched:	02-05-1962
Draft:	13' 6"	Commissioned:	14-09-1963
Displacement:	2380 tons	Paid Off:	31-07-1992

Armament: 4 x 3"/50 HA/LA guns, 2 x Limbo ASW mortar, homing torpedoes

Built by Davie Shipbuilding Ltd of Lauzon, Quebec, HMCS *Qu'Appelle* differed from her sisters in that she was constructed without the 3"/70 forward gun mount the previous ships of the *Restigouche* and *Mackenzie*-classes had carried; instead shipping a 3"/50 in its place—thereby reverting to the same forward weapons fit as the original *St. Laurent*-class destroyers. She was the fourth, and final member of her class to complete and commission. She entered service with Pacific Command in the spring of 1964 as a member of the 2nd Canadian Escort Squadron.

In August of 1971 she and the supply ship HMCS *Provider* spent two weeks tracking and providing surveillance of a squadron of three Soviet warships, during a cruise form the Aleutian Islands to Hawaii. A year later on August 28th, 1972 the two Canadian ships, in company with HMCS *Gatineau* this time, departed Esquimalt and spent the next four months completing their cruise of the South Pacific, undertaking exercises with American, Australian, and New Zealand naval units. The Canadians visited ports in Hawaii, Tonga, Western

Samoa, Fiji, Australia, and New Zealand, before they completed their 33,000-mile trek with their return to Vancouver Island.[20]

Qu'Appelle entered dry-dock at Burrard Yarrow in Esquimalt for her DELEX life extension refit on May 25, 1983. Like her sisters she saw much-needed maintenance to her hull and machinery to bring them back to nearly-new condition. Electronics and sensors that were obsolete or no longer supported were replaced or updated to meet original requirements, but save for the addition of Mk 32 Lightweight ASW torpedo tubes, no new equipment was mounted. By mid-January of 1984 she had returned to service.

The summer of 1986 saw her joined by sisters HMCS *Yukon* and HMCS *Saskatchewan* to sail to Australia to take part in the Royal Australian Navy's 75th Anniversary celebrations. Upon her return *Qu'Appelle* was once more assigned to Training Group Pacific, where she would spend the remainder of her career training junior officers of the Canadian Forces Maritime Command (MARCOM)[21].

The last of the *Mackenzie*-class destroyers to commission, she was the first to be paid off the end of July 1992. Sold to a Chinese company for scrapping in 1994, a portion of her still remains in Canada—her bell is currently held by the CFB Esquimalt Naval & Military Museum, in Esquimalt, British Columbia, and one of her two distinctive 3"/50 twin gun mounts is held by the Canadian War Museum in Ottawa, Ontario.[22]

---

[20] (Barrie & Macpherson, 1996) p. 54

[21] MARCOM was what the RCN became known as after Unification in 1968, only returning to its original name on August 16th, 2011

[22] (MacPherson & Barrie, Ships of Canada's Naval Forces: 1910-2002, 2004) p. 257

As noted above the last two *Mackenzie*-class destroyers were delayed in construction to allow for changes in design to align the final two Cadillac destroyers with their earlier brethren's DDH configuration. The design changes were as radical as the conversions of the *St. Laurent*'s had been, but it was clear that this was the direction anti-submarine warship design was going—indeed the direction it should go if they were to keep an edge over the submarines they hunted.

Their final fit was nearly identical to the *St. Laurent*-class DDH conversion. They reverted fully to the older 3"/50 twin gun mount, but they were the first Canadian warships to be fitted with the new Mk. 32 triple ASW torpedo launcher. Two of these mounts were fitted, one port and one starboard on the quarterdeck under the flight deck overhang.

This class of destroyer were also unique amongst the Cadillacs, as they would be given the most extensive DELEX life extension refit, but at the same time additional modifications would be made to make the *Annapolis* and *Nipigon* the most modern and capable of any of the *St. Laurent*-derived destroyers. This would be known as the DELEX/265 class conversions, and in many ways made the two *Annapolis*-class destroyers a merging of the *St. Laurent*-class DDH destroyer helicopter escort and the *Restigouche*-class IRE anti-submarine escort.[23]

---

[23] (Lynch, Twilight of the St Laurents, 1990) p. 190

HMCS Nipigon (*Annapolis*–class)

Length:	371'	Laid Down:	05-08-1960
Beam:	42'	Launched:	10-12-1961
Draft:	13' 8"	Commissioned:	30-05-1964
Displacement:	2400 tons	Paid Off:	01-07-1998

Armament: 2 x 3"/50 HA/LA guns, 1 x Limbo ASW mortar, homing torpedoes, 1 Sea King ASW helicopter

HMCS *Nipigon* was the second vessel to carry the name and the 35th ship built by Marine Industries Ltd. at its Sorel, Quebec shipyard.[24]

Of all the Cadillacs, only *Nipigon* and her sister HMCS *Annapolis* had been designed and built as helicopter-carrying destroyers (DDH) from the outset. She was the first of the two final Cadillacs to be built and commissioned—despite this, these vessels were considered the *Annapolis*-class; the sub-class having been named for her younger sister. Commissioned in May of 1964, she arrived in Halifax to take up her duties on June 7th.

The next year *Nipigon* was on exercises with the aircraft carrier HMCS *Bonaventure*, when on October 18th a serious fire broke out in a fuel handling room. One crewman was killed and eight others were evacuated to the *Bonaventure* with serious

---

[24] (Barrie & Macpherson, 1996) p. 63 The first HMCS *Nipigon* had been a World War Two-vintage *Bangor*-class minesweeper. Built in 1941 and in service until 1946, she was retained by the RCN until 1957 when she was transferred to the Turkish Navy as *Bafra*, until her disposal in 1972—both old and new *Nipigon* were in service at the same time between 1964 and 1972.

burns.

Much of her service was with Maritime Forces Atlantic (MARLANT) where she primarily served as a training ship. The discovery of cracks in HMCS *Ottawa*'s boilers saw all the *Annapolis*-class destroyers temporarily taken out of service for an inspection in 1981; luckily no cracks were discovered in *Nipigon*. She undertook search and rescue operations for survivors from the doomed *Ocean Ranger*; a well-publicized tragedy where the semi-submersible oil platform that had sunk in heavy seas.

The first of her class to commission, *Nipigon* was also the first of her class to undergo the full DELEX/265 refit. She entered dockyard hands at the Davie Shipyard in Lauzon, Quebec on June 27th, 1983. The modifications to the destroyer were so extensive, that when she emerged she looked quite dissimilar to her sister *Annapolis*.

Included in the modifications were the removal of the Limbo anti-submarine mortars and the variable depth sonar—both replaced by the new Canadian Towed Array Sonar System (CANTASS), first taken to sea by the destroyer HMCS *Fraser* in 1986. Four Mk 36 Super Rapid Bloom Offboard Countermeasures Chaff and Decoy Launching System (SBROC) mountings were fitted—two in the former Limbo well and two on the bridge superstructure. Where the VDS stern cutout had been was plated over to allow for the CANTASS gear, as well as the installation of NIXIE anti-torpedo countermeasures. Additionally, the PRAIRIE/MASKER system was installed. This consisted of a pair of underwater belts—one forward of the boiler room and one forward of the engine room—which used compressed air to generate a blanket of sound-deadening bubbles while deployed. This was known as MASKER and was meant to reduce or eliminate radiated noise from the machinery spaces. PRAIRIE was similar, but used bleed air through the leading edges of the propeller blades to reduce cavitation noise.

Another major change was the replacement of the former mast structure with a new lattice mast which looked quite similar to the one stepped aboard the *Restigouche*-class destroyers that had undergone the IRE refit. On *Nipigon* this carried the Marconi AN/SPS-503 radar, amongst other electronics. A new Mk. 60 gunnery control system was installed forward of the new mast.

What wasn't immediately visually apparent were the changes to her sonar fit and her operations room. Below the waterline, a new AN/SQS-505 sonar in a C3 dome replaced the three previous sonar systems. This new sonar was tightly integrated with the new Team Architecture Signal Processor (TASP), to provide enhanced sonar signal processing—producing what was known as a 'Smart 505' or the AN/SQS-510 system. Integrated into the reconfigured ops room alongside TASP was a pair of Automatic Data Link Plotting System (ADLIPS) stations, which allowed for greater sharing of data between ships so equipped, and thus a better overall situational awareness for the ship's commanding officer and those fighting the ship. [25]

It took fourteen months to complete Nipigon's refit, at a cost of some $19 million. In addition to all the above modifications, when she emerged in August of 1984 she had aboard 200 tons of ballast as compensation for the redistribution of weights with the new equipment (much of which was higher up than that which had been removed). The added weight had added a foot to her draft.

When the fishing vessel *Lady Majorie* caught fire off Halifax in April of 1985, *Nipigon* rendered assistance in taking the crew off, and then—having determined the still burning, now abandoned trawler was a hazard to navigation—sank it by gunfire. The owner of *Lady Majorie* questioned the decision to sink his vessel when he believed it could have been salvaged—going so far as to sue the Department of National Defense over the loss. *Nipigon* was cleared by a Canadian Coast Guard

---

[25] (Lynch, Twilight of the St Laurents, 1990) p. 190

report, and apparently the lawsuit was settled out of court for nearly a million dollars.

The same year *Nipigon* was taken into dockyard hands in Halifax, to repair cracks in the plating near her forefoot. Later that year she was in the hands of the Ship Repair Unit (Atlantic) after suffering weather damage while at sea. In moderately rough weather the whipping action of the lattice mast—the weight and strain of which the ship had not been originally designed to handle—strained an athwartship joint in the operations room deck to the extent that over 200 aluminum rivets were sheared off. This opened a nearly 40-foot gap that appeared between the steel and aluminum plates. Although the ultimate cause of the problem was rivets of an unusually small diameter—permanent repairs were made with bolts rather than rivets, to gain sufficient strength—the DELEX/265 refit for her sister ship *Annapolis* would include the addition of a new structural cruciform to handle the added stresses of the lattice mast. In addition to repairs to the plating (which had also buckled in 'A' Mess) *Nipigon*'s mast was further strengthened and an additional 55 tons of ballast were added (and another 40 tons redistributed). The repairs and modifications cost $95,000, but that wasn't the end of it. Late in the year, after exercises with NATO's Standing Naval Force Atlantic (STANAVFORLANT), it was found that a bulkhead behind the commanding officer's cabin had buckled and several small holes had appeared in the hull.

On 27 February 1987 *Nipigon* was once again at sea rendering aid—this time her Sea King helicopter was used to rescue crewmen from the tug *Gulf Gale* which had caught fire off Cabo Rojo, Puerto Rico. In September of 1987 she became the second warship to have a mixed-gender crew in the Canadian Forces—the first being the diving support vessel HMCS *Cormorant*. *Nipigon* was equipped with separate gender facilities and supported a crew which by 1991 was made up of 25% female sailors.

Nipigon was in refit at Port Weller, Ontario from August 30, 1988 to February 16th, 1990. In August of the next year, she was deployed once more to STANAVFORLANT. On May 16th, 1993, *Nipigon* in company of the New Zealand vessels HMNZ *Endeavour* and HMNZ *Canterbury*, departed Halifax bound for British waters. The Canadian destroyer was in Liverpool and off the Welsh coast as Canada's representative marking the 50th anniversary of the Battle of the Atlantic.

In 1995, *Nipigon* took part in the NATO exercise Strong Resolve off the coast of Norway in February and March. She then was deployed into the Atlantic to support Canadian Coast Guard ships off Newfoundland during the 'Turbot War'[26] with Spain. On June 14th, she intercepted the Spanish trawler *Patricia Nores*, and boarded her just outside Canada's exclusive economic zone. In a secret compartment aboard the *Patricia Nores* was found some eleven tons of unrecorded turbot catch.

She took part in the exercise MARCOT 1/95 in mid-June as part of Maritime Operations Group One. These maneuvers took place in St. Margaret's Bay and along the southern coast of Nova Scotia. In March of 1996 she was ordered to the aid of the submarine HMCS *Okanagan* after the *Oberon*-class sub's emergency beacon went off. As it turned out, no aid was needed as the deployment of the beacon had been accidental—and the crew of *Okanagan* were unaware that it was transmitting.[27]

Nipigon was paid off on Canada Day 1998 in Halifax, Nova Scotia—the same day as her sister HMCS *Annapolis* which paid off in Esquimalt. She left Halifax for the last time on October 16th, 2001, while under tow to Rimouski, Quebec where she was sunk as an artificial reef in July of 2003.[28]

---

[26] For a fuller description of the Turbot Dispute between Canada and Spain see footnote on page 211.

[27] (Barrie & Macpherson, 1996) p. 64

[28] (MacPherson & Barrie, Ships of Canada's Naval Forces: 1910-2002, 2004) p. 261

HMCS Annapolis (II) (*Annapolis*–class)

Length:	371'	Laid Down:	02-09-1961
Beam:	42'	Launched:	27-04-1963
Draft:	13' 8"	Commissioned:	19-12-1964
Displacement:	2400 tons	Paid Off:	01-07-98

Armament: 2 x 3"/50 HA/LA guns, 1 x Limbo ASW mortar, homing torpedoes, 1 Sea King ASW helicopter

The second HMCS *Annapolis* was built by Halifax Shipyard Ltd. in Halifax, Nova Scotia. When commissioned into the Royal Canadian Navy she was the twentieth, and final of the Cadillacs to enter service. With *Annapolis*, Canada's first post-war construction program was complete.

In the summer of 1970 *Annapolis* and half-sister HMCS *Skeena* joined the supply vessel HMCS *Protecteur* on a deployment to northern Canadian waters. The intent of the deployment was to gain operational experience in high-latitude waters and show the flag at distant Canadian communities during the province of Manitoba's Centennial. The Canadian ships made port in Fort Churchill, Rankin Inlet, Chesterfield Inlet, and Wakeham Bay before returning home in September.

Annapolis was serving as flagship for NATO's Standing Naval Force Atlantic (STANAVFORLANT) in June of 1974 when she took part in the rescue and recovery of a downed Canadian Sea King ASW helicopter. The Sea King had been about to land on the American *Brooke*-class frigate USS *Julius A. Furer* when it lost engine power. Once the helicopter's crew was aboard *Annapolis*, the Canadian destroyer began recovery of the Sea King—which was still afloat thanks to its inflated emergency flotation bags. *Annapolis* towed the helicopter (now on a barge) to Den Helder, Holland where it was brought aboard ship for transfer to the Naval Air Station in Shearwater,

Nova Scotia to be repaired.[29]

In December of the same year, *Annapolis* made headlines again when she sent boarding parties to board five Soviet fishing vessels in the Atlantic, which were believed to have been fishing illegally.[30]

HMCS *Annapolis* underwent a major overhaul in 1978/79 and underwent her DELEX/265 refit at Saint John Shipbuilding in Saint John, New Brunswick starting on August 19, 1985. Initially expected to take thirteen months, experience with her sister *Nipigon*'s DELEX (which had been taken fourteen months between June 27th, 1983 and August 22th, 1984) brought changes to the refit process, which extended her time in shipyard hands until January 8th, 1987.

This extensive conversion included the removal of the Variable Depth Sonar and its handling gear, and the removal of the Limbo anti-submarine mortar, to be replaced at the tern with the new Canadian Towed Array Sonar System (CANTASS) which had been experimentally tested aboard HMCS *Fraser* in 1986/87. Also placed in the former Limbo well were two of the ship's four new Mk 36 Super Rapid Bloom Offboard Countermeasures Chaff and Decoy Launching System (SBROC) mountings—the other two being on the bridge superstructure.

Additional countermeasures included the Nixie torpedo decoy system, and the PRAIRIE/MASKER system, which used compressed air bubbles to reduce the noise of the ship's machinery and propellers. A new gunnery control director was added, as was a new lattice mast similar to the *Restigouche*-class ships that underwent an IRE conversion.

Structurally, a large cruciform was constructed which spanned the ship's beam at frame 21 on deck two, to support the weight and strain of the new mast, which hadn't been

---

[29] (MacPherson & Barrie, Ships of Canada's Naval Forces: 1910-2002, 2004) p. 260

[30] (Montreal Gazette, 1974)

allowed for in the original design calculations of the 1960s.[31] Overall cost of the refit was $20 million—more than half the cost of her original construction.

Once back at sea in the summer of 1987, she took part in the major NATO exercise Ocean Safari '87. Later that year, from September 27th to October 3rd she served as an escort for the Royal Yacht HMY *Britannia* during the latter's royal visit to the Great Lakes. In March of the following year she underwent trials of the CANTASS system, which was projected to be installed aboard the new Patrol Frigates then under construction.

She left Halifax on August 14th, 1989 bound for Esquimalt, and on her arrival became the first towed-array equipped unit based on Canada's west coast. The next year she joined the Canadian destroyers HMCS *Huron* and HMCS *Kootenay* on a visit to Vladivostok, Russia, arriving on June 3rd and departing on June 7th 1990.

While deployed to Haiti for Operation Forward Action, on April 12th, 1994 *Annapolis* experienced an explosion in her portside boiler. Luckily no injuries were sustained and she was able to resume her duties. Having left Esquimalt on March 25th, she was relieved after 30 days on patrol by the frigate HMCS *Ville de Quebec*, after which *Annapolis* returned home. In early 1995, as a member of Maritime Operations Group Two, she took part in an American Battlegroup training exercise off Southern California.[32]

Despite expectations that she would remain in service until 2000, *Annapolis* was placed in an 'extended state of readiness' in December of 1996. She and her sister *Nipigon* were paid off on

---

[31] (Lynch, Twilight of the St Laurents, 1990) p. 190. HMCS *Nipigon* had not been refitted with this added structure initially, and as a consequence suffered extensive weather damage while in a moderately rough sea in early 1985. Almost 210 aluminum rivets were sheared off and a 40-foot gap was exposed.

[32] (Barrie & Macpherson, 1996) p. 61

July 1st, 1998—*Nipigon* in Halifax and *Annapolis* in Esquimalt.[33] Sold to the Artificial Reef Society of British Columbia in 2008, it ultimately took seven years of fighting legal challenges from environmental groups before she would be declared safe to sink in Halkett Bay Marine Park to create British Columbia's eighth artificial reef.

On April 4th, 2015 at around 1330h the former Canadian destroyer quietly and quickly slipped below the calm waters of Howe Sound—so quickly in fact it drew comment from Larry Reeves, a director with the ARSBC, who was live-blogging the event at the time.[34]

HMCS *Annapolis*, was the last of the Cadillacs to commission and the last to linger on, having gone seventeen years between paying off and being sunk as an artificial reef. With her scuttling, the last of the Cadillacs was gone.

The story of those twenty ships of the *St. Laurent-*, *Restigouche-*, *Mackenzie-*, and *Annapolis*-classes had spanned sixty years—from 1955 to 2015—a landmark accomplishment for any family of warships.

In 1960 a post-*Annapolis* follow-on class was announced. These were intended as General Purpose Frigates[35], with eight planned beginning in 1963. They would carry 'Tribal' names, and were to be similar—if smaller than—the US Navy's contemporary *Brooke*-class guided missile frigates (DEG).

---

[33] (MacPherson & Barrie, Ships of Canada's Naval Forces: 1910-2002, 2004) p. 260

[34] (CBC News, 2015)

[35] They have also been referred to as General Purpose Missile Frigates, see (Friedman, Network-centric Warfare: How Navies Learned to Fight Smarter Through Three World Wars, 2009) p. 311

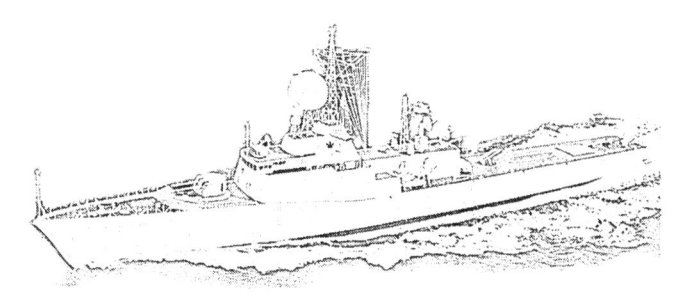

Despite the smaller size, they were projected to carry substantially more weaponry, including a twin 5-inch/38 mount (although a single 5-inch/54 Mk. 42 gun was apparently also an option), a Mk. 22 Tartar missile launcher with 16 missiles, two Sea Mauler short-range missile launchers (based on the US Army's Mauler missile then under development) with 72 missiles, two triple Mk. 32 torpedo launchers, and a single Limbo anti-submarine mortar with 60 projectiles. As follow-ons from the *Annapolis*-class DDHs, these new Tribals would carry a light helicopter[36] for standoff ASW.

Sensors for this weapons fit would include a Signaal N26 fire control system for the 5-inch gun(s), two Mk. 47 directors for the Tartars, and a variable depth sonar (VDS) as fitted on the *St. Laurent*-class vessels converted to DDHs.

Propulsion would be a two-shaft geared steam turbine arrangement with a projected speed of 30 knots.[37] They would have a complement of 236. Unusually, one requirement was that they be able to house and transport two hundred embarked troops for up to 15 days. An emphasis was placed on centralized command and control, human engineering and

---

[36] That is, a light helicopter comparable to the US Navy's Sea Sprite or the Royal Navy's Wessex—the General Purpose Frigate was not intended to support a heavier helicopter like the Sea King, although the design could provide for landing one in emergencies. (Mayne, 2008)

[37] (Gardiner, 1996) p. 46

automation—they were intended to be able to continue steaming even with their machinery spaces unmanned.

The Tartar missile was adopted in the hope that the U.S. Navy would develop an ASW version (which was, at the time, proposed but unfunded). It was intended that such a variant would carry either a homing torpedo or a depth bomb as its warhead.[38]

It was expected that these ships would cost nearly $35 million to purchase, but a fair amount of the equipment specified had yet to be developed—in fact the RIM-46A Sea Mauler would never see service, as the entire Mauler missile program was axed by the Pentagon in November 1965.[39]

These ships were cancelled in 1963 just prior to orders being placed, but much of the intended capabilities of this Tribal-class would appear five years later when the new *Iroquois*-class helicopter destroyers (DDH) were ordered.

---

[38] (Friedman, Network-centric Warfare: How Navies Learned to Fight Smarter Through Three World Wars, 2009) p. 311

[39] (Friedman, U.S. Destroyers: An Illustrated Design History, 1982) p. 360. This also negatively impacted the USN's *Knox*-class Destroyer design. Interestingly enough the US Army's selected replacement Forward Area Air Defense system was the Canadian-designed and built ADATS, which entered service with the Canadian Forces in 1989. (The Pentagon cancelled the US Army acquisition of ADATS when the Cold War ended.)

8

A NEW TRIBE
ENTER THE BUNNY-EARS

In the 1960s the Royal Canadian Navy felt the need for larger and more powerful destroyers—ships that could better integrate into a NATO taskforce, and more importantly, into a USN carrier group. The program was announced by the government in December of 1964 (a year after the abortive General Purpose Frigate had been canceled—see the previous chapter).[1] They would carry two helicopters, a surface-to-air missile system, new sonar, and a 5-inch gun. They were still seen as ASW platforms, but of a more general purpose variety with more mission flexibility than the previous generation of destroyers.

The contract costs were initially calculated as $192.7 million for the entire class but design changes and a revised

---

[1] The story of the General Purpose Frigate's cancellation when it was on the verge of being ordered and the subsequent internal battle over the fleet's composition going into the 1970s, all of which resulted in a repeat *Annapolis*-class design (which was thought of at the time as less than ideal) is documented in (Mayne, 2008) and shows just how fractured naval procurement decision making was prior to unification.

contracting process drove the price to between $25.2 million and $62.5 million per ship. Being a small class—only four vessels—made it difficult to maintain any economies of scale in their development or construction.[2]

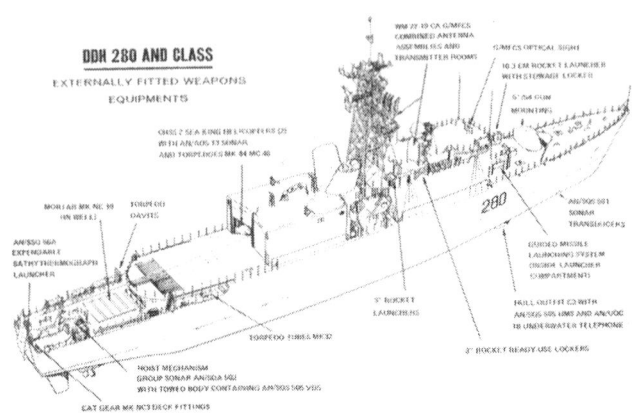

DDH 280 Class design and layout as originally built, prior to TRUMP (Official)

These new Tribals—also known as the 280s, after the pendant number of the lead ship HMCS *Iroquois*—were as cutting edge in their own way as the Cadillacs before them. They were the first major warship class to rely solely on gas turbine engines—used in a COGOG[3] arrangement, where two separate sets of turbines were used, depending on the ship's required speed. This made the 280s fast and maneuverable for their size, yet they still carried themselves with a weight and handsomeness inherited from the previous Tribal-class of the 1930s.

---

[2] (Barrie & Macpherson, 1996) p. 13

[3] COmbined Gas Or Gas – The main power plant is a pair of Allison 570 KF cruise gas turbines with another pair of Pratt & Whitney FT4A2 boost gas turbines cutting in for high speed sprinting or combat maneuvering.

This was enhanced by the location and fitting of some of the weapon systems. Unlike many contemporary destroyers which mounted their guided missiles in the open, the 280s had their Sea Sparrows enclosed in a deckhouse forward of the bridge and stored horizontally athwart ships. As the first Canadian ship mounting point-defense missiles, it was recognized that a more open mount might find itself encrusted in ice from freezing Artic or North Atlantic spray and thus unable to function. The launching arm(s) extended from the deckhouse to port and starboard to launch the missiles, and when on the launchers the missiles could fire within 33 seconds from warm-up to launch arm extension. Reloading was between 90 and 120 seconds.

The *Iroquois*-class was fitted with flume-type anti-rolling tanks to stabilize the ship at low speeds (and likely to assist in ship stability when under an ice load—a consideration in the design of the Cadillacs before them) and also like the Cadillacs this class had a pre-wetting facility to wash down NBC agents. Other NBC precautions included an enclosed citadel and control of the machinery spaces from the bridge.

The two sets of gas turbines drove two five-bladed Controlled Reversible Pitch Propellers through a pair of Swiss double-reduction gearboxes—each shaft being driven by one cruise and one boost gas turbine through one of the gearboxes. The propeller allowed for generation of reverse thrust without reversing the shaft it was on, and the *Iroquois*-class could reportedly reverse from 29 knots ahead to full reverse in 46 seconds. They could also apparently stop from full speed within 750 feet.[4]

During their service lives of over 30 years, the 280s saw many changes, not just in terms of geopolitics—the ending of the Cold War and the collapse of the USSR saw the Tribals facing former enemies as friends, and new threats emerge out

---

[4] (Barrie & Macpherson, 1996) p. 14

of the middle east and pacific rim—but also in their branch of service. In 1968 the three branches of Canada's military were unified into the Canadian Forces. Unification brought challenges large and small—including the loss of the traditional naval uniform in preference for Army green camouflage and berets. Distinctive Environmental Uniforms (DEU) brought back a more Naval-like attire in 1986. A larger challenge was the amalgamation of the RCN's aircraft into the new Canadian Forces Air Command in 1975. Names changed as well; gone was the Royal Canadian Navy, to be replaced by Maritime Command (MARCOM).[5] Throughout the tumultuous times the Tribals sailed on.

A typical period of service for the Tribals early in their career would be similar to HMCS *Iroquois'* NATO deployment in 1978. She left Halifax in April, sailing for fleet exercises off Portugal, followed by operations with French units in the Bay of Biscay and more exercises off the coast of Denmark—this time with German units. She visited NATO Headquarters staff off Portland, UK which was followed by a visit by the Supreme Allied Commander, Europe (SACEUR). Between those two friendly visits she undertook less-friendly surveillance of several Soviet vessels. Returning home *Iroquois* made Halifax harbour in early July. She had put around 14,300 miles under her keel in less than 3 months.[6]

In the 1990s there was a need to update the 280s to carry more modern sensors and armament, and with the Canadian Patrol Frigate Program's ships taking over the role of front-line ASW, the need for area air-defense was taken up as the 280s were re-

---

[5] MARCOM would be re-named the Royal Canadian Navy on August 16th, 2011. At the same time Air Command returned to being the Royal Canadian Air Force and Land Forces Command became the Canadian Army (which many of us had called it regardless)

[6] (MacPherson & Barrie, Ships of Canada's Naval Forces: 1910-2002, 2004) p. 265

roled to better serve Canada's NATO commitments. This refit of the modern Tribals was quite extensive. Called TRUMP (TRibal-class Update and Modernization Project), it saw the removal of the forward 5-inch gun (to be replaced by a smaller 76mm (3-inch) OTO Melara right under the bridge), as well as the addition of a variety of modern Surface to Air missiles and associated electronics. The most drastic change to the ship's profile came with the replacement of the original twinned, bunny-ear stacks with a single 'Low-IR' stack which looked nearly identical to those used on the *Halifax*-class frigates. While larger than the twin-stacks in terms of physical size, it is designed to reduce the heat emissions of the gas-turbine exhausts as they vent from the COGOG plant (the split stack design was originally meant as a way to avoid exhaust interference with flight operations of the Sea Kings, but in practice this was never an issue). Not so obvious were changes to the COGOG plant itself, with Allison 570 KF gas turbines replacing the original Pratt & Whitney FT12AH3 gas turbines in the cruise element. The Pratt & Whitney FT42A2 boost gas turbines were retained.

HMCS Iroquois (II) (*Iroquois*-class)

Length:	426'	Laid Down:	15-01-1969
Beam:	50'	Launched:	28-11-1970
Draft:	15'	Commissioned:	29-07-1972
Displacement:	4500 tons	Paid Off:	01-05-2015

Armament:

Original: 1 x 5" HA/LA gun, 1 Limbo ASW mortar, homing torpedoes, 2 Sea Sparrow SAM, 2 Sea King helicopters

After TRUMP: 1 x 3" HA/LA gun, 1 Phalanx CIWS, Vertical Launch System (29 cells), 6 21" Torpedo Tubes. 2 Sea King helicopters

The second HMCS *Iroquois* was built by Marine Industries Ltd. in Sorel, Quebec. Commissioned in July of 1972, she was the first of four new Tribal-class destroyers who would lend both her name and number for use when the class was spoken of—these destroyers were also known as the *Iroquois*-Class or the 280s.

Later that same year she paid a visit to Boston, and upon her return in December she ran into a storm. While battling the seas *Iroquois* was caught by a broadside gust when the wind suddenly shifted to her beam. According to her first Commanding Officer, Commander D.N. MacGillivray, the wind forced *Iroquois* to roll to the point where the inclinometer hit its limit stop—at 55 degrees—and stayed there for several minutes until she slowly righted herself.[7]

Apart from typical duties undertaken by a Canadian destroyer, *Iroquois* spent her first few years as a trials ship for her class, testing equipment or fitting improvements destined for use with her sisters.

December of 1983 saw *Iroquois* on a fishery patrol on the Grand Banks, when she responded to a request for assistance by the Panamanian-registered freighter *Ho Ming 5*. The freighter was in danger of capsizing after her cargo had shifted, changing her center of mass and causing her to list heavily. Despite heavy seas and gale-force winds *Iroquois* deployed a Sea King helicopter and was able to bring off eleven of the freighter's twenty-strong crew. The remaining nine were rescued by the destroyer's rigid-hulled inflatable boat (RHIB).[8] This rescue earned the Star of Courage for twelve of the destroyer's crew, and another six were presented the Medal of Bravery. During the daring rescue *Iroquois* experienced another 55 degree roll and recovered similarly—making her the only vessel of her class to experience not just one, but two such rolls.

In 1986 *Iroquois* joined ships from 25 other countries at an International Naval Review in New York as part of the celebration of the Statue of Liberty's centennial year.

She decommissioned and entered dockyard hands for her TRUMP refit on November 1st, 1989 and would re-emerge a different vessel on July 3rd, 1992. After this she sailed to Charleston, South Carolina to embark her full complement of 29 Standard missiles for her Vertical Launch System (VLS). She then made her way to Roosevelt Roads, Puerto Rico for test firings of the Sea Sparrows later that month.

She deployed to join a NATO fleet off the coast of the former Yugoslavia in September of 1993. There she replaced

---

[7] (Barrie & Macpherson, 1996) p. 73

[8] More commonly known by the name of the manufacturer: 'Zodiac'.

her sister HMCS *Algonquin* in enforcing UN sanctions against the warring factions. *Iroquois* returned to Halifax April 25th, 1994, having been relieved by the first of the *Halifax*-class frigates, HMCS *Halifax* herself.

On March 7th, 1995 she sailed to Yorktown, Virginia to embark updated versions of her Standard missiles. Iroquois then departed for the Roosevelt Roads missile test range for trials of the new missiles. On March 19th she successfully launched a missile against a sea-skimming target, being the first Canadian warship to successfully test fire the SM2 Block 3 missile. On March 21 she launched an SM2 at a target at 50 nautical miles, achieving another successful interception. Additional anti-submarine, boarding and chaff exercises were undertaken before returning home. She arrived in Halifax in early April.

HMCS *Iroquois* was appointed flagship of Maritime Operations Group 1 (MOG 1) June 17th, 1995, taking over from the destroyer HMCS *Terra Nova* in St. John's, Newfoundland. MOG 1 departed Halifax on February 22nd, 1996 for work-ups in the Caribbean, followed by the NATO exercise Unified Spirit off the east coast of the United States. On her way to the Caribbean she stopped in Granada to play host to then Prime Minister of Canada Jean Chrétien and a number of Caribbean heads of state. She returned to Halifax after Unified Spirit the middle of December.[9]

In 1996 she was one of three designated francophone units in the fleet.[10]

Iroquois joined a Canadian Task Group and departed Halifax in March of 2000 to head south for spring exercises. On their way southward they were diverted to render assistance to the bulk carrier *Leader L* which had sunk northeast of Bermuda. Of the crew, thirteen were rescued and six bodies were

---

[9] (MacPherson & Barrie, Ships of Canada's Naval Forces: 1910-2002, 2004) p. 265

[10] (Barrie & Macpherson, 1996) p. 73

recovered. A further twelve sailors had gone missing. *Iroquois* delivered the bodies and survivors to Bermuda, before sailing to rejoin the task group.

On October 17th, 2001 she departed Halifax as the flagship of the Canadian Task Group of Operation Apollo, in support of Operation Enduring Freedom—the American-led intervention in Afghanistan. *Iroquois* sailed with HMCS *Charlottetown* and HMCS *Preserver* for the Arabian Sea, the task force returning to Halifax on April 27th of 2002; they had been deployed for 193 days.[11]

In February of the next year *Iroquois* would depart Halifax to assume duties as flagship of Task Force 151, the multinational naval force in the Persian Gulf region. Departing on the 24th, her deployment was aborted three days later when a Sea King helicopter crashed on her flight deck. Two of the four helicopter crewmembers sustained minor injuries in the crash and *Iroquois* was forced to return to Halifax.[12] *Iroquois* would finally redeploy in March with the frigate HMCS *Fredericton*. She returned from her second OP Apollo deployment on July 27th, 2003. In her nearly-six months on station she stopped 1,200 vessels and boarded and inspected 44.

Iroquois was on deployment to the Mediterranean in November of 2006, when she responded to a request for assistance from an allied vessel of the US Navy. The rudder had fallen off the *Perry*-class frigate USS *Boone* while on deployment in the western Mediterranean. HMCS *Iroquois* responded—providing divers who were able to inspect the

---

[11] Supply ship HMCS *Preserver* spent 171 days at sea—51 days of that consecutively. During that time she traveled some 44,000 nautical miles, transferred 1,380 cargo pallets (over 200 metric tons) and almost 27 million liters of fuel. She conducted 120+ Replenishment At Sea (RAS) operations with ships from Canada, US, France, Australia, UK, Netherlands, and Italy.

[12] (Gimblett, 2004) p.115

frigate's underside.

In spring of 2008 she arrived in San Juan, Puerto Rico, to rendezvous with the frigate HMCS *Calgary* and the supply vessel HMCS *Protecteur*. The three Canadian vessels trained with several allied nations in multinational ASW scenario, transiting through the Mediterranean Sea. *Iroquois* was once again bound for the Arabian Sea.

On June 3rd, 2008 Commodore R.A. Davidson, RCN took over command of CTF 150, and at this time *Iroquois* became CTF 150's flagship. Between June and September of 2008 CTF 150 would make 190 visits to vessels, carrying out four operations, and be involved in nine rescue efforts. In mid-September *Iroquois* took part in disrupting a pirate attack.

On September 16th Denmark's Commodore Chirstensen took over command of CTF 150. *Iroquois*, *Calgary*, and *Protecteur* began the journey back to Canada. *Iroquois* traveled via Strait of Hormuz, Gulf of Aden, and the Suez Canal on her way to Halifax, while the other two ships headed east, stopping to visit India and Malaysia en route to Esquimalt.

Between May 9th and 12th, 2013 *Iroquois* visited Hamburg, Germany during port's 824th birthday celebrations. She followed this up with a visit—between May 24th and 28th—to Liverpool, UK, for the 70th Anniversary of the Battle of the Atlantic—which her predecessor *HMCS Iroquois (I)* had taken part in.

In early May of 2014 fatigue cracks were found in the ship's hull while she was visiting Boston. By that time she had been in service for forty-two years—and her first keel plates had been laid some forty-five years before. She returned to Halifax and was laid up for inspection, being placed out of service indefinitely.

Finally on May 1, 2015 HMCS *Iroquois* was paid off. She was the first of her class—a pioneer in many ways—but the second to decommission. Her sister HMCS *Algonquin* would follow her little more than a month later.

HMCS Huron (II) (*Iroquois*–class)

Length:	426'	Laid Down:	01-06-1969
Beam:	50'	Launched:	09-04-1971
Draft:	15'	Commissioned:	16-12-1972
Displacement:	4500 tons	Paid Off:	2005

Armament:
Original: 1 x 5" HA/LA gun, 1 Limbo ASW mortar, homing torpedoes, 2 Sea Sparrow SAM, 2 Sea King helicopters
After TRUMP: 1 x 3" HA/LA gun, 1 Phalanx CIWS, Vertical Launch System (29 cells), 6 21" Torpedo Tubes. 2 Sea King helicopters

HMCS *Huron* was the second of the *Iroquois*-class destroyers, and was the second (and last) to be built by Marine Industries Ltd. at its Sorel, Quebec shipyard. She had been laid down six months after her sister *Iroquois*, launched six months later, and commissioned six months later as well.

Her first couple of years of service were almost laconic, but she did have her moments of glory. She was Canada's representative at the Silver Jubilee naval review at Spithead, UK on June 28th, 1977. In the fall of 1979 she entered dock for a refit which included the removal of her sonar dome retraction facility. The edges of the dome, in its retracted position, had been causing turbulence noise on the sonar, so the C3 dome was fixed in the 'down' position and faired into hull.

In March of 1980 she was patrolling off the coast of Nova Scotia when she responded to an SOS from the freighter MV

Maurice Desgagnes. The freighter's cargo of railway ties had shifted and punctured the hull. *Huron* was able to rescue the 21 crew members before the freighter sank.

The next month saw *Huron* in the Mediterranean for the first time. There she took part in exercises during the last week of April.

In February of 1981 she sailed to Roosevelt Roads, Puerto Rico, to act as a trials ship for the vertical-launched Sea Sparrow missile. This weapons system would eventually be permanently fitted to *Huron* (and her sisters) during the TRUMP refit. In May and June of the same year she carried the then-Governor General Edward Schreyer on a tour of five Scandinavian ports.

On July 17th, 1987 *Huron* was sent west to join Pacific Command, assigned to the 2nd Canadian Destroyer Squadron in Esquimalt. She was the first modern Tribal to be assigned to that coast. The destroyer HMCS *Gatineau* was sent eastward to take *Huron's* place in Halifax.

In November of 1989, *Huron* underwent a refit in the Port Weller Drydock in St. Catherines, Ontario. It had been some time since a Great Lakes shipyard had refit a warship. At this time new propellers were installed, underwater fittings were replaced, and the shafts and rudder re-sleeved. Additional modifications to her stability tanks turned them into extra fuel tanks, and some watertight doors were fitted. Finally her tanks and bilges were cleaned, other miscellaneous repairs made, and the whole ship repainted. The price tag was $2 million.

In the summer 1990 she led a Canadian Task Force—which also included destroyers HMCS *Annapolis* and HMCS *Kootenay*—on a visit to Vladivostok, USSR. They were the first Canadian warships to enter the Soviet port since before the Second World War.

Early in 1991 *Huron* departed Halifax destined for the Persian Gulf. There she would relive her sister HMCS *Athabaskan*. Like her sister she was specially fitted with a 20mm Phalanx CIWS atop her Limbo mortar well and two 40mm Bofors AA mounts; one to port and the other to starboard on her boat deck. She returned to Esquimalt on August 2nd.

In 1993 *Huron* undertook an Adriatic Sea deployment in support of the United Nations naval embargo of the former Yugoslavia. This would be her final deployment in her original configuration.

Her TRUMP refit took place at Marine Industries Ltd.'s Davie shipyard in Lauzon, Quebec between July 1993 and November 1994. She was the last of her class to undergo this refit, and left Lauzon on November 25th to begin trials in Halifax. Upon their successful completion in June of 1995, she left Halifax and headed west once more, stopping in Curaçao, Puerto Vallarta, and San Diego before arriving in Esquimalt on July 21st.[13]

The next five years would see *Huron* taking part in major exercises across the Pacific Ocean, along with other maritime duties. In September 1999, *Huron* embarked personnel from the Royal Canadian Mounted Police and Canadian Immigration officers and departed Esquimalt. She spent two days tracking a coaster which was carrying 146 Chinese migrants. Once hailed, *Huron* escorted the vessel to Nootka Sound where it was inspected and found unfit for further travel. The migrants were brought aboard *Huron* and taken to Esquimalt.

Not all of her service was hum-drum. *Huron* took a star-turn (like HMCS *Terra Nova* and HMCS *Mackenzie* would after their own decommissionings) when she portrayed a new class of US Navy ship in an episode of the TV Series "Seven Days" which aired January 5th, 2000.[14] Sadly, this was the end of the road for the destroyer as an operational vessel.

---

[13] (Barrie & Macpherson, 1996) p. 71

[14] At the end of the episode the following acknowledgement is noted: "The producers would like to thank the Admiral and officers of the Canadian Naval Base CFB Esquimalt, and the officers and crew of the HMCS *Huron*, for their cooperation during the filming of this episode."

While she had been the most recently refitted of the 280s, defense cutbacks in the 1990s and personnel shortages saw her placed under a care and maintenance party in December of 2000.[15] In 2005 she was the first of the *Iroquois*-class to be paid off, and she was left awaiting disposal at Esquimalt—but the her end wouldn't be by a cutter's torch. In 2006 Maritime Forces Pacific (MARPAC) elected to undertake a sink-exercise (SINKEX) for the first time. Exercise Trident Fury would use a range of MARPAC and US Navy ships as well as Canadian Forces aircraft to attack *Huron* with a variety of ordinance, to judge the effectiveness of such weaponry on modern destroyers (and how survivable a modern warship was against such weaponry). Should it be necessary, *Huron* would finally be sunk by a submarine-launched torpedo.

During the winter of 2006/2007 *Huron* was stripped of all weaponry and useful equipment (including her propellers), and any remaining fuel and other potentially hazardous environmental contaminants were also removed. Then on May 14th, 2007 she was towed to the offshore weapons range 200 km west of Vancouver Island. When the balloon went up, *Huron* was on the receiving end of attacks from Sea Sparrow missiles as well as gunfire from a variety of surface vessels—including the 57mm Bofors carried by *Halifax*-class frigates. She weathered it all until her sister HMCS *Algonquin* got her turn. Proving that the 76mm (3-inch) gun carried a punch, *Algonquin* holed *Huron* several times, sinking her. Perhaps fittingly, the 76mm OTO Melara mount carried by *Algonquin*—the one to strike the fatal blow to *Huron*—was *Huron's* own gun. It had been removed when *Huron* was awaiting disposal and mounted to her sister vessel.[16]

---

[15] (MacPherson & Barrie, Ships of Canada's Naval Forces: 1910-2002, 2004) p. 264

[16] The 76mm OTO Melara mount had replaced the earlier 5-inch gun during the TRUMP refit. There had been some suggestion at the time that even the 76mm gun was too large and that the destroyers should be provided the same 57mm Bofors gun the *Halifax*-class frigates shipped. As shown during the SINKEX

This was the first operational sinking of a Canadian warship in Canadian waters.[17] It was also *Huron's* television swansong—footage of the SINKEX was used in the 2007 History Television documentary "Sinking a Destroyer."

Subsequently *Huron's* port propeller was placed on display at the Naval Museum of Alberta in Calgary. Unveiled June 3, 2012 it is a monument dedicated to the men and women who served in the boiler and engine rooms of RCN warships during the 20th century. The propeller itself is mostly brass, with a diameter of almost 14 feet and weighing over 3 tons.

---

however the smaller calibre Bofors might not be able to sink a modern destroyer with just a couple of shots.

[17] HMCS *Huron's* final location is reportedly 49° 58.5' N, 127° 58.6' W where she rests at a depth of over 1000 meters.

HMCS Algonquin (II) (*Iroquois*–class)

Length:	426'	Laid Down:	01-09-1969
Beam:	50'	Launched:	23-04-1971
Draft:	15'	Commissioned:	03-11-1973
Displacement:	4500 tons	Paid Off:	11-06-2015

Armament:
Original: 1 x 5" HA/LA gun, 1 Limbo ASW mortar, homing torpedoes, 2 Sea Sparrow SAM, 2 Sea King helicopters
After TRUMP: 1 x 3" HA/LA gun, 1 Phalanx CIWS, Vertical Launch System (29 cells), 6 21" Torpedo Tubes, 2 Sea King helicopters

While all three of her sisters were named after vessels built as part of the 1930s Tribal-class, HMCS *Algonquin* was different—her predecessor had been a V-class War Emergency destroyer; its only link to the Tribals was the name the RCN gave her: *Algonquin*.

This new *Algonquin* was built by Davie Shipbuilding Ltd. at its shipyard in Lauzon, Quebec. Launched on April 23rd, 1971, she was the last of her class to take to the water—her sister HMCS *Huron* having left the stocks at the Marine Industries Ltd. shipyard in Sorel, Quebec only two weeks before.[18] *Algonquin* was commissioned the end of 1973, and was subsequently based out of Halifax.

---

[18] (MacPherson & Barrie, Ships of Canada's Naval Forces: 1910-2002, 2004) p. 263

A year after her commissioning, she was on hand to rescue seven crew from the fishing vessel *Paul & Maria* which had foundered 80 miles east of Halifax.

In January 1975, *Algonquin* departed Halifax—along with the American frigate USS *Edward McDonnell*—destined for Portland, UK, to take over as the flagship for the NATO Standing Naval Force Atlantic (STANAVFORLANT). Later in May, She sailed with her sister ship HMCS *Iroquois*, the supply vessel HMCS *Protecteur*, and the *St. Laurent*-class destroyers HMCS *Skeena* and HMCS *Margaree*, bound for Bermuda to take part in the MARCOT 75 exercises.[19]

Algonquin took part in a search and rescue (SAR) operation in late summer of 1976, looking for the fishing vessel *Peggy's Cove* which had collided with the freighter *Arosia*. Once again, in November, *Algonquin* was ordered to sea to render assistance. This time however it was to help the fisheries protection vessel *Chebucto* in arresting a pair of Cuban fishing vessels who were apparently violating Canadian Costal Fisheries laws in the Halifax approaches.[20]

In January of the following year, as flagship of the 1st Canadian Destroyer Squadron, *Algonquin* joined HMCS *Margaree* and HMCS *Protecteur* to take part in the CARIBEX 1-77 exercises, which were part of a larger US Navy training operation known as Springboard 77, which were taking place near Puerto Rico.[21] During this time she also visited Rio De Janeiro, Brazil, and in doing so became the first of the new Tribal-class to cross the equator.[22]

May of 1978 saw *Algonquin* successfully defend her titles for

---

[19] (Department of National Defense/Canadian Forces) 1975 Report

[20] Ibid. 1976 Report

[21] Ibid. 1977 Report

[22] (Barrie & Macpherson, 1996) p. 67

the L.W. Murray Trophy for gunnery excellence and the 20 Knot Mortar Firing Trophy. In late August, she departed Halifax for the NATO Exercise Northern Wedding, and a month later *Algonquin* once again joined the seven-ship squadron of STANAVFORLANT, assuming the role of flagship of the Canadian Commander from sister ship *Huron*. Throughout November, the ship conducted ASW operations in the Baltic Sea as part of STANAVFORLANT. She would remain part of this force until the end of 1978, while continuing to track and shadow Warsaw Pact submarines in the North Atlantic.[23]

Algonquin suffered a class 'A' fire in her forward decontamination compartment on January 26th, 1981. The fire was believed to have been caused by toilet paper—being stored temporarily in that compartment—coming in contact with a steam radiator. In November she took part in ASW exercises; torpedo firing and other similar evolutions with the submarine HMCS *Okanagan*.[24]

The destroyer entered dock the first of the following year, to undertake a refit that had been postponed from the previous January. The work undertaken included installation of additional monitoring equipment for her gun and missile fire control systems, and the addition of 84 tons of permanent ballast. The refit lasted until July, and she left dockyard hands as scheduled to undertake work-ups throughout August and September. In November she took part in the MARCOT 2/81 naval exercises.[25]

In 1982 *Algonquin* was deployed once again to STANAVFORLANT as fleet flagship for five months. She also has a two-month deployment for the CARIBOPS 82

---

[23] (Department of National Defense/Canadian Forces) 1978 & 1979 Reports

[24] Ibid. 1980 Report

[25] Ibid. 1981 Report

exercises earlier that year. In the CARIBOPS 82 deployment in February she was ordered to assist the diving support vessel HMCS *Cormorant*, which had lost all propulsion and was drifting 24 kilometers west of Martinique. Once she had rendezvoused with the stricken vessel, it was decided that *Algonquin* would tow her into Bridgetown, Barbados. She also took part in the SAFEPASS 82 exercise the next month, where NATO was testing convoy procedures.

Her STANAVFORLANT deployment began in August, and the following month she was operational near the Shetland Islands during Exercise Northern Wedding 82, where she was providing ASW close escort to an American amphibious taskforce executing a landing on the coast of Jutland, Denmark. In October she undertook joint operations with the Danish Navy in the Western Baltic, and a month later joined the Royal Navy exercise JMC 824. Finally in December she took part in a French transit exercise, where she led a French Naval force across the English Channel. [26]

1983 saw *Algonquin* coming up on a decade's worth of service. She took part in the CARIBOPS 83, MARCOT 1/83, and MARCOT 2/83 exercises, along with a shallow-water ASW exercise in the Gulf of St. Lawrence in October. By her 10-year anniversary she had put over 200,000 nautical miles under her keel, with a cumulative time-at-sea of three years. She'd taken part in over twenty multinational exercises, and had been deployed to STANAVFORLANT four times—three of them as flagship.[27]

The following February, *Algonquin* was at sea for 36 days straight, guarding the American aircraft carrier USS *Independence*. In April she went into dry dock in Montreal until August. Then, in October *Algonquin* sailed to Bermuda. 1984 also marked the final posting of a Helicopter Air Detachment as

---

[26] Ibid. 1982 Report

[27] (MacPherson & Barrie, Ships of Canada's Naval Forces: 1910-2002, 2004) p. 262

part of *Algonquin*'s ship's company—it would be a decade before she was to embark on one again.[28]

1985 was the 75th Anniversary of the founding of the Naval Service of Canada. As part of the celebrations *Algonquin* joined 32 other ships at anchor in the Bedford Basin in Halifax, Nova Scotia, followed by a June trip up the St. Lawrence River. Beyond a series of patrols and trials, *Algonquin* also joined the NATO fleet exercise Ocean Safari '85 in August.

The following March, a Panamanian fishing trawler ignored orders to put into St. John's harbor and attempted to run from the fisheries protection vessel *Cape Rogers* into international waters. Still aboard the fleeing *Peonia 7* were a pair of Canadian Department of Fisheries and Oceans officers. *Algonquin* was duly dispatched to intercept and overtake the trawler and join *Cape Rogers* in escorting her to St. John's, Newfoundland, where her hostages could be recovered.[29]

Algonquin was slated to start her TRUMP refit in October 1997 at the same Lauzon, Quebec shipyard where she had been laid down 16 years previously. Before she entered her refit however, she did take part in the CARIBOPS 87 exercise in February and returned to STANAVFORLANT as flagship between March and May. She was also at the Open Gate exercise in the Strait of Gibraltar, followed by the NATO North Sea exercise Vendetta a month later. Finally, on October 26th she docked in Lauzon to get TRUMP-ed.

Unfortunately the process was anything but smooth, and it took four years of hard work, labour problems, contract disputes, and specification changes before she was returned to the RCN in October of 1991, after which she continued to undergo trials until the summer of 1992. During one of these—an inclining experiment while alongside at Halifax in November of 1991—she took on excess water and heeled over

---

[28] (Department of National Defense/Canadian Forces) 1984 Report

[29] (Barrie & Macpherson, 1996) p. 67

to 25 degrees, which was 5 degrees more than the trials had been designed for. Once righted, it was discovered that she had been flooded in some of the machinery and living spaces.[30]

Finally declared fully operational, on March 29th she departed Halifax to take up flagship duties with STANAVFORLANT once more. On June 24th she transited the Strait of Otranto and into the Adriatic Sea as part of the NATO and allied forces blockade of the former Yugoslavia—a blockade intended to interdict arms and other war supplies, preventing their delivery to any of the warring factions within the region. She returned to Halifax after her six-month deployment on October 15th 1993, having spent four months of that in the Adriatic.

Upon her arrival in Halifax she was taken in hand to receive replacement computers and software, a pair of new navigational radars, as well as undergo some structural repairs to her mast and fuel system, and a new set of propeller blades. Following her successful completion of inspections and sea trials, *Algonquin* was reassigned to join the other west coast destroyers in Esquimalt. At the time she was one of three ships in the fleet designated as French language units.

In the first half of 1995, *Algonquin*—as a member of Maritime Operation Group Two (MOG2)—took part in an American Battle Group training exercise off the coast of southern California. That fall, during a visit to the Pacific Missile Test Range in the Hawaiian Islands, she became the first west coast unit to fire the Standard Mk 2 Block 2 surface-to-surface missile. The next spring she took up flagship duties with a group of Canadian vessels taking part in exercise WESTPLOY 96. This three-month exercise with a group consisting of the frigates HMCS *Regina* and HMCS *Winnipeg*, and the supply ship HMCS *Protecteur*, took the Canadian warships to Japan, South Korea, and the Soviet Union; after

---

[30] Ibid.

which they joined the RIMPAC 96 exercises in Hawaiian waters, returning to Esquimalt in June.[31]

During another exercise later in the year, *Algonquin* was tasked with escorting a Russian merchant vessel to the entrance of Juan de Fuca Strait. This was intended as an intelligence gathering mission. The end of the year saw *Algonquin* preparing to enter dock for a refit, which started mid-January of 1997. She re-entered service in May of 1998, the work having cost some $25 million.[32]

On August 24th of 1999 a privately-owned Mig-21 went down at sea, and *Algonquin* was to undertake SAR operations. After 24 hours, having found nothing more than an oil-slick and some debris, the search was terminated. Later the same week *Algonquin* joined the Canadian Coast Guard in intercepting, tracking and boarding an illegal Chinese migrant vessel. The ship was escorted to Gold River, British Columbia and the 159 migrants aboard were transferred to the RCMP for medical and legal processing.

Algonquin started the new millennium with a deployment to the WESTPLOY 00 exercise in April of 2000. She and the frigate HMCS *Winnipeg* conducted the first western nation exercise with a Chinese ship, when they departed Qingdao. Two months later she was one of the 54 ships (altogether over 20,000 crew) from Australia, Canada, Chile, Japan, Korea, and the United States to take part in RIMPAC 00. The following year she continued her role as Canadian Fleet Pacific flagship, taking part in various exercises and work-ups leading up to Operation Apollo—the Canadian naval deployment in support of the Afghanistan war. Her deployment for Op Apollo began in March 2002 as part of Roto One, with frigates HMCS *St. John's* and HMCS *Ottawa* and the supply ship HMCS *Protecteur*.[33]

---

[31] Ibid. p. 68

[32] (MacPherson & Barrie, Ships of Canada's Naval Forces: 1910-2002, 2004) p. 262

[33] (Gimblett, 2004) p. 80

Her seven-month deployment ended in September 2002 and she arrived home in Esquimalt on October 14th. She had sailed over 55,000 nautical miles during that time. She had undertaken over 1,700 hailings and 55 boardings, and was able to apprehend several suspected terrorists.

She was in Victoria Shipyards dry dock for a refit between March and August of 2003, once again taking up the role of flagship when she rejoined the Pacific fleet. In October of 2005 she visited San Francisco with HMCS *Protecteur*, and frigates HMCS *Vancouver* and HMCS *Calgary*, after the four ships completed west coast naval exercises. By 2008 she was once more in dock at Victoria Shipyards for refit. She wouldn't reenter service until the next year.

On August 30th, 2013, *Algonquin* was involved in a collision at sea with the supply ship HMCS *Protecteur*, while practicing towing operations en route to Hawaii. There were no injuries and the ship was able to return to Esquimalt for a full damage assessment. From publicly available photos however, it was clear that *Algonquin* suffered extensive damage to her port side hangar, and so remained alongside in Esquimalt. A planned deployment to the Asia-Pacific region was cancelled.

By this time *Algonquin* had been in service for 40 years. Her sister HMCS *Huron* had already been expended as a target six years before, and the other two remaining 280s were getting long in the tooth as well—they were projected to retire in 2019. *Algonquin* was deemed beyond economic repair, and in September of 2014 it was announced that *Algonquin* would be paid off. On June 11th, 2015 Rear Admiral M.F.R. Lloyd RCN,[34] Deputy Commander of the Royal Canadian Navy— who had commanded HMCS *Algonquin* from September 2004

---

[34] RAdm. Lloyd's first shipboard posting was as navigator aboard HMCS *Iroquois*, a sister to *Algonquin*. He commanded the frigate HMCS *Charlottetown* during Operation Apollo in the Persian Gulf in 2000, prior to taking command of *Algonquin*. In 2016, promoted to the rank of Vice-Admiral, he became Chief of the Naval Staff and Commander of the Royal Canadian Navy.

to May 2006—led the formal decommissioning ceremony for the destroyer at A1 Jetty, HMC Dockyard Esquimalt.[35]

Both *Algonquin*, and *Protecteur* (also determined to be beyond economic repair) were sold to R.J. MacIsaac Ltd. of Antigonish, Nova Scotia for scrapping on November 27th, 2015. *Algonquin* departed Esquimalt for the last time on May 10th, 2016. She left under tow, bound for Liverpool, Nova Scotia and the torch.

HMCS Athabaskan (III) (*Iroquois*–class)

Length:	426'	Laid Down:	01-06-1969
Beam:	50'	Launched:	27-11-1970
Draft:	15'	Commissioned:	30-09-1972
Displacement:	4500 tons	Paid Off:	In Service

Armament:
Original: 1 x 5" HA/LA gun, 1 Limbo ASW mortar, homing torpedoes, 2 Sea Sparrow SAM, 2 Sea King helicopters
After TRUMP: 1 x 3" HA/LA gun, 1 Phalanx CIWS, Vertical Launch System (29 cells), 6 21" Torpedo Tubes. 2 Sea King helicopters

The third HMCS *Athabaskan* was the first of the two 280s to be built by Davie Shipbuilding Ltd. Laid down at the Lauzon, Quebec shipyard three months before her sister HMCS *Algonquin*, she would enter service nearly fourteen months earlier than *Algonquin*, when she was commissioned on

---

[35] (Pugliese, Retirement ceremony for HMCS Algonquin to be held Thursday, 2015)

September 30th, 1973.

Like some of her sisters, 'Athabee'—as her crew called her—had a reasonably quiet time during her early couple of years of service, seeing costal patrol duties mixed with a variety of Canadian and multinational exercises.

In November of 1981 *Athabaskan* was dispatched, along with sister HMCS *Algonquin* and supply vessel HMCS *Preserver*, to respond to a distress call from the MV *Euro Princess*. The ship had been badly holed and was drifting towards the oil platform *Rowan Juneau* off Sable Island. The *Euro Princesses'* crew were recovered by rescue helicopters and *Athabaskan's* Sea King braved 60 knot winds to remove 44 people from the *Rowan Juneau*. Landings aboard the destroyer were ticklish, as the recovery cable to the 'Beartrap' helicopter haul-down winch had failed in the Sea State 5 conditions. The abandoned merchant vessel was recovered later by the Coast Guard vessel CCGS *Alert*.

Despite routine punctuated with the occasional high drama, by her tenth year in service *Athabaskan* had racked up some 267,000 miles at sea.

Late in 1988, while trying to assist the Belgian frigate BNS F913 *Westhinder*, which had grounded in Vestfjord, Norway, *Athabaskan* herself grounded.[36] Ultimately both vessels were freed, but *Westhinder* would unfortunately be lost after a similar grounding accident in 1993 during another NATO exercise.

August 24th, 1990 saw *Athabaskan* depart Halifax on deployment to the Persian Gulf during Operation Friction—the Canadian Naval commitment to the first Gulf War. Prior to departure she had undergone some weaponry revisions, with a 20mm Phalanx CIWS being added over top of her (closed) Limbo mortar well, and two 40mm Bofors Boffin mounts added to her boat deck, one to port and one to starboard. She sailed in company with the destroyer HMCS *Terra Nova* (which

---

[36] (Barrie & Macpherson, 1996) p. 69

also had armament added) and the supply vessel HMCS *Protecteur*.[37]

Athabaskan acted as the Canadian taskforce flagship, assisted in enforcing UN sanctions against Iraq, and participated in the liberation of Kuwait. In January 1991, once ground and air combat began, *Athabaskan* and her Task Group acted as escorts for auxiliary vessels of coalition forces such as supply ships and hospital ships.

On the morning of February 18th, USS *Princeton*—a *Ticonderoga*-class guided missile cruiser—triggered two bottom-laid influence mines while patrolling off Falka Island in the Persian Gulf. The first of the Italian-made MN103 Manta mines went off under the port quarter (right below the port rudder) while the second—which could have been a sympathetic detonation—exploded just off of the starboard bow. The *Princeton* suffered severe damage, with cracks in the superstructure, hull damage, a jammed port rudder, and a damaged starboard propeller shaft. The Number 3 switchboard room was flooded through cracked chilled water piping and several crewmembers were injured.

While not assigned to the area, *Athabaskan* responded to a specific request for assistance from the American vessel and moved north from her then-current position, through the minefield, to stand by *Princeton* and transfer damage control supplies to the stricken cruiser.

The ability to operate both of her Sea King helicopters simultaneously provided *Athabaskan* the capability of using them as long-distance mine hunters (not unlike the sub-hunting they had been designed for) and allowed *Athabaskan* to guide *Princeton* through a portion of the minefield, until the American minesweeper USS *Adroit* could join them and lead the cruiser out of the minefield. During that time—some thirty hours in total—the Canadian destroyer stayed beside

---

[37] (MacPherson & Barrie, Ships of Canada's Naval Forces: 1910-2002, 2004) p. 263

Princeton, and even undertook to deliver several cases of beer to the American ship—an act that was certainly welcome under the situation, notwithstanding the fact that US Navy canteens are dry (i.e. serve no alcohol). After seeing *Princeton* safely out of danger, *Athabaskan* resumed her station and continued her escorting duties.

She was relieved by her sister HMCS *Huron* in early spring of 1991, and arrived home to Halifax in April. Despite having the weapons upgrades (which consisted of some of the additions for TRUMP), she would be taken in hand by Marine Industries Ltd. in Lauzon, Quebec in October 1991, to have her additions removed and a full TRUMP refit undertaken. Upon completion she sailed to Halifax on June 9th, 1994 and was provisionally accepted by MARCOM on August 3rd. She was almost immediately scheduled for additional enhancement which hadn't been part of her TRUMP fit—including added radar, anti-torpedo decoys, reverse osmosis distillers, and an interim black-water management system.

On completion of extensive trials she was accepted back into the fleet in May of 1995. In June the destroyer was off to Roosevelt Roads, Puerto Rico where she undertook missile trials, successfully tracking and engaging an inbound sub-sonic drone with one of her new Standard Missile Mk. 2 Block 3 missiles. That October, she and the destroyer HMCS *Kootenay* took part in the two-month UNITAS exercise off Uruguay. Ships from the United States, Uruguay, Argentina, Brazil, Chile, and Spain also took part. This deployment was the first time in 17 years that Canadian warships had visited South America, and the first time they had ever joined the annual exercise.[38]

In 1999 *Athabaskan* had a six-month deployment to NATO's Standing Naval Force Atlantic (STANAVFORLANT); and again in 2000. On August 3rd of

---

[38] (Barrie & Macpherson, 1996) p. 70

that year a boarding party from *Athabaskan* boarded the GTS *Katie*, which was 160 km off Newfoundland. This was done to compel the delivery of Canadian military equipment, which had been shipped from Kosovo to be delivered to Bécancour, Quebec. The *Katie* was refusing to land the equipment due to a payment dispute. *Athabaskan* entered Halifax shipyard in October of 2001 to start a $9.4 million refit.

In November of 2004, HMCS *Athabaskan* joined the frigates HMCS *St. John's*, HMCS *Halifax*, and HMCS *Toronto* to form part of Task Group 301.1. These ships left Halifax to take part in Combat Readiness Operations—the largest concentration of Canadian naval assets since Operation Apollo. In September of 2005, *Athabaskan* was one of several Canadian vessels serving with MARLANT to be deployed to Mississippi and Louisiana, to assist in relief efforts in the wake of Hurricane Katrina. The following January, *Athabaskan* departed Halifax en route to Keil, Germany, to join the Standing NATO Response Maritime Group One (SNMG1). In February, while off the Denmark coast, one of her Sea Kings crashed while attempting a landing—luckily there were no casualties or injuries. On April 21st 2006, SNMG1 with *Athabaskan* as flagship, arrived at Devonport, Great Britain to celebrate the 80th birthday of Queen Elizabeth II. In September of 2009, while in the UK for Exercise Joint Warrior, *Athabaskan* passed though Scapa Flow to pay her respects to the British battleship HMS *Royal Oak*, sunk there early in the second world war by a German U-boat that had penetrated into the anchorage. During this visit, *Athabaskan* made calls to the ports of Glasgow and Edinburgh.

In 2009, a Nova Scotia man stumbled across one of *Athabaskan's* original Pratt & Whitney FT12AH3[39] gas turbines in a shipping container he had bought for $400. He was using

---

[39] These original cruise gas turbines were replaced by a pair of Allison 570 KF engines during the TRUMP refit.

the container as a bridge on his property when he made the engine discovery. The gas turbine—essentially a jet engine—was originally valued at $2 million.[40]

January 2010 saw *Athabaskan* and the frigate HMCS *Halifax* rapidly fitted out for a humanitarian deployment to Haiti in the wake of a 7.0 magnitude earthquake. *Athabaskan* focused relief efforts on the city of Léogâne, where the crew assisted the Canadian Medical Assistance Team with triage efforts and cleared rubble within the Notre Dame Asylum. The city of 135,000 inhabitants had been nearly flattened by the earthquake and it had been slow to receive relief efforts, so the Canadian response—which also consisted of building three orphanages and lending aid to five more—was crucial in assisting the city's 20,000 to 30,000 casualties.

In June of 2010 HMCS *Athabaskan* was selected as command ship for Queen Elizabeth II's International Fleet Review in Halifax harbor—this being the highlight of the Canadian Naval Centennial celebrations of that year.

In 2012, *Athabaskan* put into St. Catharines, Ontario for a $21 million refit at the former Port Weller Dry Docks (now Seaway Marine & Industrial Ltd.) in the Welland Canal. While being towed to Halifax for the winter, *Athabaskan* broke loose from her tow near Scatarie off the coast of Cape Breton. She suffered hull damage in the incident and had to tie up in North Sydney, Nova Scotia. It had been intended that the refit would have been completed by November of 2012, but maintenance delays and other issues left the destroyer unable to transit to Halifax under her own power.

Once repairs were completed, *Athabaskan* returned to sea, visiting Baltimore, Maryland in September of 2014, to celebrate the bi-centennial of the US National Anthem 'The Star-Spangled Banner'. Afterwards she sailed to the Caribbean as part of Operation Caribbe, a multinational campaign against

---

[40] (CBC News, 2009)

drug trafficking and organized crime. While on this deployment she took part in the interdiction and seizure of some 820 kg of Cocaine, which had an estimated value of $24.5 million. *Athabaskan* returned to Halifax in October having spent 37 days at sea during Operation Caribbe.[41]

Athabaskan suffered weather damage during a storm in mid-February of 2015. The destroyer was in Sea State 9, with winds of 65 knots driving waves over 14 meters. Due to the hazard to exposed personnel, crew were kept off the weather decks for a period of 36 hours. During this time ten drums of oil totaling some 3,000 liters, a rack of gasoline-filled jerry cans, and four drums of hazardous waste (mainly oil-soaked rags) were washed overboard. This was reported by the Navy as being due to failure of some upper-deck fittings and straps during the storm.[42]

In July of 2015, having experienced a series of engine failures and maintenance issues, *Athabaskan* was recalled from her 2015 Operation Carribe deployment to Halifax for repairs. The most significant issues related to the ability to control the engines; indications were that secondary means were required to run the ship's propulsion systems. The ship's age was noted as one factor in the ongoing problems, but Rear Admiral John Newton also commented on her weapons systems, saying, "I don't think it's a surprise to anyone, based on the age of the ship, that some of her primary warfare systems—we would not rely on them in this modern era." Although some critics suggested that *Athabaskan* wouldn't sail again due to the ongoing reliability concerns around her engines, the ship underwent repairs in preparation for an October deployment on twin NATO exercises.[43]

---

[41] (CBC News, 2014)

[42] (Pugliese, HMCS Athabaskan received minor damage in storm, 2015)

[43] (CBC News, 2015)

On September 1st, a fire broke out in the ship's port engine enclosure, while she was off Halifax undertaking training exercises. No serious damage was caused, as it was reported that only some engine lagging had caught fire and not the engine itself. There were no injuries reported, and while *Athabaskan* returned to port briefly, she was back to sea the next day.[44]

On September 8th, *Athabaskan* set sail for the NATO naval exercises Joint Warrior and Trident Venture in company with HMCS *Windsor*, HMCS *Halifax*, HMCS *Montréal*, HMCS *Goose Bay*, and HMCS *Summerside*. Unfortunately, the starboard cruise engine failed while crossing the Atlantic. She sailed to the United Kingdom where she was joined by a mobile repair team which replaced the engine.[45]

Having completed repairs over the winter, HMCS *Athabaskan* was once again making public appearances in the spring of 2016. In March she took part in ceremonies marking the 25th Anniversary of the liberation of Kuwait during the first Gulf War. *Athabaskan* had been flagship of the Canadian Task Group deployed on Operation Friction in the Persian Gulf during that war.[46]

In May she and two *Kingston*-class MCDVs—HMCS *Kingston* and HMCS *Moncton*—visited New York City for Fleet Week 2016 which ran from May 25th to 31st. The three Canadian ships were the only foreign participants in the annual gathering—which in its modern form has been running since 1984. It was an especially interesting visit for two of *Athabaskan*'s engineering room crew—the pair of New Zealand sailors on a five-month exchange tour had the opportunity to see 14 US Navy ships sail into New York

---

[44] (Withers, 2015)

[45] (CBC News, 2015)

[46] (The Chronicle Herald, 2016)

Harbor as a highlight of their time with the RCN.[47]

As part of the Fleet Week 2016 celebrations, on May 27th, *Athabaskan*'s command team and crew were on Wall Street, where they rang the bell at the NASDAQ stock exchange-- thereby opening the day's trading.[48]

As of June 2016, HMCS *Athabaskan* is the last of her class, and the last Canadian destroyer in active service. She is expected to be decommissioned in 2017.

---

[47] (Gilmore, 2016)

[48] (Matheson, 2016)

9

CAPABILITIES FOR THE FUTURE?
FROM CADRE TO SCSC & CSC

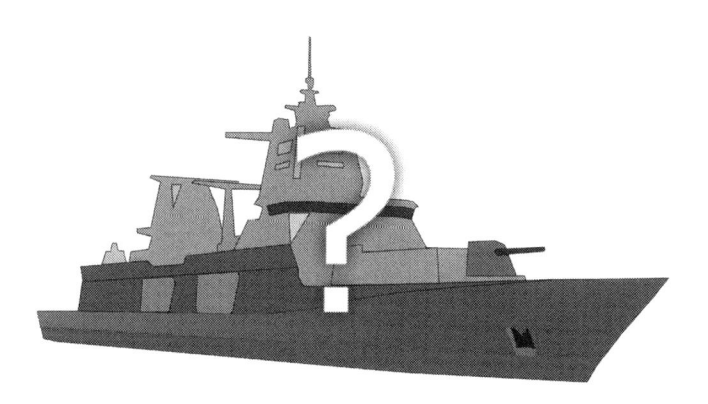

While the *Iroquois*-class destroyers have served remarkably well both at home and abroad, by the second decade of the 21st century it was obvious that they needed replacement. By then HMCS *Huron* had already been sunk in Exercise Trident Fury in 2007. The other 280s soldiered on, but their age began to catch up with them not long after.

In August of 2013, HMCS *Algonquin* collided with the replenishment oiler HMCS *Protecteur* and HMCS *Iroquois* was laid up after severe cracking was discovered in her hull. Both vessels were subsequently paid off. By 2015 only HMCS

Athabaskan was still in service, and in July of that year when she was sidelined by engine difficulties, Rear-Admiral J.F. Newton, RCN, Commander of Maritime Forces Atlantic expressed concern about the vessel's material state and her deferred maintenance. There was some question if she would make it to her planned retirement date in 2017[1]. The search for a replacement to the *Iroquois*-class destroyers however, has grown and evolved over several decades into an effort to resolve gaps in fleet requirements and force structures rather than simply defining and building destroyers to replace aging hulls on a one-to-one basis.

Modern warships are a complex collection of weapons, sensors, defense and propulsion systems—and that doesn't even take into account the variety of 'hotel' services required to support a crew on a deployment. Nor do modern warships act alone—they are part of a larger tactical and strategic environment which includes other types of warships as well as support and maintenance facilities (ashore and afloat) and communications and control infrastructure all unified with other fighting assets to provide as close to a real-time understanding and management of combat forces as possible.

One naval officer put it this way: "It is an important point to note that we now refer to a 'surface combatant' and not a 'destroyer' or 'frigate' because as capabilities of ships have grown and technologies shrunk and converged, it's not so much about a particular ship (by name or numbers of them) but rather the capabilities provided toward accomplishing assigned missions."

A major planning document produced by the Department of National Defence in 2010, entitled *Horizon 2050: A Strategic Concept for Canada's Navy*, appears to be the foundation upon which the next generation of surface combatants' mission

---

[1] (Pugliese, Canada's last destroyer, HMCS Athabaskan, sidelined by engine problems amid fears for its future, 2015)

capabilities will be defined.[2] The Royal Canadian Navy's current and future requirements are for a balanced, combat-effective, multi-purpose fleet. Major units need to be fully interoperable with the US Navy, Arctic capable while globally deployable and responsive to crisis, and sufficiently survivable to continue effective operation regardless of hostile action, weather conditions or other hazards. Finally, such units need to have the mission agility to re-role in the middle of a deployment without returning to a major naval facility. The Navy's force structure grows from those required capabilities.

Naval Force Structure isn't something that can be sketched out on the back of a napkin—if it's not done with due care and consideration, at best you have a navy with the wrong ships to meet the next global threat; at worst you have chaos in the halls of Naval Headquarters as proponents of different technologies and platforms duke it out over their preferred means of projecting naval power. Either way the Navy can find itself in a position where it's unable to respond effectively to the criticism that its costs are out of control. Worse yet, it can find itself facing a government and a citizenry that are hostile to the whole idea of purchasing warships—especially the costly but potentially more effective ones advocated by various proponents. A unified voice comes from a unified purpose and unified goals.

The struggle at Naval Headquarters in the early 1960s over prospective force structure—that is, to keep and/or expand the RCN's aircraft carrier force as well as a potential foray into nuclear submarines—saw the cancellation of the General Purpose Frigate as well as the scuttling of the hope for a Guided Missile Destroyer. Much of the strife came from

---

[2] *Horizon 2050* has not been released publicly, but some indication of its contents can be found in Elinor Sloan's "US-China military and security developments: Implications for Canada," (2010-2011) International Journal, Vol. 66 No. 2, p. 276-277.

aircraft carrier and nuclear submarine 'advocates' who set out to undercut any project that might threaten their desired acquisitions.[3]

No less damaging, even if it was less acrimonious, was the fleet rationalization of the 1980s. The Senate's 18-month enquiry into Canada's Maritime Defence resulted in a report which called for extensive new capabilities and a radically expanded 'ideal fleet.' This was to include 20 modern submarines and 12 missile-armed fast patrol boats. Without a commensurate increase in the defence budget, this was a fleet which only looked good on paper—and then likely only when viewed by a naval enthusiast. DND's more rational *Capabilities Planning Guide* of 1984 outlined a status quo fleet. The 1984 election of the Conservative Mulroney Government was thought to signal a more aggressive Naval policy, and some believed it was time to balance NATO and North American defence commitments with Arctic sovereignty. The 1987 Defence Whitepaper suggested (once again) a fleet of nuclear submarines for such duties. It was considered that these subs could be Phase III of the Ship Replacement Project (SRP).

SRP was a four-phase plan which included two flights of the *Halifax*-class frigates as Phases I and II. Phase III would be a third flight of frigates (or alternatively nuclear submarines) and Phase IV was a replacement for the *Iroquois*-class destroyers. The proposal of nuclear submarines rather than more frigates ended up being a poor choice—Canadians neither wanted to pay for the purchase of, nor own and support nuclear vessels. When the submarine concept died, so too did SRP III and IV. The SRP program was completed with the commissioning of the frigate HMCS *Ottawa* in 1996. There would be no replacement for the 280s in the foreseeable future.[4]

---

[3] (Mayne, 2008)

[4] (Haydon, Choosing the Right Fleet Mix: Lessons from the Canadian Patrol Frigate Selection Process, 2008)

The dawn of the 21st century saw an apparent renewed interest in defining what naval capabilities Canada required. Between the end of the Cold War and the attacks of September 11th, 2001 there wasn't a much clarity on what major threats and operations might surface requiring Canadian naval response.[5] Humanitarian assistance was certainly one, and from the 1960s the response to a limited war oversees had seen both peacekeeping deployments as well as coalition warfighting on the part of the Canadian Forces. In some ways the war in Afghanistan was more of the same—but it helped focus Canadians on the need for, and support of the Canadian military as a whole. It also made clear the costs of fighting a war—and how cutting the military budget to the bone to save on monetary costs only increased the human costs of warfare.

Most importantly though, it made clear to Canada's citizens and politicians that what Canada's Navy needed were ships that could be flexible and versatile and a fleet large enough to support multiple deployments.[6] This, of course, was no revelation to senior Naval officers, who surely felt like voices in the wilderness crying this out for the previous three decades.

Although *Horizon 2050* dated from 2010, defining Canada's next major surface combatant extends back to at least February 1994 with the establishment of the Command/Control and Air Defence Replacement (CADRE) project. CADRE focused on addressing the need to replace the air defence and command and control capabilities provided to the fleet by the recently TRUMP-ed 280s. CADRE's clear purpose was the replacement of these two capabilities, crucial for the effective

---

[5] (Haydon, What Naval Capabilities Does Canada Need?, 2001)

[6] Not the least of which was the need to automate manpower-intensive shipboard activities like damage control to reduce the crew size and the provision of secure communications infrastructure to allow crew to feel closer to home on long deployments

deployment of the Canadian Task Group—it was not intended to replace the four destroyers per se. Potential options for CADRE could have included a CADRE-specific platform designed and built in Canada, an off-the-shelf foreign platform built under license in Canada (or offshore) or the incorporation of the required capabilities into existing Canadian ships like the *Halifax*-class frigates or the next generation of support ships designed to replace HMCS *Protecteur* and her sisters.

An off-the-shelf design, potentially modified for Canadian requirements, has been an option that tends to elicit heated debate, both for and against—at least in civilian circles. Canada has never really been adverse to this approach—see the original Tribal-class destroyers or HMCS *Saguenay* and HMCS *Skeena* from the 1930s; both designs modified for and built to Canadian requirements in British shipyards (at least the first batch of Tribals). During the contentious debate within the Navy in the mid-1960s on the best approach to acquiring guided missile ships, the American *Charles F. Adams*-class was mooted as a possible solution to be built in Canada.

The strength of off-the-shelf designs are that they have been tried and tested—and hopefully that has worked out the kinks. They also tend to be cheaper. The major weakness are that they are often behind the technology curve—some are even obsolete before they slide down the ways. Cutting-edge technology carries risk—of cost over-runs and disappointing performance—but so does the status quo. It's a fine line to sail—and woe unto the Navy that can't steer that course.

CADRE may well have inspired a sketch design based on MIL Systems Engineering's *Concept Design for a Baseline Air Defense and Command Ship, Book Two Point Concept Design Report*—a study released in February 1995 and a sketch which looked similar to modern European frigate/destroyer designs like the Royal Navy Type 45 or the French *La Fayette*-class.[7]

---

[7] (Burke, 1998)

Type 45 guided missile destroyer HMS *Dauntless*
Construction of prefabricated module blocks
HMNB Portsmouth Shipyard
Adrian Jones; 2 July 2005

In the September 1999 document *MARCOM Capability Planning Guidance 2000*, the Chief of the Maritime Staff (CMS)[8] made clear that CADRE was first on the Navy's capital project priorities list. As CADRE progressed, its scope of investigation expanded from 'traditional' Cold War area air defence and looked at the potential to handle threats from ballistic and cruise missiles, shore-based weapons, kinetic weapons (traditionally, those which fired shells) and directed energy or beam weapons.[9] Canadian Task Group command needs expanded to cover upgrading command, control, communications, computers, intelligence, surveillance and reconnaissance capabilities, as well as the ability to fight co-

---

[8] The position was held at the time by Vice Admiral G.R. Maddison, who had commanded HMCS *Athabaskan* from May 1986 to April 1988.

[9] While the latter may sound like Science Fiction, the US Navy is known to have spent much time over the last several decades exploring such directed energy weapons and it's likely that other major powers have as well.

operative engagements. CADRE also recommended additional general purpose capabilities like naval gunfire support (NGS) which would allow the resulting warship to provide support to joint and combined forces ashore[10].

After consideration of both the affordability of the project and the defined needs, CADRE was cancelled in June of 2002. In April of 2004 the Frigate Transition plan was added to the Strategic Capability Investment Plan (2004) and by May, 2007 the Department of National Defence endorsed the CMS'[11] intention for a destroyer replacement—now known as the Destroyer Replacement Project (DRP)—and the use of a common platform/hull for both the DRP and the future frigate replacement project.

DRP was officially launched on July 12th, 2007, and was tasked with recapitalizing the fleet's Area Air Defence and Task Group Command and Control (AAD/TG C2) capabilities provided by the three remaining *Iroquois*-class destroyers. DRP became part of the Single Class Surface Combatant (SCSC) initiative, which would also include the replacement of the *Halifax*-class frigates once they reached the end of their useful lives. At the time it was thought that frigate replacement might start as early as 2016, with replacement for the 280s occurring even earlier. In April of 2008, the SCSC project received a new name, becoming the Canadian Surface Combatant (CSC) project. The following month saw the release of the Canada First Defence Strategy. In it, the Canadian Government stated its intent to acquire 15 new ships as replacements for the Navy's destroyers and frigates—all based on a common hull design.

Between 2008 and 2012, 35 separate studies were commissioned by the Navy to explore payload systems,

---

[10] (GlobalSecurity.org)

[11] The position was held by this time by Vice Admiral D. W. Robertson, who had also commanded *Athabaskan*, from August 1999 to January 2000.

platform systems, commonality and crew requirements, project support capabilities, and acquisition support. Also included were Maritime Operational Research Team (MORT) studies.

The CSC project charter was approved on January 29th, 2009 and focused the project's priorities on the most pressing need—the replacement of the remaining 280s and their AAD/TG C2 capabilities. The intent was for CSC to start with an initial flight of three ships to replace the existing destroyers, and would act as a basis for a follow-up group of general purpose, multi-threat capable warships. The goal for platform commonality would be to reduce costs throughout the service lives of the ships as the use of a common hull, weapons and equipment would simplify maintenance, support and training.

Seven months later however, a Market Survey report from the CSC Project Management Office was released which concluded that 15 ships with the capabilities defined in the draft CSC requirements could not be acquired within the existing budget limit. The report recommended additional analysis to determine the correct mix of capabilities. In March of 2010 change approval was requested for 'up to 15' vessels. This was reiterated in November of 2010 with a change of scope recommendation, where it was also recommended that the number and variants of CSC ships should be determined in the project's Definition Phase—in this way the precise costs could be determined in cooperation with industry.

The Government of Canada launched the National Shipbuilding Procurement Strategy (NSPS) on June 3rd, 2010. Projected to take 20 years, the NSPS would consist of several 'packages', the first and largest was for the procurement of 21 warships for the RCN—these would include 5-6 Arctic Patrol Vessels and 'up to' 15 Canadian Surface Combatants. The second was for 17 non-combatant ships for the RCN and Canadian Coast Guard (CCG)—these would include 2 Joint Support Ships for the RCN and 15 other vessels for the CCG. The third was for smaller vessels not included in the previous two packages of work. The first two packages and their details were announced on October 11th of the same year. On October 19th, 2011 the Government of Canada selected Irving Shipbuilding Inc. (formerly Saint John Shipbuilding) as the lead on the first package of work worth $25 billion.

The CSC project's Definition Phase 1 was kicked off on January 31st, 2012, and on August 29th project leadership was transferred from the RCN to the Assistant Deputy Minister (Material) who is responsible for the acquisition, maintenance and support of all the equipment that the Canadian Forces requires and uses. That same year, in a series of 15 industry engagements the CSC project began the process of informing industry about the project as well as soliciting industry feedback. At the same time Irving Shipbuilding was contracted by the CSC Project Management Office to undertake an initial review of the project. Irving's contracted Systems Planning and Analysis Inc. and A.T. Kearney to conduct a requirements review and assessment as well as an assessment of costs to meet the preliminary project requirements. Based on the results of these assessments, recommendations were made to refine the ships' capabilities in such a way as to reduce procurement and lifetime costs without compromising or risking mission profiles. The RCN's review of these recommendations showed that ship cost could potentially be reduced with an acceptable level of additional operational risk.

In May of 2015 the newly-released Canadian procurement strategy specified that Irving Shipbulding, as prime contractor, would bring together and work with—as first-tier subcontractors—a warship designer and a systems integrator to design, build, and integrate the Canadian Surface Combatant's many and varied systems. That September, once the RCN's initial reconciliated requirements were completed, these were presented to the Independent Review Panel for Defense Acquisitions and the Deputy Ministers Governance Committee for review. Both were satisfied with the process thus far. Finally, in November of 2015, seven companies were pre-qualified for the warship designer role. These included, Alion-

JJMA Corp. who has been involved in the USN's Littoral Combat Ship project; ThyssenKrupp Marine Systems, builder of the MEKO A-200 frigate, and BAE Systems Surface Ships Ltd. who designed and are building the British Type 45 destroyer. ThyssenKrupp also made the shortlist for the combat systems integrator role, which included Lockheed Martin Canada, Saab Australia Pty Ltd., and Thales Nederland B.V.[12]

Mid-2016 saw the new Liberal government announce a refined procurement strategy, which was to consist of a design-then-build methodology to select a total ship design that would include an integrated platform and combat systems. Based on this new methodology, on October 27th, 2016 a Request for Proposal (RFP) was issued for a Total Ship Reference Point.

As of the end of 2016, the Royal Canadian Navy has made significant progress in developing the next generation surface combatant. For many outside the Navy, this may have been mostly invisible—or at least obfuscated by the scope of a modern warship selection process which speaks of force structures, characteristics, capabilities and integrated combat systems more than simply 'building ships.' That isn't to say that building ships won't be the end result—but for a Navy which has often found itself struggling against government parsimony, especially in the area of ship acquisition, the lessons from a painful past have been well-learned. These lessons drive the current acquisition strategy: determine what missions the Navy needs to fulfill, determine what capabilities required to fulfill those missions look like, and fit them into a solution that is cost effective both now, and in the future.

---

[12] Also making both shortlists was the French industrial group DCNS SA which is 64% owned by the French state and 35% owned by the French Thales Group. DCNS might best be known for being at the center of France's 'Frigates-to-Taiwan' scandal as detailed in *Taïwan Connection : Scandales et meurtres au cœur de la République* by Thierry Jean-Pierre.

If one were to look at the Navy's warship procurements since the 1990s, things would seem pessimistic. Since the commissioning of the final *Halifax*-class frigates in the middle of that decade, only a dozen minesweepers (the last of which, HMCS *Summerside*, was commissioned in 1999) and the *Victoria*-class submarines have entered the fleet.[13] In that time however, between CADRE, the SCSC and today's CSC projects the Navy has spent a lot of time studying and planning for the next generation of Canadian destroyers—or at least the next generation of surface combatants. Soon—very soon it is hoped—that methodical planning will pay dividends for the Royal Canadian Navy, and for the Canadian taxpayer, both of whom can be proud of a new series of combat- and cost-effective warships to carry the Canadian destroyer tradition into the mid- to end of the 21st century.

With a little bit of luck, a lot of hard work, and a firm hand on the tiller, steel may be cut on the next RCN tin-can by 2020—perhaps the most fitting way of marking a century of Canadian destroyers.

---

[13] The *Orca*-class patrol boats—eight of which were constructed between 2004 and 2008 for service on the Canadian West Coast—are not commissioned warships and don't carry the prefix HMCS; for that reason they are not listed here.

AFTERWORD
LOST AND GAINED

I started this project in 2012 when I was first taken in by the story of HMCS *St. Croix* and her sinking by U-305. Initially it was research for a model of a four-stack destroyer, prompted by the gift of a hull of said ship from a friend. Needless to say, it didn't end when the model was complete.

The men and women who serve on Canadian warships today may come from the modern world of email and cellphones, where they can communicate with friends and family easily and in real-time, when deployed. They are sailors who ply peaceful (and not so peaceful) waters close to home or far afield. Yet, for all that, they are no different from their forefathers who sailed aboard the much smaller tin-cans of an earlier age. They take upon themselves a duty—and often a heavy burden—of watching out for the defense of Canada and all her citizens. Even in peace time there are risks to sailing in destroyers—as there are in all warships.

Some 925 lives have been lost in the last century in RCN Destroyers; Canadian ships and crews lost in war and in peace (HMCS *Kootenay's* gearbox explosion was one of the worst peace-time disasters in the history of the Royal Canadian

Navy[1]).

Since November 1st, 1920, 62 destroyer-type ships have served in the Canadian navy. Throughout they have served our fighting men and women—and all whom they protected, be it Canadian or otherwise—with pride and with distinction.

In many ways the destroyer has been the backbone of Canadian Naval defense policy. While the Navy always saw larger ships (cruisers, carriers etc.) as highly valuable fleet assets, the RCN has generally preferred destroyers and frigates as the main combat element. This has often revolved around cost—destroyers and other small units cost less to procure and maintain.

It has however been stated policy that destroyers were "unambiguous warships" which could provide the greatest flexibility and are "the very finest ship for defence [sic] or attack within our means" according to the Chief of the Naval Staff in 1934. Destroyers also provided the ability to work closely with the Royal Navy battle fleet (and later the United States Navy and other NATO allies), and avoided the perception of the RCN as an insignificant coastal force. Indeed prior to the war, Admiral Nelles had hoped to use Canadian Tribal-class destroyers as "a free-ranging flotilla hunting down commerce raiders."[2]

While some have pointed out that the Canadian destroyers of the Second World War were not as effective as pre-war doctrine had hoped—British destroyers (and thus Canadian destroyers) became well known for both limited AA capabilities and short range—they proved their worth in the Battle of the Atlantic, thanks in large part to the crews who fought them and kept them in fighting trim.

They also proved, however, that the 'Destroyer Myth'— that destroyers alone were enough for Canada to fight a war—

---

[1] (Bartlette & Reber, 2009)

[2] (Hansen, 2006)

was true. Although they rarely worked with the British fleet, on convoy duty they were often paired with corvettes and frigates who could better deal with U-boats at close range, due to their smaller turning circle and lower-mounted guns. That said, in many cases Canadian destroyers were the SOE for the convoy they escorted, and their ability to sprint allowed them to be johnnie-on-the-spot when needed, in a manner that dedicated convoy escorts such as sloops, corvettes, and frigates could not. The true lesson it seems is that a balanced fleet needs more than just one type of warship to meet its combat commitments—and that the destroyer is a key part of that mix. It just shouldn't be the only part of that force structure.[3]

From the 1920s, when the Royal Canadian Navy's only warships afloat were a pair of destroyers, to WW2 and Korea, when our destroyers hunted submarines and bombarded enemy positions on shore, through our Cadillacs which, with the 280s saw service in two Gulf wars decades apart, the destroyer has served Canada well. The destroyer has been our protector, our defender, our peace-keeper, and when required, our enforcer. Some may say the pen is mightier than the sword, but while the pen has written the naval history of this country, the Canadian destroyer—our sword—has been making it.

What will the next century hold for Canadian destroyers? Right now it's hard to say—procurement policy makes for a clouded crystal ball. Certainly there will be challenges, and while a new generation of Canadian warships may not be termed 'destroyers', the Royal Canadian Navy will sail on; and whatever ships fly the Canadian ensign, the crews will stand to their duty and brave danger, because that is what they do. That is who they are. Perhaps being a tin-can sailor is more a state of mind than a ship assignment.

It is thanks to these men and women and the ships they

---

[3] Ibid

crew that Canada has seen a safe and secure democracy for the last century that we have been protected by our destroyers. While we have lost much—in ships and lives—we have also gained much, and our place on the world stage and our leadership in world events owes much to their service in the Royal Canadian Navy.

Finally, I think I'll quote once again, Bertrand Twinn's verse—because, to me, it sums up the spirit of the destroyer and her never-say-die Tin-Can Canucks:

"Our duty's clear and it SHALL BE DONE."

The crew of HMCS *Grilse*
CWM 19790653-007
George Metcalf Archival Collection
Canadian War Museum

BIBLIOGRAPHY

"On Patrol" rare HMCS Grilse 1916 poem. (2016, 09 28). Retrieved 01 16, 2016, from Canadian War Poetry WW1 Era 1900 1950: https://canadianwarpoetryww1.wordpress.com/

Audette, L. C. (1982). The Lower Decks and the Mainguy Report. In J. A. Boutilier, *RCN in Retrospect: 1910 - 1968* (pp. 235 - 249). Vancouver: The University of British Columbia Press.

Barnaby, K. C. (1964). *100 Years of Specialized Shipbuilding and Engineering.* London: Hutchison & Co. (Publishers) Ltd.

Barrie, R., & Macpherson, K. (1996). *Cadillac of Destroyers: HMCS St. Laurent and Her Successors.* St.

Catharines, Ontario: Vanwell Publishing Ltd.

Bartlette, S., & Reber, S. (2009, October 21). *Taking stock of Canada's worst peacetime naval disaster.* Retrieved January 11, 2016, from CBC News: http://www.cbc.ca/news/canada/taking-stock-of-canada-s-worst-peacetime-naval-disaster-1.852261

Bercuson, D., & Herwig, H. H. (2011). *Deadly Seas: The Duel Between The St.Croix And The U305 In The Battle Of The Atlantic.* Vintage Canada.

Bowie, D. (2010). *Cruising Turbines of the 'Y100' Naval Propulsion Machinery.* Retrieved January 16, 2016, from Haze Gray: The Canadian Navy of Yesterday & Today: http://www.hazegray.org/navhist/canada/systems/propulsion/y100/y100.pdf

Burke, M. U. (1998). The Command/Control and Air Defence Replacement (CADRE) Project. *Canadian Defence Quarterly*(Summer 1998), 25 - 28.

Burrow, L., & Beaudoin, E. (1987). *Unlucky Lady: The Life & Death of HMCS Athabaskan.* Toronto, Ontario: McClelland & Stewart Inc.

Canadian Forces Directorate of History and Heritage. (n.d.). *Details/Information for Canadian Forces (CF) Operation Haiti 1963.* Retrieved January 16, 2016, from Operations Database: http://www.cmp-cpm.forces.gc.ca/dhh-dhp/od-bdo/di-rieng.asp?IntlOpId=59&CdnOpId=68

Canadian Press. (1970, July 16). *Canadian Destroyer Aground*. Retrieved January 16, 2016, from The Montreal Gazette: https://news.google.com/newspapers?nid=1946&dat=19700716&id=LIwyAAAAIBAJ&sjid=J7kFAAAAIBAJ&pg=3913,3787060&hl=en

Canadian Press. (2013, April 20). *French pitch new warships for next Canadian navy vessels.* Retrieved January 16, 2016, from CBC News: http://www.cbc.ca/news/politics/french-pitch-new-warships-for-next-canadian-navy-vessels-1.1301575

CBC News. (2009, September 8). *Cargo container yields $2M surprise*. Retrieved January 15, 2016, from CBC News: http://www.cbc.ca/news/canada/nova-scotia/cargo-container-yields-2m-surprise-1.821211?ref=rss

CBC News. (2014, October 30). *HMCS Athabaskan returns home*. Retrieved January 16, 2016, from CBC News: http://www.cbc.ca/news/canada/nova-scotia/hmcs-athabaskan-returns-home-1.2818216

CBC News. (2015, April 4). *HMCS Annapolis sunk to make artificial reef.* Retrieved January 16, 2016, from CBC News: http://www.cbc.ca/news/canada/british-columbia/hmcs-annapolis-sunk-to-make-artificial-reef-1.3021329

CBC News. (2015, July 20). *HMCS Athabaskan sent back to Halifax for major engine repairs*. Retrieved January 16, 2016, from CBC News: http://www.cbc.ca/news/canada/nova-scotia/hmcs-athabaskan-sent-back-to-halifax-for-major-engine-repairs-1.3160864

CBC News. (2015, October 6). *HMCS Athabaskan tied up in U.K. after engine fails*. Retrieved January 15, 2016, from CBC News: http://www.cbc.ca/news/canada/nova-scotia/hmcs-athabaskan-engine-fails-1.3258059

Chappelle, D. (1995, January). Building a Bigger Stick: The Construction of Tribal Class Destroyers in Canada, 1940 - 1948. *The Northern Mariner/Le Marin du nord, V*(1), 1 - 17.

Cleaves, H. (1981, July 2). *Destroyer aground in ints home port*. Retrieved January 16, 2016, from Bangor Daily News: https://news.google.com/newspapers?nid=2457&dat=19810702&id=qhVbAAAAIBAJ&sjid=jE4NAAAAIBAJ&pg=6225,594751&hl=en

Department of National Defense, The Government of Canada. (2016, June 13). *Canadian Surface Combatant*. Retrieved June 15, 2016, from National Defense and the Canadian Armed Forces: http://www.forces.gc.ca/en/business-equipment/canadian-surface-combatant.page

Department of National Defense/Canadian Forces. (n.d.).
UIC 7714 HMCS Algonquin Annual Historical Report
.

Digiulian, T. (2012, February 12). *Britain 3"/70 (7.62 cm) Mark 6.* Retrieved January 16, 2016, from NavWeaps.com: http://www.navweaps.com/Weapons/WNBR_3-70_mk6.htm

Dorschner, J. (2014, March). *Over The Horizon – Next Generation Multi-role Absalon Destroyers: A Modest Proposal.* Retrieved August 5, 2015, from Canadian American Strategic Review : http://www.casr.ca/mp-dorschner-rcn-absalon-ddh.htm

Douglas, W. A., Sarty, R., & Whitby, M. (2004). *No Higher Purpose: The Official Operational History of the Royal Canadian Navy in the Second World War, 1939-1943* (Vols. II, Part I). Vanwell Pub Ltd.

Douglas, W. A., Sarty, R., & Whitby, M. (2007). *A Blue Water Navy: The Official Operational History of the Royal Canadian Navy in the Second World War, 1943-1945* (Vols. II, Part II). Vanwell Publishing Limited.

Easton, A. H. (1966). *50 North: Canada's Atlantic Battleground.* Toronto. Ryerson.

Ellensburg Daily Record. (1962, February 21). Retrieved January 11, 2016, from Google News Archive:

https://news.google.com/newspapers?nid=860&dat=19620221&id=YH9OAAAAIBAJ&sjid=VEsDAAAAIBAJ&pg=6162,1884685&hl=en

English, J. (1993). *Amazon to Ivanhoe: British Standard Destroyers of the 1930s.* Kendal: World Ship Society.

English, J. (2001). *Afridi to Nizam: British FleetDestroyers 1937 - 43.* Gravesend, Kent: World Ship Society.

English, J. (2008). *Obdurate to Daring: British Fleet Destroyers 1941 - 45.* World Ship Society.

Friedman, N. (1982). *U.S. Destroyers: An Illustrated Design History.* Annapolis, Maryland: Naval Institute Press.

Friedman, N. (2008). *British Destroyers and Frigates: The Second World War and After.* Barnsley: Seaforth Publishing.

Friedman, N. (2009). *British Destroyers: From Earliest Days to the Second World War.* Barnsley: Seaforth Publishing.

Friedman, N. (2009). *Network-centric Warfare: How Navies Learned to Fight Smarter Through Three World Wars.* Annapolis, Maryland: Naval Institute Press.

Future Destroyers and Frigates: The Canadian Surface Combatant. (2012, November). Retrieved August 5, 2015, from Canadian American Strategic Review: http://www.casr.ca/doc-loi-navy-csc-project.htm

Gainsville Sun. (1982, July 18). *News Media Airplanes Buss Soviet Spy Vessel.* Retrieved January 16, 2016, from Gainsville Sun: https://news.google.com/newspapers?nid=1320&dat=19820718&id=7ztWAAAAIBAJ&sjid=iukDAAAAIBAJ&pg=6962,1211965

Gardiner, R. (1996). *Conway's All the World's Fighting Ships, 1947-1995* (Rev Sub ed.). Annapolis, Maryland: Naval Institute Press.

German, T. (1990). *The Sea is at Our Gates: The History of the Canadian Navy.* Toronto: McClelland & Stewart Inc.

Gilmore, B. (2016, 06 12). *RCN ships attend New York City Fleet Week.* Retrieved 06 15, 2016, from The Chronicle Herald: http://thechronicleherald.ca/other/1371771-rcn-ships-attend-new-york-city-fleet-week

Gimblett, R. (1999, July). "Too Many Chiefs and Not Enough Seamen:" The Lower-Deck Complement of a PostwarCanadian Navy Destroyer –. *The Northern Mariner, IX*(3), 1 - 22.

Gimblett, R. (2004). *Operation Apollo: The Golden Age of the Canadian Navy in the War Against Terrorism.* Ottawa: Magic Light Publishing.

GlobalSecurity.org. (n.d.). *Canadian Surface Combatant (CSC).* Retrieved November 25, 2016, from

GlobalSecurity.org: http://www.globalsecurity.org/military/world/canada/hmcs-csc.htm

Gough, B. M. (2001). *HMCS Haida: Battle Ensign Flying.* St. Catharines, Ontario: Vanwell Publishing.

Hadley, M. L., & Sarty, R. (1991). *Tin-Pots and Pirate Ships: Canadian Naval Forces and German Sea Raiders 1880 - 1918.* Montreal & Kingston, Quebec, Canada: McGill-Queen's University Press.

Hague, A. (1990). *Destroyers for Great Britain: A History of 50 Town Class Ships Transferred from the United States to Great Britain in 1940* (Revised and Expanded ed.). London: Greenhill Books.

Hansen, K. (2006, Fall). The "Destroyer Myth" in Canadian Naval History. *Canadian Naval Review, 2*(3), pp. 5-9.

Haydon, P. T. (2001). What Naval Capabilities Does Canada Need? *Canadian Military Journal, 2*(1), pp. 21-28.

Haydon, P. T. (2008). Choosing the Right Fleet Mix: Lessons from the Canadian Patrol Frigate Selection Process. *Canadian Military Journal, 9*(1), pp. 65 - 75.

Hodges, P. (1971). *Tribal Class Destroyers.* London: Almark Publishing Co. Ltd.

Hofman, E. (1970). *The Steam Yachts: An Era of Elegance.* Tuckahoe, N.Y.: John De Graff Inc.

Jenson, L. B. (2000). *Tin Hats, Oilskins & Seaboots: A Naval Journey, 1938 - 1945.* Toronto, Ontario: Robin Brass Studio Inc.

Johnston, W., Rawling, W. G., Gimblett, R. H., & MacFarlane, J. (2011). *The Seabound Coast: The Official History of the Royal Canadian Navy, 1867–1939* (Vol. I). Dundurn.

Lambie, C. (2009, November 4). *That's a lot of scrap metal.* Retrieved January 16, 2016, from The Chronicle Herald: https://web.archive.org/web/20091107104920/http://thechronicleherald.ca/Business/1150984.html

Lay, H. N. (1982). *Memoirs of a Mariner.* Stittsville, Ontario: Canada's Wings Inc.

Leach, N. S. (2008). *Broken Arrow: American's First Lost Nuclear Weapon.* Calgary, Alberta: Red Deer Press.

Lynch, T. G. (1990). Twilight of the St Laurents. (R. Gardiner, Ed.) *Warship*, 175 - 197.

Lynch, T. G., & Lamb, J. B. (1984). *Gunshield Graffiti.* Halifax: Nimbus Publishing Ltd.

MacDonald, A. (2015, May 27). *Canada first: DND's procurement and industrial strategy [CAN2015D1].* Retrieved January 16, 2016, from IHS Jane's 360: http://www.janes.com/article/51694/canada-first-dnd-s-procurement-and-industrial-strategy-can2015d1

MacIntyre, L. R. (1997, Spring/Summer). Sinking into History: The Wreck of HMCS Assiniboine. *Island Magazine*(41), pp. 10 - 13.

MacKenzie, S. C., & Tuteja, R. (2006). *Modular Capabilities for the Canadian Navy's Single Class Surface Combatant: A Perspective on Flexibility.* Consulting and Audit Canada. Defense Research and Development Canada.

MacPherson, K., & Barrie, R. (2004). *Ships of Canada's Naval Forces: 1910-2002* (3 ed.). Vanwell Publishing Ltd.

MacPherson, K., & Butterley, K. (2008). *River Class Destroyers of the Royal Canadian Navy* (2 ed.). Vanwell Publishing Ltd.

Madgwick, E. (2003). *Tribal Captain.* Helston, Cornwall, UK: Blue Island Books.

Marland, P. (2015). Postwar Weapons in the Royal Navy. In J. Jordan (Ed.), *Warship 2015* (pp. 142 - 160). Annapolis, Maryland: Naval Institute Press.

Matheson, L. (2016, 06 12). *HMCS Athabaskan visits NASDAQ during Fleet Week New York City.* Retrieved 06 15, 2016, from The Chronicle Herald: http://thechronicleherald.ca/other/1371780-hmcs-athabaskan-visits-nasdaq-during-fleet-week-new-york-city

Mayne, R. O. (2008). *The Annapolis Riddle: Advocacy, Ship Design and the Canadian Navy's Force Structure Crisis, 1957-1965.* Doctoral Dissertation, Queen's University, Department of History, Kingston, Ontario.

McClearn, S. (2009). *HMCS Kootenay Gearbox Explosion.* Retrieved January 16, 2016, from Haze Gray & Underway: http://www.hazegray.org/navhist/canada/postwar/restigou/kootenay-explosion/

McClearn, S. (2010). *Y100 Machinery.* Retrieved January 16, 2016, from Haze Gray & Underway: http://www.hazegray.org/navhist/canada/systems/propulsion/y100/

McKee, F. (1983). *The Armed Yachts of Canada.* Boston Mills Press.

McKee, F., & Darlington, R. (1998). *The Canadian Naval Chronicle 1939-1945.* St. Catharines, ON: Vanwell Publishing Ltd.

Milner, M. (1990). *North Atlantic Run.* Markham, Ontario: Penguin Books Canada Ltd.

Milner, M. (1999). *Canada's Navy: The First Century.* Toronto: University of Toronto.

Montreal Gazette. (1946, August 9). *Latest Tribal Destroyer Nootka Starts Sea Trials From Halifax.* Retrieved

January 16, 2016, from Montreal Gazette: https://news.google.com/newspapers?nid=1946&dat=19460810&id=VC4rAAAAIBAJ&sjid=NZkFAAAAIBAJ&pg=2514,6157786&hl=en

Montreal Gazette. (1947, July 18). *Micmac Probe Should be Open.* Retrieved January 16, 2016, from https://news.google.com/newspapers?nid=1946&dat=19470718&id=iDQrAAAAIBAJ&sjid=ipgFAAAAIBAJ&pg=5833,3028859&hl=en

Montreal Gazette. (1973, July 4). *No Drugs Found Yet on Old Warship.* Retrieved January 16, 2016, from Montreal Gazette: https://news.google.com/newspapers?nid=1946&dat=19730704&id=SlwlAAAAIBAJ&sjid=Z6EFAAAAIBAJ&pg=5954,413770

Montreal Gazette. (1974, December 4). *Destroyer Crew Boards 5 Soviet Fishing Vessels.* Retrieved January 16, 2016, from The Montreal Gazette: https://news.google.com/newspapers?nid=1946&dat=19741204&id=25AjAAAAIBAJ&sjid=v6EFAAAAIBAJ&pg=1908,550333

Montreal Gazette. (1984, August 15). *Aging Canadian Vessel Tracking Soviet Spy Ship.* Retrieved January 16, 2016, from The Montreal Gazette: https://news.google.com/newspapers?nid=1946&dat=19840815&id=QlkxAAAAIBAJ&sjid=naUFAAAAIBAJ&pg=3196,573935

Mooney, James L; Naval Historical Center, et al. (n.d.). *Dictionary of American Naval Fighting Ships* (online). Washington, D.C.: U.S. Department of the Navy : Naval Historical Center.

Niestlé, A. (2007, January 7). *Re-assessment of German U-boat losses in World War II: The loss of U 305, U 377 and U 641.* Retrieved January 16, 2016, from Uboatwaffe.net: https://web.archive.org/web/20120729072311/http://www.ubootwaffe.net/research/reports.cgi?a=7;p=1

Ode to the Grilse. (n.d.). Retrieved 01 16, 2016, from Wartime Canada: http://wartimecanada.ca/document/world-war-i/poetry/ode-grilse

Perkins, J. D. (2000). *The Canadian Submarine Service in Review.* St. Catherines, Ontario: Vanwell Publishing Ltd.

Proc, J. (2014). *Nootka's History.* Retrieved January 16, 2016, from HMCS Nootka: http://jproc.ca/nootka/history.html

Pugliese, D. (2015, July 20). *Canada's last destroyer, HMCS Athabaskan, sidelined by engine problems amid fears for its future.* Retrieved August 5, 2015, from National Post: http://news.nationalpost.com/news/canada/canadas-last-destroyer-hmcs-athabaskan-sidelined-by-engine-problems-amid-fears-for-its-future

Pugliese, D. (2015, March 24). *HMCS Athabaskan received minor damage in storm*. Retrieved January 16, 2016, from Ottawa Citizen: http://ottawacitizen.com/news/national/defence-watch/hmcs-athabaskan-receives-minor-damage-in-storm

Pugliese, D. (2015, June 10). *Retirement ceremony for HMCS Algonquin to be held Thursday*. Retrieved January 16, 2016, from Ottawa Citizen: http://ottawacitizen.com/news/national/defence-watch/retirement-ceremony-for-hmcs-algonquin-to-be-held-thursday

Raven, A. (1972). Royal Navy camouflage of WW2. (E. C. Jr., Ed.) *Warship International, Volume IX*(Number 1), 54-57.

Raven, A., & Roberts, J. (1976). *Ensign 6: War Built Destroyers O to Z Classes.* London: Bivouac Books Ltd.

Royal Canadian Navy. (1962, June). Vice-Admiral H. E. Reid Dead. *The Crowsnest, 14*(8), p. 6.

Sarty, R. (1988). Hard Luck Flotilla: The RCN's Atlantic Coast Patrol, 1914 - 18. In W. A. Douglas (Ed.), *RCN in Transition 1910 - 1985* (pp. 103 - 125). Vancouver: The University of British Columbia Press.

Schleihauf, W. (Summer 2000). "Necessary Stepping Stones..." The Transfer of Aurora, Patriot and Patrician to the Royal Canadian Navy after the First World War. *Canadian Military History, 9*(3), 21 - 28.

Schull, J. (1987). *Far Distant Ships: An Official Account of Canadian Naval Operations in World War II.* Toronto, Ontario: Stoddart Publishing Co. Ltd.

Smith, P. (1971). *Hard Lying; The Birth of the Destroyer 1893 - 1913.* London: William Kimber and Co. Ltd.

Snowie, J. A. (1987). *The Bonnie (HMCS Bonaventure).* Erin, ON: Boston Mills Press.

Spokane Chronicle. (1982, July 17). *Soviet Spy Ship patrols just off coast.* Retrieved January 16, 2016, from Spokane Chronicle: https://news.google.com/newspapers?nid=1345&dat=19820717&id=1VUaAAAAIBAJ&sjid=UicEAAAAIBAJ&pg=2795,389582

Spokane Daily Chronicle . (1962, March 12). Retrieved January 11, 2016, from Google News Archive: https://news.google.com/newspapers?nid=1338&dat=19620312&id=VVVYAAAAIBAJ&sjid=i_cDAAAAIBAJ&pg=5056,2611022&hl=en

The Chronicle Herald. (2016, March 7). *HMCS Athabaskan celebrates 25th anniversary of Kuwait liberation.* Retrieved June 15, 2016, from The Chronicle Herald: http://thechronicleherald.ca/trident/1347257-

hmcs-athabaskan-celebrates-25th-anniversary-of-kuwait-liberation

The Engineering Journal. (1931, October). The Canadian Torpedo-Boat Destroyers Saguenay and Skeena. *The Engineering Journal*, pp. 518 - 521.

The Milwaukee Journal. (1989, December 13). *Canadian Navy, US Fishing Boat Clash*. Retrieved January 16, 2016, from The Milwaukee Journal: https://news.google.com/newspapers?nid=1499&dat=19891213&id=N64cAAAAIBAJ&sjid=_SsEAAAAIBAJ&pg=6897,4920792&hl=en

The Spokesman Review. (1968, October 16). *Canadian ship captain found guilty*. Retrieved January 16, 2016, from The Spokesman Review: https://news.google.com/newspapers?nid=1314&dat=19681016&id=c3szAAAAIBAJ&sjid=aukDAAAAIBAJ&pg=4946,500866

The Turbine Driven Yacht Winchester. (1912, December 27). *Engineering, XCVIII*, p. 879 and 882.

Thorgrimsson, T., & Russell, E. C. (1965). *Canadian Naval Operations in Korean Waters 1950 – 1955.* Ottawa: National Defence and the Canadian Armed Forces.

Tremblay, C. (2009, Fall 2009/Winter 2010). HMCS Kootenay — 40 Years of Lessons. *Maritime Engineering Journal*(65), 16 - 20.

Tutton, M. (2016, June 13). *Federal government opts for off-the-shelf design to cut costs of new warships.* Retrieved June 15, 2016, from CTV News: http://www.ctvnews.ca/politics/federal-government-opts-for-off-the-shelf-design-to-cut-costs-of-new-warships-1.2943307

Twinn, B. L. (1916). The Assassin by Night.

Watson, J. V. (2001). *Shipwrecks & Seafaring Tales of Prince Edward Island.* Halifax, NS: Nimbus Publishing Limited.

Whinney, B. (1986). *The U-Boat Peril: A Fight for Survival.* London: Cassel.

Whitby, M. (1992, July). Instruments Of Security: The Royal Canadian Navy's Procurement Of The Tribal-Class destroyers, 1938-1943. *The Northern Mariner/Le Marin du nord, II*(3), 1 - 15.

Withers, P. (2015, September 04). *HMCS Athabaskan fire 'minor,' says navy.* Retrieved January 16, 2016, from CBC News: http://www.cbc.ca/news/canada/nova-scotia/hmcs-athabaskan-fire-minor-says-navy-1.3215720?cmp=rss

Zimmerman, D. (1989). *The Great Naval Battle of Ottawa.* Toronto, Ontario: Toronto University Press.

INDEX

** **Bold** items indicate main ship history entry.*

Baldwin, F. W. 17
Bancroft, George 74
Bancroft, Mary W 74
Bell, Alexander Graham 17
Bell, Allan 215
Bentley, Doris. 66
Bernays, Max 37
Borden, Robert 3, 5
Boudreau, W.A. 215
Bourett, Pierre 215
Brodeur, Victor Gabriel 30
Churchill, Winston 28, 36, 44, 122
Cox & Stevens (Naval Architects) 9
Crabbe, T.G. 215
Creery, Wallace Bouchier 41
Davidson, R.A. 258
de Champlain, Samuel 22
Diguilian, Tony 224
Dobson, Andrew Hedley 48, 95
Duvalier, Francois 230
Dyer, Kenneth Lloyd 33, 37, 153
Edwards, William W. 77
Establishments & Bases, Royal Canadian Navy
    CFB Esquimalt ... 201, 202, 205, 206, 210, 218, 219, 220, 222, 231, 232, 235, 236, 242, 245, 246, 258, 260, 261, 262, 269, 270, 271, 272
    CFB Halifax. 178, 184, 185, 194, 195, 207, 210, 214, 241, 245, 256, 257, 258, 260, 264, 269, 273
    HMCD Esquimalt . 6, 20, 30, 32, 41, 43, 47, 51, 130, 141, 143, 146, 147, 148, 150, 151, 152, 157, 158, 161, 162, 163, 165, 167, 174, 177, 179, 180, 182, 183, 187, 188, 190, 193, 201, 203, 209, 221, 224, 227, 228, 230, 233
    HMCD Halifax ... 6, 10, 12, 44, 58, 60, 61, 67, 68, 69, 70, 73, 76, 78, 122, 123, 129, 130, 131, 133, 134, 135, 137, 138, 140, 142, 153, 157,

    161, 162, 175, 205
    HMCS Cornwallis 28, 62, 65, 73, 76
    HMCS Point Edward 164
    HMCS Royal Roads 96
    HMCS Stadacona 100
Exercises
    CARIBEX1-77 265
    CARIBOPS 82 266
    CARIBOPS 83 267
    CARIBOPS 87 268
    JET 64 227
    JETEX 62 190
    JMC 824 267
    Joint Warrior 276, 279
    Linked Seas 207
    Magic Lantern 200, 203, 215
    MARCOT 1/83 267
    MARCOT 1/95 .... 207, 211, 242
    MARCOT 2/81 266
    MARCOT 2/83 267
    MARCOT 75 265
    Northern Wedding 78 266
    Northern Wedding 82 267
    Ocean Safari 85 268
    Ocean Safari 87 245
    Ocean Safari 91 .... 181, 189
    Open Gate 268
    RIMPAC 00 270
    RIMPAC 86 218
    RIMPAC 94 219
    RIMPAC 96 270
    SAFEPASS 82 267
    SAMPLOY 89 228
    Springboard 77 265
    Strong Resolve 211, 242
    Teamwork 76 .... 188, 191
    Trident Fury 262, 281

Trident Venture 279
  Unified Spirit 256
  UNITAS 220, 275
  Vendetta 268
  WESTPLOY 00 270
  WESTPLOY 96 269
Fisher, William Allen 71
Frewer, F.C. 53
Furey, William Jr. 185
Galloway, Nelson 216
German, Anthony (Tony) B.C. 226
Hardy, M.A. 215
Harman, E.G. 215
Hennessy, R.L. 37
Hibbard, J.C. 121
Holmes, W.B.L. 121
Hutton, G.W. 215
Jackson, N.F. 231
Jenson, Latham Brereton 50
Kennedy, A.F. 215
Kingsley, H. 69
Kingsmill, Charles Edmund 4
Kretschmer, Otto 52
Landymore, William Moss 90
Laurier, Wilfred 3, 5
Lay, Horatio Nelson 30, 31, 43
Leir, R.H. 180
Lloyd, Maurice Frank Ronald 271
Luppis, Giovanni 1
MacKinnon, John 215
Maddison, Gregory Ralph 287
Madgwick, E.T.G. 121, 134
Mainguy, Edmund Rollo 166
Miles, G.R. 27
Nelles, Percy Walker 27, 294
Newton, John 278, 282
O'Brien, John Charles 213

Operations
- Apollo 257, 270, 271, 276
- Athletic 160
- Caribbe 277, 278
- Dredger 99, 104
- Enduring Freedom 257
- Excess 113
- Forward Action 194, 207, 219, 245
- Friction 273, 279
- Gearbox III 122, 125
- Halberd 113
- Hats 112
- Holder 122
- Kinetic 33, 99
- Overlord 27
- Post Horn 122, 133
- Tiger 113
- Tungsten 159
- Urban 156
- Vigorous 103, 107
- Wilfred 112
- Winch 102

Partanen, V.A. 215
Phillips, R. C. 26
Piers, Desmond William 45
Prentice, James Douglas 109
Pullen, Hugh Francis 53, 107
Pullen, Thomas Charles 49
Reid, Howard Emerson 17, 30, 31, 192
Richter, H.R. 67
Robertson, Drew W. 288
Rockwell, F W. 66
Rouss, Peter Winchester 9
Roy, J.W.R. 90
Rutherford, C.A. 49
Schreyer, Edward 260
Shipbuilders

317

Bethlehem Shipbuilding Corporation 68, 74, 77
Burrard Drydock Ltd. 179, 192, 233
Canadian Vickers Ltd. 173, 186, 199, 226
Davie Shipbuilding Ltd. 209, 235, 264, 272
Fore River Shipyard 63, 66
Halifax Shipyard Ltd. 136, 141, 146, 150, 182, 190, 202, 221, 243
J. Samuel White & Co. 35, 155
John Brown & Co. Ltd. 97, 101, 159, 162
John Isaac Thornycroft & Co. 2, 6, 15, 18, 20, 22, 26, 29
Laird, Son & Co. 2
Marine Industries Ltd. 176, 213, 238, 254, 259
Newport News Shipbuilding 59
Palmers Shipbuilding Co. Ltd. 88
Portsmouth Naval Dockyard 42, 46
Swan Hunter & Wigham Richardson 96
Union Iron Works 61, 71
Vickers Armstrong Ltd. 40, 51, 105, 111, 120, 124, 128, 132
Victoria Machinery Depot Ltd. 229
Yarrow & Co. 2, 9, 26, 170

Ships, Canadian Coast Guard
  CCGS Alert 273
  CCGS Simon Fraser 195
  CCGS Tupper 183

Ships, Other
  Aavril Sarychev 227, 231
  Admiral Hipper 107, 112
  Admiral Scheer 75
  Afanasiy Nikitin (tug) 191
  Alpha Omega II (fishing vessel) 195
  Amphailos (tanker) 153
  Arosia (freighter) 265
  Bak Dusan (sub-chaser) 143
  Bansurf (tug) 47
  Barma (freighter) 178
  Bismarck 36, 72
  BNS Westhinder 273
  California (troop transport) 120

Cape Perry (fish packer) 147
Cape Rogers (fisheries protection vessel) 268
Cedarwood (oceanographic survey vessel) 152
Chebucto (fisheries protection vessel) 265
Clam (oiler) 73
Concordia (fishing vessel) 184
Elbe (tug) 217
Elisabeth van Belgie (freighter) 49
Estai (trawler) 211
F.J. Wolfe (tanker) 49
Fausang 89
Foundation Vigilant (tug) 209
Gilbert Jr (passenger vessel) 138
Glendon (tug) 152
GTS Katie 276
Gulf Gale (tug) 241
Harvey And Sisters (fishing vessel) 145
Ho Ming 5 (freighter) 255
Independence Hall (merchantman) 67
Jean D'Arc 122
Kingston Beryl (trawler) 121
Kronprins Olav 105
Kurdistan (tanker) 191
Lady Majorie (fishing vessel) 240
Leader L (freighter) 256
Maille-Breze 131
Maja Romm (sailing vessel) 195
Manchester Port (freighter) 199
Marques (sailing vessel) 178
Marshal Ustinov 211
Melrose Abby (freighter) 48
MS Stensby 23
MV Arandora Star 52
MV Euro Princess 273
MV Foundation Security 65
MV Glenshiel 103
MV Hannover (merchant vessel) 36

MV Marysville (former minesweeper) 227
MV Maurice Desgagnes (freighter) 259
MV Nord Pol 219
MV Pacifico 207
MV Port Fairey (I) (troop transport) 89, 90, 91, 109, 120, 121
MV San Franscisco 54
Nyholt (merchantman) 73
Ocean Ranger (oil platform) 239
Odin Salvatore (tug) 175
Orania 98
ORP Blyskawica 32, 133
ORP Krakowiak 156
Pamir 164
Patricia Nores (trawler) 242
Paul & Maria (fishing vessel) 265
Peggy's Cove (fishing vessel) 265
Peonia 7 (trawler) 268
Princess Marguite (troop transport) 115
Puffin 203
Redwitch (yacht) 192
Rio Blanco (freighter) 67
RN Bartolomeo Colleoni 112
Rotesand (tug) 149
Rowan Juneau (oil platform) 273
Sapfir (tug) 189
Semen Chelyushkin 201
SS Aquitania (troop transport) 137
SS Azra (freighter) 28
SS Conch 52
SS Duchess of York (troop transport) 120
SS Empire Bond 38
SS Eurymedon 47
SS Mauretania (troop transport) 137
SS Mauritania (troop transport) 141
SS Sulairia 47
SS Yarmouth County (freighter) 134, 137
St. Irene (fishing vessel) 194

Strathnaver (liner) 105
Sveve (tanker) 49
SY Trillola .... *See* HMCS *Grilse*
SY Winchester (3rd) .... *See* HMCS *Grilse*
SY Winchester (4th) .... *See* HMCS *Renard*
T-24 .... 126, 127
T-24 122
T-27 .... 126, 127, 133
T-29 .... 126, 129
Terra-Nova (Antarctic Vessel) 204
Tirpiz 155, 156, 160
Tongshu (tanker) 152
Tony McKay (tug) 196
USCGC Hornbeam 65
Warrior (fishing vessel) 195
Yaqui Queen 192

Ships, Royal Australian Navy
   HMS Perth 43
   HMS Stuart 85
   HMS Sydney 85, 112
   HMS Warramunga 143, 158

Ships, Royal Canadian Navy
   HMCS Algerine 5
   HMCS Algonquin (I) 137, 155, **159**, 160, 161, 162, 167, 168, 221
   HMCS Algonquin (II) .. 256, 258, 262, **264**, 265, 266, 267, 268, 269, 270, 271, 272, 273, 281
   HMCS Annapolis (I) 49, **61**, 76
   HMCS Annapolis (II) ... 180, 195, 206, 214, 219, 237, 238, 239, 241, **243**, 245, 260
   HMCS Antigonish 213
   HMCS Assiniboine (I) **35**, 36, 37, 38, 39, 43, 55, 96, 100
   HMCS Assiniboine (II) **176**, 177, 178, 186, 190, 195, 215
   HMCS Athabaskan (I) 122, **124**, 125, 126, 127, 129, 133, 152
   HMCS Athabaskan (II) 119, 146, 147, 148, **150**, 151, 152, 153, 157, 166, 188
   HMCS Athabaskan (III) . 25, 206, 220, 260, **272**, 273, 274, 275, 276, 277, 278, 279, 280, 281, 287, 288

HMCS Aurora 14, 15, 16
HMCS Battleford 53
HMCS Bonaventure 153, 186, 213, 215, 216, 238
HMCS Bras d'Or 17, 176
HMCS Brockville 176
HMCS Buckingham 131, 144
HMCS Buxton 58, **77**
HMCS Calgary (I) 176
HMCS Calgary (II) 176, 258, 271
HMCS Canada 5
HMCS Cape Scott 213
HMCS Cayuga 119, 139, 140, 142, 145, **146**, 147, 148, 149, 151, 157
HMCS Chaleur 183
HMCS Chambly 32, 109
HMCS Champlain 15, 20, **22**, 23, 27
HMCS Charlottetown (III) 257, 271
HMCS Chaudière (I) ... 45, 48, 54, 55, 85, 86, 87, 95, 100, 108, 109, **111**, 115, 116, 117, 213
HMCS Chaudière (II) **202**, 203, 204, 219
HMCS Chilliwack 53, 115
HMCS Columbia (I) 44, **59**, 60
HMCS Columbia (II) 200, 215, **221**, 222
HMCS Constance 5
HMCS Cormorant 241, 267
HMCS Crescent 154, 162, 163, 164, **165**, 166, 168, 221
HMCS Crusader 154, **162**, 165, 168
HMCS Curlew 5
HMCS Esquimalt 176
HMCS Fraser (I) 32, **40**, 41, 42, 43, 47, 51, 52, 88, 89, 165
HMCS Fraser (II) 179, 180, **192**, 193, 195, 196, 211, 215, 244
HMCS Fredricton (I) 176
HMCS Fredricton (II) 257
HMCS Gatineau (I) 54, 86, **92**, 108, 115
HMCS Gatineau (II) 208, **209**, 211, 212, 217, 235, 260
HMCS Goose Bay 279
HMCS Grilse 7, **8**, 9, 10, 11, 12, 13, 22, 296
HMCS Grilse (II) 213

HMCS Haida 118, 119, 122, 124, 126, 127, 129, **132**, 133, 134, 135, 137, 142, 144, 145, 153
HMCS Halifax (II) 207, 256, 276, 277, 279
HMCS Hamilton 58, **63**, 64, 65
HMCS Huron (I) . 119, 122, 123, 126, **128**, 129, 130, 131, 133, 138, 139, 144
HMCS Huron (II) . 210, 229, 245, **259**, 260, 261, 263, 266, 271, 275, 281
HMCS Iroquois (I) **119**, 139, 144, 163, 258
HMCS Iroquois (II) 250, 252, **254**, 255, 256, 257, 258, 259, 265, 271, 281
HMCS Kingston 279
HMCS Kitchener 176
HMCS Kootenay (I) 45, 54, **83**, 85, 86, 87, 89, 95, 108, 109, 115
HMCS Kootenay (II) ... 170, 172, 202, 204, **214**, 218, 220, 231, 245, 260, 275, 293
HMCS La Malabie 176
HMCS Mackenzie **226**, 227, 228, 229, 231, 233, 261
HMCS Magnificent 138, 142, 166
HMCS Margaree (I) 41, **88**, 89, 91
HMCS Margaree (II) 176, 188, **189**, 191, 215, 265
HMCS Margaret 5
HMCS Micmac **136**, 145, 149
HMCS Moncton (II) 279
HMCS Montreal 279
HMCS Moosejaw 109
HMCS Napanee 53
HMCS New Liskeard 142
HMCS Niagara 66
HMCS Niobe 5, 15
HMCS Nipigon 214, 231, **238**, 239, 241, 242, 244, 245
HMCS Nootka (II) 119, 140, 144, 148, 149, 158
HMCS Okanagan..... ....242, 266
HMCS Ontario 138, 151
HMCS Ottawa (I) 32, 43, 44, 45, **46**, 50, 51, 62, 69, 107, 162
HMCS Ottawa (II) 54, 55, 86, 95, 100, 105, 110, 115, 116
HMCS Ottawa (III) 174, 182, **186**, 187, 188, 190, 215, 233, 239
HMCS Ottawa (IV) 270, 284

HMCS Outremont 144
HMCS Owen Sound 54
HMCS Patrician 14, 15, 16, 17, **18**, 19, 20
HMCS Patriot 14, **15**, 16, 17, 18, 19, 20, 30
HMCS Preserver 206, 211, 257, 273
HMCS Protecteur 180, 190, 243, 258, 265, 269, 270, 271, 272, 274, 281, 286
HMCS Provider 210, 213, 218, 227, 233, 235
HMCS Qu'Appelle (I) 33, 45, 55, **97**, 99, 100, 104, 112, 116
HMCS Qu'Appelle (II) 210, 225, **235**, 236
HMCS Quebec 144
HMCS Rainbow 5, 15
HMCS Regina (I) 176
HMCS Regina (II) 269
HMCS Renard 9
HMCS Restigouche (I) 32, 36, 40, 41, **42**, 44, 46, 47, 51, 55, 99, 100, 104, 110
HMCS Restigouche (II) **199**, 200, 201, 202, 214, 218
HMCS Saguenay (I) 20, 22, 23, 24, 25, 26, 27, 29, 30, 31, 34, 36, 51
HMCS Saguenay (II) 131, 152, 174, **182**, 183, 184, 185, 187, 214, 215
HMCS Saskatchewan (I) 45, 82, 96, 99, **101**, 104
HMCS Saskatchewan (II) 97, 227, **229**, 230, 231, 232, 236
HMCS Shearwater 5
HMCS Shediac 70
HMCS Sherbrooke 49, 176
HMCS Sioux 143, 147, 151, **155**, 157, 168
HMCS Skeena (I) 20, 21, 22, 24, 25, 26, **29**, 30, 31, 32, 33, 34, 37, 38, 43, 45, 51, 55, 99, 104, 116
HMCS Skeena (II) **179**, 180, 181, 205, 214, 243, 265
HMCS St. Catherines 115
HMCS St. Clair **71**, 72
HMCS St. Croix (I) 48, 62, **68**, 74, 95, 293
HMCS St. Croix (II) 178, 205, **212**, 214
HMCS St. Francis 44, 65, 69, **74**
HMCS St. John's 270, 276
HMCS St. Laurent (I) 27, 32, 35, 43, 47, **50**, 54, 86, 95, 100, 108, 115
HMCS St. Laurent (II) 152, 170, 171, **173**, 175, 182, 186, 187, 215

    HMCS Stettler 213
    HMCS Stratford 110
    HMCS Summerside (II) 279, 292
    HMCS Terra Nova 201, **204**, 205, 206, 208, 212, 213, 215, 218, 219, 229, 256, 261, 273
    HMCS Thunder 183
    HMCS Toronto (I) 144
    HMCS Toronto (II) 276
    HMCS Transcona 176
    HMCS Trois-Rivieres 176
    HMCS Vancouver (I) 15, **20**, 21, 22, 23, 30
    HMCS Vancouver (II) 271
    HMCS Ville de Quebec (II) 207, 245
    HMCS Warrior 141
    HMCS Wetaskawin 33
    HMCS Windsor 279
    HMCS Winnipeg (II) 269, 270
    HMCS York 39
    HMCS Yukon (I) 225, 227, 228, **233**, 234, 236
Ships, Royal Navy
    EFA Olynthus 105
    HMS Acheron 214
    HMS Amazon 80
    HMS Ambuscade 80
    HMS Amethyst 165
    HMS Anson 132
    HMS Arethusa 106
    HMS Argus 102
    HMS Ariel 5
    HMS Ark Royal 98, 102
    HMS Ascania 52
    HMS Ashanti 126, 129, 133
    HMS Audacity 36
    HMS Bargate 125
    HMS Bedouin 112
    HMS Berwick 102, 134
    HMS Black Prince 126, 129

HMS Bonaventure	113
HMS Breconshire	103
HMS Brocklesby	164
HMS Calcutta	41, 90
HMS Celadine	50
HMS Comet (1931)	*See* HMCS *Restigouche*
HMS Constance	143
HMS Cossack	112
HMS Courageous	46
HMS Crescent (1931)	*See* HMCS *Fraser*
HMS Crescent (1944)	*See* HMCS *Crescent*
HMS Crusader (1931)	*See* HMCS *Ottawa*
HMS Crusader (1944)	*See* HMCS *Crusader*
HMS Cumberland (1902)	10
HMS Cygnet (1931)	*See* HMCS *St. Laurent*
HMS Dainty	85
HMS Daring (1894)	2
HMS Dauntless	287
HMS Decoy (1894)	2
HMS Decoy (1932)	*See* HMCS *Kootenay (I)*
HMS Defender	85
HMS Diana	86
HMS Diana (1932)	*See* HMCS *Margaree (I)*
HMS Dominion	4
HMS Douglas	120
HMS Dreadnaught	3
HMS Duncan	84
HMS Dunedin	36
HMS Egret	125
HMS Emerald	35, 52
HMS Encounter	94, 113
HMS Eridge	114
HMS Esk	93
HMS Eskimo	112, 129, 133
HMS Express (1934)	*See* HMCS *Gatineau (I)*
HMS Faulknor	98, 102
HMS Fearless	102

HMS Ferret (1893) 2
HMS Firedrake 98
HMS Forester 112
HMS Fortune (1934) .... See HMCS Saskatchewan (I)
HMS Foxhound (1934) .... See HMCS Qu'Appelle (I)
HMS Fraser 43
HMS Furious 160
HMS Fury 102
HMS Gallant 106
HMS Gipsy 106
HMS Glasgow 102
HMS Glorious 42
HMS Glory 163
HMS Glowworm 107
HMS Goldfinch 4
HMS Good Hope 220
HMS Graph 67
HMS Grenville 125
HMS Greyhound 105
HMS Griffin (1935) .... See HMCS Ottawa (II)
HMS Hardy 112
HMS Harvester 48
HMS Hasty 85, 113, 114
HMS Havock (1893) 2
HMS Havock (1936) 114
HMS Hereward 111, 113
HMS Hero (1936) .... See HMCS Chaudière (I)
HMS Hornet (1893) 2
HMS Hostile 112
HMS Hotspur 103, 106
HMS Hunter 112
HMS Hurworth 114
HMS Icarus 112, 115
HMS Illustrious 94
HMS Indefatigable 160
HMS Intrepid 93
HMS Itchen 71

HMS Ivanhoe	93
HMS Jaguar	113
HMS Janus	93
HMS Javelin	129
HMS Jed	125
HMS Jervis Bay	75
HMS Jupiter	93, 94
HMS Kelvin	93
HMS Kempenfelt (1931)	See HMCS *Assiniboine*
HMS Kenya	157
HMS Kimberly	112
HMS Lance	114
HMS Latona	113
HMS Leander	170
HMS Legion	114
HMS Lightning	2
HMS Lively	114
HMS Lynx (1893)	2
HMS Mashona	72
HMS Mauritius	122
HMS McCook	See HMCS *St. Croix (I)*
HMS Medway	114
HMS Mohawk	112
HMS Moyola	120
HMS Nabob	160
HMS Norfolk	132
HMS Onslaught	128
HMS Onslow	122, 128, 159
HMS Orion	85, 113
HMS P514	62
HMS Patrician	See HMCS *Patrician*
HMS Patriot	See HMCS *Patriot*
HMS Pelican	77
HMS Prince of Wales	28, 36, 44, 94
HMS Protector	105
HMS Punjabi	112
HMS Queen Elizabeth	113

HMS Repulse 36, 94
HMS Rodney 86
HMS Rother 125
HMS Roxborough 58
HMS Royal Oak 46, 276
HMS Savage 154
HMS Seahorse 97
HMS Searcher 160
HMS Shark 102
HMS Shikari 106
HMS Sikh 114
HMS Stattice 87, 108
HMS Tartar 72, 133
HMS Theseus 151, 158
HMS Torbay (1919) .... *See* HMCS *Champlain*
HMS Toreador (1918) .... *See* HMCS *Vancouver (I)*
HMS Transylvania 102
HMS Troubridge 131
HMS Trumpeter 160
HMS Ursa 122
HMS Valentine (1943) .... *See* HMCS *Algonquin (I)*
HMS Viper 171
HMS Vixen (1943) .... *See* HMCS *Sioux*
HMS Wanderer 70
HMS Warspite 38, 86, 98, 112
HMS Witch 49
HMS Zambesi 156
HMS Zealous 122
HMS Zest 122, 156
HMS Zulu 114
HMT Mackenzie 226
HMY Britannia 152, 188, 213, 245
Ships, Royal New Zealand Navy
   HMS Canterbury 242
   HMS Endeavour 242
   HMS Rotoiti 163
Ships, Submarines & U-boats

Ajax	102
Argo	27, 52
Deutschland	12
Faa Di Bruno	48
HMS Acheron	214
HMS Graph	67
HMS P514	62
HMS Seahorse	97
HMS Shark	102
Lafole	106
O-15	64
U-138	98
U-155	12
U-156	11
U-17	184
U-190	141, 142
U-210	37, 38
U-234	45
U-27	101
U-270	55
U-305	70
U-354	160
U-356	53
U-39	98
U-427	123
U-44	101
U-50	98
U-501	109
U-558	125
U-559	115
U-56	102
U-568	114
U-569	53
U-570	67
U-588	33
U-621	45, 87, 109, 116
U-678	109

U-69	16
U-732	114
U-744	95, 115
U-845	54
U-87	70
U-90	70
U-91	49, 62
U-96	49
U-971	133
U-984	87, 116
U-99	52
USS Ohio	231

Ships, United States Navy

USS Adroit	274
USS Argus	77
USS Bancroft (1919)	See HMCS *St. Francis*
USS Bataan	163
USS Bogue	53
USS Boone	257
USS Edward McDonnell	265
USS Edwards (1918)	See HMCS *Buxton*
USS George Washington	77
USS Haraden (1918)	See HMCS *Columbia (I)*
USS Independence	267
USS Julius A. Furer	243
USS Kalk (1918)	See HMCS *Hamilton*
USS Kearsarge	182, 187
USS Kendrick	104
USS Mackenzie (1918)	See HMCS *Annapolis (I)*
USS McCook (1919)	See HMCS *St. Croix (I)*
USS Ohio	231
USS Princeton	274
USS Ranger	132
USS Richard E. Byrd	181
USS Thatcher (1919)	See HMCS *Niagara*
USS Tigley	11
USS Valdez	191

USS Williams (1918) .... *See* HMCS *St. Clair*
Stephen, G.H. 54
Stephens, G.L. 30
Stringer, John 216
Stubbs, J.H. 37
Thatcher, Henry K. 66
Thornycroft, John Isaac 2
Timbrel, R.W. 109
Tisdale, P. 193
Turbot War 211, 242
Twinn, Bertrand Lawrence 7
Units, Kreigsmarine
   4th Motor Torpedo Boat Flotilla 156
   4th Torpedo Boat Flotilla 126
Units, NATO
   'Matchmaker' Squadron 200
   Standing Naval Force Atlantic (STANAVFORLANT) 178, 181, 188, 189, 190, 191, 194, 200, 201, 209, 210, 211, 231, 241, 242, 243, 265, 266, 267, 268, 269, 275
Units, Royal Air Force
   269 Squadron (Coastal Command) 67
   42 Squadron 115
Units, Royal Canadian Navy
   1st Canadian Destroyer Squadron 183, 265
   1st Canadian Escort Squadron 161, 176
   2nd Canadian Destroyer Squadron 182, 192, 210, 260
   2nd Canadian Escort Squadron 148, 167, 177, 179, 187, 190, 221, 235
   3rd Canadian Destroyer Squadron 180, 182, 186, 190, 213
   3rd Canadian Escort Squadron 149, 164, 176
   4th Canadian Destroyer Squadron 227
   5th Canadian Destroyer Squadron 184, 203, 213
   5th Canadian Escort Squadron 226
   Canadian Escort Group 1 (EG C-1) 36, 53
   Canadian Escort Group 2 (EG C-2) 94, 95, 115
   Canadian Escort Group 3 (EG C-3) 38, 104
   Canadian Escort Group 4 (EG C-4) 45
   Canadian Escort Group 5 (EG C-5) 86, 107

Canadian Special Service Squadron 130, 138, 147, 151
VX-10 (Aircraft Experimental) 177
WLEF Escort Group 1 (EG W-1) 79
WLEF Escort Group 10 (EG W1-0) 60
WLEF Escort Group 10 (EG W-10) 67
WLEF Escort Group 2 (EG W-2) 67, 73
WLEF Escort Group 4 (EG W-4) 60, 64
WLEF Escort Group 9 (EG W-9) 67

Units, Royal Navy
10th Destroyer Flotilla 84, 122, 126
12th Destroyer Flotilla 94
13th Destroyer Flotilla 18, 106, 112, 113
14th Destroyer Flotilla 16, 106
14th Emergency Destroyer Flotilla 162, 165
1st Destroyer Flotilla 83, 88, 105, 106
20th Destroyer (Minelaying) Flotilla 93
20th Destroyer Flotilla 84
21st Destroyer Flotilla 84, 89
22nd Destroyer Flotilla 114
26th Destroyer Flotilla 155, 159
2nd Batallion Royal Marines... 102
2nd Destroyer Flotilla 35, 40, 42, 46, 51, 85, 99, 103, 107, 111, 112
3rd Destroyer Flotilla 89, 120, 128, 132
4th Destroyer Flotilla 99, 102
5th Destroyer Flotilla 92, 93
6th Destroyer Flotilla 97, 101
8th Cruiser Squadron.. 47
8th Destroyer Flotilla 84, 88, 98, 101
British Escort Group 6 (EG B-6) 78
Escort Group 10 (EG 10) 27, 32
Escort Group 11 (EG 11) 95, 104, 115
Escort Group 12 (EG 12) 104
Escort Group 14 (EG 14) 104
Escort Group 21 (EG 21) 69
Escort Group 6 (EG 6) 99
Escort Group E-4 (EG E-4) 59

Units, United States Navy

    Destroyer Squadron 2 (DESRON2) 61
    Destroyer Squadron 3 (DESRON3) 63
    Destroyer Squadron 4 (DESRON4) 61
Vancouver, George 20
Vian, Phillip Louis 112
Warwick, R.B. 28
Whitehead, Robert 1
Wilson, P.L. 77
Wilson, Woodrow 77
Windeyer, G.S. 53
Yarrow, Alfred 2

TIN CAN CANUCKS

"The Assassin by Night"

With rolling hull and quivering stem,
Our decks a'littered with iron-nerved men;
For storm or foe, fear there is none—
Hard graft's ahead and IT'S GOT TO BE DONE!

Eyes are piercing the darkness of Hell,
While stern lifts and crashes in wave-split well;
Guns are loaded, torpedoes gleam bright,
With "bone in our teeth" we plunge through the night.

Up on the bridge, rail clenched in his hands,
Legs a' straddled, stands he Who commands;
Helmsman with wheel in vise-like grip;
Signalman keen for sight of a ship.

Down by the boilers like Imps from below,
Beaten by rolling and scorched by the glow,
Firemen like demons, keep steam on the run—
Hard graft's ahead and IT'S GOT TO BE DONE!

The Engineroom staff, bespattered with oil,
As nurse to her charges, they stick to their toil;
Eyes to the gauges and ears for the gong,
To hum of the engines sing many a song.

Down in the Wireless room, wearied and worn;
Oft thrown from his seat by pranks of the storm,
In touch with headquarters by night and by day
Old "Sparks" hears all that other ships say.

It may be a raider we're out to locate,
Or guarding a Trooper from Submarine's hate;
For storm or foe fear there is none—
Hard graft's ahead and at GOT TO BE DONE!

S.D. Campbell

Pitching and rolling and plunging along—
The work may be hard but we've time for a song,
A song of our Empire, so Great and to Free:
Oh! who would not fight for the King on the Sea?

So here's to the "Grilse" "Assassin by Night"!
We're doing our bit for King and the Right.
Hard graft's ahead and it may take long—
But what has to be done WE'LL DO WITH A SONG!

Bertrand L. Twinn / 1916

ABOUT THE AUTHOR

Sean Campbell is a former reservist with the Canadian Forces, with a deep love of Canadian military history. Hailing from Prince Edward Island, Sean's interest in the RCN was first piqued in 1995 with the commissioning of the patrol frigate HMCS *Charlottetown (III)*, but it was the 2010 Canadian Naval Centennial that truly caught his imagination.

He is a competitive scale modeler, having won awards for his work, and has several models of Canadian naval vessels on public display. Some of Sean's prior written work on the history of Canadian destroyers has appeared in *Canadian Naval Review*.

A software engineer turned digital marketing consultant, Sean currently resides in Calgary, Alberta with his daughter and an overweight guinea pig.

Made in the USA
San Bernardino, CA
23 August 2017